About the Author

Ian Whitcomb was born in Surrey, England, in 1941. While studying modern history and political science at Trinity College, Dublin, he recorded a song that reached Top Ten in America in June, 1965: "You Turn Me On," a novelty rocker. After two years of touring, TV, and concerts, he was given up by the rock life and he turned his attention to early American popular music, especially ragtime. Since 1966 he has recorded over 20 albums ranging from ragtime to rock, including spoken word tracks, tangos, music hall numbers, and country and western. He also produced Mae West's album "Great Balls Of Fire" (MGM). He has hosted his own radio show in Los Angeles for KROQ and KCRW.

He began his career as author with *After the Ball: Pop Music from Rag to Rock,* reissued by Limelight Editions in 1986. His other books include *Tin Pan Alley, LotusLand* (a novel), *Whole Lotta Shakin'—A Rock 'n' Roll Scrapbook,* and *Rock Odyssey.* He was an associate producer of *Repercussions—A Celebration of African-American Music,* and a contributor to *The New Grove Dictionary of American Music.*

Ian lives in Altadena, California, and Putney, London. He continues to appear in concerts, mainly at ragtime and traditional jazz festivals in the USA, Canada, Switzerland, Australia, and Ireland.

IRVING BERLIN AND RAGTIME AMERICA

Ian Whitcomb

LIMELIGHT EDITIONS

NEW YORK

First Limelight Edition October, 1988
Copyright © by Ian Whitcomb 1987

All rights reserved under international and Pan-American Copyright
Convention. Published in the United States by Proscenium Publishers
Inc., New York and simultaneously in Canada by Fitzhenry &
Whiteside, Limited, Toronto.

Library of Congress Cataloging-in-Publication Data

Whitcomb, Ian, 1941–
Irving Berlin and ragtime America.

Reprint. Originally published: London:
Century-Hutchinson, 1987.
Bibliography: p.
Includes index.
1. Berlin, Irving, 1988– . 2. Composers—
United States—Biography. I. Title.
ML410.B499W5 1988   784'.092'4 [B]   88–17897
ISBN 0–87910–115–6

Contents

1 A Day in the Life of a Mouldy Fig   1

2 The Yiddishe Yankee Doodle   14

3 Origins of the Alley   39

4 Come on and Hear!   64

5 The Strange Myth of the Hot Coon   83

6 Everybody's Doing it now   138

7 Russian Rag   182

8 Mr Jazz Himself   194

Bibliography   212

Index   214

1

A Day in the Life of a Mouldy Fig

They are not long, the days of wine and roses:
  Out of a misty dream
Our path emerges for a while, then closes
  Within a dream.

Ernest Dowson

During the 1980s, with me in my forties, I started reading short poems before going to sleep. They had a soothing effect. But the Dowson poem made me think of the old saying: 'Time is of the essence.' All around, in Los Angeles and the world, people were doing things. Twenty miles from Hollywood I lay sweating in my Altadena house, looking at Dowson's warning.

It was 2 a.m. and the thought struck me that I'd had a noisy life and had achieved nothing. The poem told me the Big Dream was hovering. Meanwhile, mercifully, I was closed within a nice dream. Berlin had called me up again. Sometimes it was Isaiah – but this time it was definitely Irving. I could tell by the certainty of his high-pitched New York croak.

Irving Berlin, dean of pop-song writers, the Compleat Tin Pan Alleyman. One-time subject of the Tsar, chief architect of the great ragtime movement of the 1910s; writer of an American National Anthem ('God Bless America'). At ninety-eight this Grand Old Man of world pop was phoning *me*.

'This is Irving,' he croaked through the static and I felt

like Al Jolson, filming on the Coast, about to receive a new song from the hit-maker. But this morning he felt like telling me priceless stories about the good old days in Tin Pan Alley, about his childhood in Temun, Russia, and the sorrowful minor key melodies he heard there. And about how, exactly, and detail for detail, he'd come to write 'Alexander's Ragtime Band'.

I was about to ask whether he'd known Scott Joplin (because of a desire to knit art to commerce) when I was rudely woken up.

'EAT ME ALIVE!' commanded a voice barely riding an industrial crash of rock music cut jagged from blood-dripping sheet metal. 'EAT ME ALIVE!' The singer was forcing the girl to perform fellatio at gunpoint. 'Eat me for breakfast any time, lady,' drawled the snivelling deejay through his abused nose. I recognized the Screaming Eagle. 'That was Judas Priest at number one on the K-SMASH top forty. And now here's a message from your friendly coke dealer. That's Coca-Cola, folks – don't get me wrong!'

I had been snatched from the misty dream back onto the road of the 1980s, a road lined with ghetto blasters telling me the old, old story in high-tech electronics. A Chinese torture of continuous riffs raided from the blues larder. Those blues have a lot to answer for. So does syncopation. Maybe we should blame ragtime for stimulating the desire for non-stop syncopation – the thrust from the groins – back in the Victorian Age? We must connect the past to the present.

But I couldn't blame ragtime. Because ragtime was my sanctuary from the electrical storms of the eighties. Ragtime was my escape into the misty world of the mouldy fig.

K-SMASH, the sound of today playing the hits of tomorrow, had been activated into screaming by my bedside alarm clock/radio made by Toshiba with a simulated woodgrain finish of polystyrene. I dialed up a calmer station. Synthesizers placidly washed along a siren voice singing of having a compass and building one's house on a solid rock.

I'd landed on a religious station in pop clothing. 'Satan wins his greatest victory when he's ignored,' lectured the

2

host in the voice of God. I twiddled again and landed on a classical music station, coming in on a talk about Bach.

I wish I knew more about Bach and Beethoven and all those well-schooled composers. I wish I could read and write music. But, despite teachers, I remain a musical dyslexic, ruled by the ear. 'Don't stamp your foot to the étude,' said a bad teacher back in schooldays. 'Only Tin Pan Alley illiterates do that.'

And in reaction (and emotion) I dived into that very Alley. A world of June honeymoons, lost children looking for dead fathers, ragtime Romeos, yearnings for the old swimming hole on a hot summer day near the green, green grass of Wyoming. In the smoking city beyond the hill was Alexander, forever ragging and prancing. Stamping his foot.

Surely the beat was the pulse, was the heart of music? Surely rhythm came first? Drumbeats before melody, harmony and counterpoint. So there had been nothing wrong with beating time into a musty old piano exercise – probably written by Bach. But all the while I'd been longing to escape this spinster teacher and race to my study to play again the new record of Bill Haley & the Comets.

Ironically, the Big Beat is now a curse for me. Its current ubiquity sets my nerves jangling as it invests cars, houses, beaches, woods. Walter Brattain, eighty-two, the inventor of the transistor, is on my side: 'The only regret I have about my invention is that it's used for rock & roll. I still have my rifle and sometimes when I hear that noise I think I could shoot them all.'

The Bach programme on the classical station suddenly ended. A deep, sea-breezy voice announced a message on behalf of Investment Bankers, Inc. I felt disgusted. (But wasn't money-making a driving motive behind the Tin Pan Alley song salesmen?) I switched to a Country & Western station hoping to hear the Alley traditions continuing in this hitherto conservative repository of well-made songs.

But I heard the bland leading the bland into a land of tight formats and soft options. A dreary countrypolitan love song by Crystal Gayle with an adult-contemporary theme, fine-tuned to appeal to the 'romantically eligible family market which is the target of today's advertisers'. I read that somewhere.

I violently punched the 'Off' button on my Toshiba. Then I plumped up a pillow on the California king-size bed and, with garish local birds singing demented songs outside the window, I lay back and gazed in stupefaction at the framed reproductions on the bedroom wall.

The alarm of 1980s radio had roused me and now I was working up the right mood with which to beat a new day.

Computerized figures from the Toshiba flashed me the time: 5.15 and two millionth of a second. By 6 a.m. I had to be on the air at K-SMASH. But as the station was only a mile down the road there was still time for some picture therapy.

On the wall in front of me was Constable's *Hay Wain*, bought in a Pasadena shopping mall. Summer countryside frozen for keeps, soothing rather than provocative, confirming the past rather than creating the future. Oldies but Goodies.

To the left of my bed was a bulletin board posted with a homily I'd read in some magazine: 'Coming to terms with the past is a valid way of coming to terms with the present.' Excellent. A rationale for my mood. I'd like to live in that sure world depicted on the covers of old sheet music. I could 'Settle Down in a One-Horse Town', wearing overalls, strolling with the girl in the gingham dress—as written and copyrighted by Irving Berlin in New York, 1914.

I made a mental note to call his New York office after the radio show. The usual attempt to speak to my idol.

So here I was, stranded at the end of the twentieth century, retreating into the turn of the century ragtime and ballads, even retreating into a warm green womb of charming and harmless prints of a vanished rural England. An obsessive nostalgiac – and not even for my own youth.

After ablutions, and with my plastic case filled with eclectic records – ragtimers, comedians, and the like – I was ready for the K-SMASH show. As I opened the door of my Honda Accord my dog Beefy jumped in to claim the front passenger

4

seat. It's a ritual, like the placing of the call to Irving Berlin Music Corp. I like ritual routines, don't you?

I was backing out of the driveway when my neighbour Oliver ambled up. An early riser, too. Oil executive. Like most of my neighbours in sunny Altadena, he's black. Smiling widely, suited and tied, he signalled to me to roll down the window. You do that in these parts. He said: 'It'd be real nice to see your grass a bit trimmer.' I told him I'd booked a gardener for next week. Then I asked how his gospel church plans were going. 'We're getting close. Found a location. Hope you don't mind the sacred music from the house every now and then.'

Actually, the hymns float from his *garage*. Of an evening a heavenly white light fans from under the door and the street is filled with glad tidings. I've wondered whether he objects to the secular syncopations that my player piano gives out on such piano rolls as 'Everything in America Is Ragtime' (Irving Berlin, 1916). Oliver's too polite to tell me outright. One time his children's piano teacher suggested it might be nice to go easy on the bluesier numbers.

As I drove down Los Robles towards Pasadena and the station I thought about blacks. I often think about blacks. The stereotype of the dandy darky, the nigger minstrel of the nineteenth century, still persists today. The hot-zip coon. We still assume that blacks are born with rhythm, that they can all quite naturally tap dance, moan the blues or shout the gospel. But Oliver and his garage congregation sing straight-laced beatless hymns; his son bangs a drum kit often after school—very badly because he has no sense of rhythm. The late Eubie Blake, the black composer of 'I'm Just Wild About Harry' and ragtime pieces like 'Charleston Rag', once told me that his favourite composer was Leslie Stuart, the British church organist who wrote such demure and dainty songs as 'Tell Me, Pretty Maiden' and 'Lily of Laguna'. Eubie also loved Bach and Mozart, etc. He said Berlin was a sad man with a sharp ear.

Maybe it was us whites who invented the strutting, shuffling, syncopating darky fantasy? Maybe we needed a freewheeling alter ego, a beat-crazed outlaw who would

5

devil-dance us out of our well-ordered world of maths and business and into a dream chaos?

Pondering away as I drove through my largely black neighbourhood, with its tree-lined, tidy streets and charming spic-and-span houses, I almost ran through a red light. Shuddering next to me, and champing for the Git-Go of the green light, was a low-slung motorboat of a car commanded by a jet-black youth. He was pounding his wheel, yelping and shaking his dreadlocks to the strict mechanized bash of a rap record. Deep in a rhythm trance, eyes glassy, tarantula hair venomous, he terrified me, summoning up from Hades all my nightmares of the tinted menace. So out of the window went my theories of sweetly reasonable, law-abiding blacks.

To counter the threat from this jukebox on wheels I switched on my radio, loud. Prince, current rock hero, was finishing a song about masturbation. 'That was a commercial-free three records in a row. Sheena Easton, Cyndi Lauper and Prince – rapping on the old topic of beating the meat. Get educated on K-SMASH! Next up, at the 6 a.m. spot is Ian Whitcomb with some blasts from the past and a few cobwebs too, ha-ha!'

I made my usual stop at the AM/PM market for coffee and Danish pastry. The dog was jumping for his ritual pepperoni stick as the Armenian assistant dangled it over the counter when the black customer spoke up: 'When are you people gonna clean up your act in Lebanon?' 'I'm not from Lebanon,' replied the Armenian wearily. 'Well, wherever,' said the customer, slapping down his gas money.

Nor is the Armenian from Arabia, Palestine, Iran or Canvey Island. But what's the use? I've spent wasted time explaining that there's no bridge between Ireland and England and that baseball's roots are in the English game of rounders.

It must have been dizzying for Irving Berlin when, as the child Izzy Baline, he arrived with his family in the New York of the 1890s. No melting pot as yet. A babble of foreign languages, a mêlée of races, and a master people speaking English. But soon he'd mastered English and by his teens was writing songs drenched in slang and poking fun at the race circus: 'Oh, How That German Could Love!', 'Cohen Owes Me 97 Dollars'. Such songs cleared the air of tension. Today, they would be considered racial slurs.

K-SMASH is not a pretty station but it is dedicated to money music not visuals. Inside the shack, under a yellow light, I noted the Miller High Life beer bottle perched on the staircase bannister as I trod the sick-green carpet, avoiding contact with the sticky turd-brown compressed cardboard walls. Set into a lunar-landscape mural is the programme director's office door. It was open and soon Beefy was in there and laying a monster turd as he likes to do whenever possible. I encourage this because the P.D. has never liked my show, never seen the relevance of the old songs. Talks only in numbers, ratings, charts. Hasn't time for music for its own sake.

But had Berlin time for that? Didn't he once issue the statement: 'A good song is a hit song, a hit song is a good song'? If only I could catch him at his office. If only he'd call me.

'Hey baby, you're on!' Amid the fried-chicken cartons, pizza cases, joint papers and other junk littering the control room stood the Screaming Eagle. 'C'mon, or else Rick'll get on your case.' Rick Krupp: programme director and Scientology graduate.

But Chris Chaos, my engineer, hadn't turned up. Knowing little about electrical matters I am provided with a teenager to spin the discs, check the meters, call up the weather bureau. All I do is talk. 'You'll have to work the board yourself,' shouted Eagle as he left. I had a dreadful time getting the right tracks on. Finally, I resorted to feeding in tape cartridges, starting off with a 'Wet Bikini' contest announcement and following with a Public Service message about teenage alcoholism.

Music today can be reduced to the binary code of digital technology. Wild wood notes, heart-wrenching harmonies, jungle drums, an 'aaaargh!' – all analyzed into numbers and plusses and minuses. As a child I had run to music as an escape from inhuman maths. In music you flew around in clouds of emotion, plucking whichever mood you wanted. Behind the curtain draping the cabinet horn of the wind-up gramophone was an orchestra of tiny players waiting to play at the flick of a switch. I could work the switch, I could screw in the needles.

Still – Lenin, father of Soviet Russia, had trouble putting in a light bulb. And as for Berlin – he can't operate a record player at all. In my quest for Berlin I once got as far as the offices of the Irving Berlin Music Corporation, New York. The suite was musty and decorated in late forties style. And there were paintings of sad-eyed clowns and perfect Asian girls, all set in black velvet and framed in gold. They were each signed in big letters: 'Irving Berlin'. The record player was a forties phonograph, covered in dust. I asked the little bird-woman who presided over the office whether Mr Berlin had played my recordings of his obscurer ragtime songs. The ones I'd sent him. She said secretively: 'I'll tell you – this is off the record: I had to play your record to him over the phone. You see, he doesn't understand electrical things.' We have something in common. I felt a kinship.

In 1912 he wrote 'When I Lost You' in response to the tragic death of his wife while on honeymoon. Now, these harmonies could be binarily identified but I respond to them with an aching heart. And I was singing 'When I Lost You' *a cappella* when Chris Chaos finally arrived. I'd run out of cartridges to play. Of course, the phones were lighting up madly so I sampled some calls while Chris steered K-SMASH back onto its right course.

The phone said: 'What is this crap you're singing, man? Cut this old shit, I wanna hear what's happening *now*, I wanna hear . . .' But I cut him off by pressing the next flashing button: 'I just dropped some acid and I wanna hear Bowie.' Another button: a Buena Park girl needed some Scritti Politti or Springsteen to help her through her sales work. Another button: 'Fuck you, mouldy fig.' Another: 'There's nothing wrong with remaking the past in your own image.' Hey, I liked that. What's your name? 'Laura. I work as a seamstress and I love your accent. Keep showing us the roots of today.' She offered her home number and an ecological meal, anytime.

Taking the bull by the horns I ordered Chris Chaos to play a Scott Joplin record. Phone buttons began blinking immediately. I was getting fed up with complaints, I wasn't young and I wanted breakfast. I picked up the phone and pressed the button with the red light: 'Don't give me any more shit, I beg of you.' 'Put the Phil Collins before the Mick Jagger and then power-play Katrina and the Waves. And lay off the roller-skate rink music.' 'But that's Scott Joplin.' 'And this is Rick Krupp. I never sleep. This is ratings week. Let's put our energy together and go after the competition for a 10 per cent share of the market! Or you're fired!'

After the show I had breakfast at my regular coffee shop. My mind won't stop working; it was still pondering things like: how can I relate ragtime and Tin Pan Alley at the dawn of the century to the morass of here and now? I love Today when it's Yesterday.

The Chinese-American waitress smilingly brought me my usual dish: tuna melt on sourdough with coleslaw. At the next table two overalled workers were, typically, earnestly discussing the military-industrial complex and its relationship to the racial make-up of America. If only, one said, the government would consult them then matters might be straightened out. Over the music system a thousand and one strings were playing 'Let's Face the Music and Dance'. Berlin had written this during the Great Depression. Still relevant. In the *Herald Examiner* I was reading as I chewed tuna melt: Duluth, Minnesota – a former weathercaster person is suing her TV station bosses for $8 million, claiming she was told to wear revealing clothing and sit in a suggestive manner while delivering the weather report. She was fired when she refused to wear a microphone that accentuated her breasts. I bet Irving could have thought up a good topical song based on this item. Something on the lines of his 1909 hit, 'Sadie Salome, Go Home!' Item: a twenty-five-year-old man remains in a comatose state after swallowing parts of a broken ping-pong bat during a PCP-induced rage after losing a match to a teenage boy. Of course, there was no PCP or LSD around in Irving's youth. But down in the Bowery, in Chinatown, there was plenty of opium available.

Reliable sources tell me that many songwriters picked up the opium habit while working as singing waiters and such, down in the depths of the Bowery where self-indulgence was rampant. Of course, I'm not suggesting Irving indulged but I sometimes wonder whether the Alley's magic web of silv'ry moons and red-hot coons and frankfurters in revolt ('The Terrible War in Snider's Grocery Store', 1914) was spun within clouds of opium. But can we name the Alley dopers?

I needed to do some solid research. I needed to get my facts straight. I needed some sleep badly. When I got home I tried calling the Berlin office but the bird-woman said he wasn't there, he wasn't ever likely to be there, and even if he was there he wouldn't necessarily be talking to me. But if I wanted to record some more of Mr Berlin's songs she'd be only too glad to mail me professional copies. Everyone was recording Mr Berlin's songs, even the modern synthesizer people.

I took a Valium, looked at the Constable and sank back onto the pillows of my bed. Soon I was in Alleyland on Robinson Crusoe's Isle under a ragtime moon listening to the midnight choo-choo leaving for Alabam . . .

At 6 p.m. the radio alarm clock woke me to the peaceful drone of an all-news station. Hijackings, a jumbo disintegrates in mid-air, an old film star passes away. I jumped up and started to get ready for my impending cabaret appearance that evening at the Variety Arts Center. Pin-striped suit, Trinity College Dublin tie, and a selection of ukuleles. The uke is a very handy tool: I have wooed girls in punts with it; have kept audiences at bay when electricity failed or pianos were found to have no strings; in an underground car park in San Francisco I won a contested parking spot by aiming my uke case at a gangster-chauffeur type and telling him I was 'fully armed'. The uke is very useful.

The Variety Arts Center, dedicated to the preservation of the variety arts is a five-storey 1920s building in downtown L.A. This area, with splendid Victorian gingerbread houses and art nouveau and deco buildings, has long been abandoned to the poor, the mad and the evil. The better fed, whose ancestors once lived here, now cluster in antiseptic suburbs of pastiche: useless Tudor beams nailed to Olde Spaghetti Factories where joggers with leather patches on

10

their new tweed jackets drink ancient Irish ale from Colorado.

In the celebrated Roof Garden, atop the Variety Arts Center, a mixed bag had assembled. Some, the older folk, were my fans; some were actual members of the public. A few were members of an organization I belong to: the Maple Leaf Club, dedicated to the preservation of classic ragtime. Unfortunately, old things tend to attract social misfits and the latter were here in force tonight – tilted of body, boss-eyed, with speech impediments and body odours. This has never been good for my image as an all-round entertainer.

A rag fan buttonholed me, spitting peanut fragments, to discuss the dichotomy in the intro to Scott Joplin's 'The Entertainer'. Luckily, I was rescued by Art Deco (his stage name), the house-band leader, who wanted to talk over the accompaniment to my act.

Management, in an attempt to fill the house, had allowed the Knights of the Pythian Temple to hold their annual dinner here this evening. Before anybody could attack the salad bar the Knights insisted on a 'solemn invocation' with hands over hearts, followed by candles held aloft, as prayers were offered for the American hostages held somewhere in Beirut. I'd forgotten about that incident.

But would the Knights enjoy my cabaret trip through the sometimes arcane byways of Alleyland? I gave them my all from ragtime to rock. I showed how, 'When Alexander Takes His Ragtime Band to France' (1918), the Germans two-stepped back to Berlin, mesmerized by American syncopation. The cultural invasion of Europe (and then the world) had been started by ragtime and would soon be joined by jazz, swing and rock & roll. Finally, in the sixties, the Old World got its revenge by counter-attacking with the Beatles and the other British invaders (I had been one of them, for my sins). American bounce countered by European decadence!

The Knights and their ladies liked the act. The evening was saved and I had managed to put across my response to the late twentieth century. If only Irving had been out there to set his seal of authenticity on the show.

It was a horrible time of night. I was awake and the world was asleep but in the silence I could hear creatures scurrying about. So I turned on the bedside lamp, the one with the huntsmen all round the shade, and I looked at a framed photo on the bedside table. My father and mother in deck-chairs near Bognor with me behind them and all of us in summer holiday clothes, 1949. Left behind in London were bombsites and hot milk. Ahead was the end-of-pier show with dancing girls and comedians performing in front of the end of a painted rainbow which splashes onto the little village on the edge of the enchanted forest.

The phone knocked me out of the reverie. The radio alarm clock said 3.05 a.m.

'Hello?'

'This is Irving Berlin speaking. I heard the records you made of some of my songs. They're OK and I'm flattered but fascinated that you'd want to dig them up. They're old, very old. Too old.'

A high-pitched buzzy voice running with the choke out. I paused and then put myself on automatic pilot: 'To me they're new and timeless and . . . relevant. I love ragtime . . .'

'Ragtime? I never found out what it was.'

'But you put it on the world map!'

'Listen, I wrote about what people wanted to hear. I packaged their feelings and sold them back. They wanted to laugh, they wanted to cry, they wanted to dance. I serviced them. I met the market.'

'And you also wrote about what you felt in your heart. The memories of Russia, of your childhood. I can hear that in those minor key strains. I can hear the pain.'

'Bullshit! If the Tsar wanted to be a customer he had to pay for his song copy just like the public. You know one of his military bands had a hit with my Alexander song?'

'What year was that, sir?'

'Who's talking dates? I'm not a history book. Tell me about today, about how hearts work today. I hear you're on a rock & roll station . . .'

'I often play "Everything in America Is Ragtime", the song you wrote in 1916 . . .'

'Jesus! Dates, dates, dates! Stop trying to bury me in a Siberian winter . . .'

'Speaking of which . . .'

'Look, I gotta go before you trap me. I'll call you up some morning again, soon.'

But he never did, and so I decided to re-arrange the fire that had licked the century into shape.

2

The Yiddishe Yankee Doodle

By the 1920s American music had kidnapped the world democratically and the Jazz Age set in. Patriots like Hitler and Stalin attempted to release their respective cultures but they failed. Ironically, it had been Alexander III who had fathered this insidious invader. What a lively to-and-fro between the Old World and the New! And wriggling in the woodpile was the Afro-American—thus involving a North American Third World as well!

Here's how Alexander fits into the game: following the assassination of his liberal father in 1881, the new Tsar revived with utmost brutality the anti-Jewish pogroms.* These created a spontaneous mass exodus to America, land of the free. The pogroms were to continue until 1906 and among those who escaped were the families of George and Ira Gershwin, of Al Jolson, of Sophie Tucker, and of lesser lights such as L. Wolfe Gilbert ('Waiting for the Robert E. Lee') and Jack Yellen ('Happy Days Are Here Again'). But, most significantly of all, from Siberia came the family of Irving Berlin.

These refugee children grew up to create a body of indigenous work that seemed, to outside ears, twangy, slangy and very, very Yankee. Inside America, Jerome Kern, the great Jewish-American composer who had been nurtured in

*Pogrom is a Russian word meaning a violent mass attack on any ethnic group living within the community that is not a true offspring of Mother Russia. The first anti-Jewish pogrom was in 1871 in Odessa, birthplace of L. Wolfe Gilbert, the noted Tin Pan Alley lyricist and raconteur.

English musical comedy, pronounced in the early twenties:
'. . . Irving Berlin has *no* place in American music. HE IS
AMERICAN MUSIC.'*

As we shall see, in their new 'Promised land' the refu-
gees were to find pop music's basic ingredients already scat-
tered about: British ballads, jigs and reels; German marches
and polkas; the syncopation-soaked lifestyle of the black-
and-white under-mass—folk music from the forsaken home-
lands.

One of the great contributions of the Jewish newcomers
was to gather together these bits and pieces of an insular
society and feed them into their song factory in New
York—Tin Pan Alley. From the Alley poured streamlined
manufactured product for home consumption and the international market. One sing of their song products told the
world that the music-message was 'Made in USA'—and
proud of it, too!

Yet Irving Berlin, as one of the Tsar's rejected children,
was aware of those European roots which contributed to
ragtime and jazz. In 1920, at the top of his trade and acknowledged as spokesman for the Alley song salesmen, he
had developed a nice skill in theory-spinning. Here he is
outlining the ingredients of the great American musical
stew to Frank Ward O'Malley of *American Magazine:*

> The syncopated, shoulder-shaking type of vocal and in-
> strumental melody, which has now been dignified interna-
> tionally as 'typical American music' is not wholly, or
> even largely, of African origin as is popularly supposed.
> Our popular song writers and composers are not negroes.
> Many of them are of Russian birth and ancestry. All of
> them are of pure white blood. As in the case of every-
> thing else American, their universally popular music is
> the product of a sort of musical melting pot. Their dis-
> tinctive school is a combination of the influences of

*This quote comes at the end of a testimonial letter about Berlin. Kern
wrote it in response to a request by Alexander Woollcott who was writing the authorized biography: *The Story of Irving Berlin,* published by
Putnam, New York, in 1925.

Southern plantation songs, of European music from almost countless countries and of the syncopation that is found in the music of innumerable nationalities . . . Therefore, those who label our popular dance and song music as 'typical American music' hit the bullseye in so naming it. For it is the syncopation of several lands and centuries 'Americanized'.

Irving Berlin, self-made and self-assured young man in a hurry, defining and refining with, no doubt, all his being pricking. At the top of the heap, the Compleat Alleyman—able to join art with commerce, to hammer out songs in all genres, to tap into America and himself (often the same creature) and to sell song moods to a public that recognized these as their own. A salesman of dreams and also a prime example of the American Dream come true: from ghetto poverty to riches and fame.

His success in the teen years of the twentieth century, as the captain of the pop juggernaut, is spectacular, of course. (From the twenties onwards he gradually lost his supremacy and, as a study in perpetual motion, he is no longer so interesting.) But, though he is my central focus, I want also to examine the world of American ragtime because I consider its era to be the gunpowder plot that banged us into what we are today. In fact, ragtime was a crucial ingredient of this explosive era. Its repercussions have rolled into present-day rock, whether I like it or not. So, while I will be tracing the story of Irving Berlin, I shall also be putting him in the period picture alongside his colleagues and rivals and raw field material (the blacks, the country folk) and the song legacy of the nineteenth century. Suddenly, it all came together in a rush of feverish activity in the crucial crucible of New York at the turn of the century. And Alexander III had played his part in creating an Alexander who led a ragtime band.

Irving Berlin was born Israel Baline in Temun, Siberia, on 11 May, 1888. Temun was an illegal Jewish town because it was outside the official Pale of Settlement.* At that

*The Berlin birthplace is currently in dispute. In legal documents (as opposed to press statements) Berlin seemed unable to decide exactly where he was born. Place follows place in a merry chase for the biographer

16

time more than 50 per cent of the world's Jews lived within the Russian Empire. The Jews were a nation within a nation, subject to hundreds of harsh regulations, and lately, pogroms. They lived in closed communities, ghettos, within the cities or outside them in *shtetls*—forbidden to farm, to become civil servants, to marry gentiles, to travel abroad. Forbidden to become army officers but always a good source of cannon fodder for the Great White Silent One, the largest and worst-organized army in the world. As eldest sons were exempt from military service (an uncommon Tsarist kindness) there was much inventing of new family names by the Jews. The Balines had not had their present name very long.

Israel was one of eight children born to Leah, wife of Moses, a cantor in the synagogue of Temun. This village was a blot in the wilderness and the synagogue was a fetid shanty with animals wandering in and out, making themselves known. But when Moses sang he soared himself into another, better place. The ancient tunes buzzed around in minor modes but then, unexpectedly, they burst high in triumphant major. The rabbi wanted Moses to study more than he sang, to read the never-changing Word that assured Jews they were safe in their spiritual and cultural time-warp in Russia so long as they avoided Western thought and ways (even clocks) and prayed for the Tsar. The Little Father, as head of the Russian Orthodox Church, was required to remind his people that the Jews were Christ-killers and were thus eternal enemies of the keepers of the true faith. The decadent West had long ago left the path of righteousness.

Moses sang on, rejoicing to be above it all for the short

---

hound. However, *The New Grove Dictionary of American Music* states that he was born in Tyumen, a city about 175 miles east of Sverdlovsk. Scholars have told me that it's unlikely that any Jewish settlements existed outside of The Pale and that therefore Temun, Siberia, was an Irving Berlin fiction. But why would he invent his birthplace? And why Siberia? The Great Man remains an enigma and I like to believe in this feisty little village on fire in bone-aching ice-blue Siberia. Scholars will have to *prove* Temun never existed before I change my tune.

ecstasy time he was in the synagogue. At home he ruled like a Tsar in the strict and restrictive Judaic traditions. Life might have seemed irksome to Israel Baline: God was watching you everywhere. From the dawn bath to the night straw cot, everything was of religious significance. God was in the food and in the clothing. When Moses caught Israel pulling on his little shoes in a manner proscribed by the Talmud he beat him.

The floor of the Baline hut-home was of hard black dirt. Outside, the squiggly streets of Temun were either mud or dust according to the season. Lining the squiggles were horrid wooden huts. Sometimes wild pigs would rage into town and bite children to death.

It was not a setting to sing about. Maybe, through idealized identification, those merry darky songs about log cabins by the Swanee River might have eased the situation for the inhabitants. But American minstrel show tours, though active in the St Petersburg circuit, never reached Siberia. Instead, cantor Moses took his children to the synagogue where, in soothing sing-song readings from the Talmud, the cares of the day were eased away.

Life in Temun sounds pretty awful but, in later years, Irving Berlin said he was unaware of being raised in abject poverty. He knew no other life and there was always hot food on the table, even if it was God-riddled. To please his father he would pipe the age-old, never-changing liturgical tunes. He had a good voice and Moses pictured a cantor's life ahead for Israel.

And there he might have remained, living the old ways in this time-warp, with revolutions going by, until he became a citizen of the USSR; perhaps writing some state songs, smuggling in jazz records, reading about the Elton John concert in Moscow. But, suddenly one day, the Cossacks rampaged in on a pogrom and the cocoon was burst open.

As Temun was an illegal Jewish settlement there was no need for the Cossacks to stand on ceremony—they simply burned it to the ground. Israel and his family watched from a distant road. Israel was wrapped in a warm feather

18

quilt. Then they made a hasty exit. Knowing that they were breaking the law by leaving without a passport (Russia at that time was the only country requiring passports), the Balines smuggled themselves creepingly from town to town, from satellite to satellite, from sea to shining sea, until finally they reached their star: the Statue of Liberty.

In 1892, when the Balines (minus two of Israel's older brothers who'd decided to quit the exodus while still in Russia) arrived in New York harbour after the month-long ordeal aboard ship (though Israel had been comfy in his mother's feather bed) the infamous Ellis Island 'reception centre' was within months of opening. They were dumped at the Battery where the immigration authorities treated them like cattle. They poked at their privates with dirty rubber gloves, they chalked marks on their clothing, they awarded them a number and let them keep the family name.

New York had a reputation as the loudest, rudest and most congested of cities. The citizens worked hard to live up to the reputation and spurned welcome wagons. None of them gave a hoot for yet another bunch of raw and untreated Jews. They were blocking the sidewalk with their baggage. Then a red-haired Tammany man signed up the Balines as voters. Then a sallow-faced man in a shiny striped suit and derby hat pulled up in a horse and cart. He didn't look like a Jew but he turned out to be Moses's cousin and he'd come to take them to their new home. The messages had got through, he said in their own language, the Yiddish of well-ordered Russia. Soon they were all up on the cart and heading for Manhattan.

To Americans up the ladder, both Early Colonial and Late Jewish, the Lower East Side of Manhattan was a contemptible neighbourhood. A malodorous kitchen with a bubbling, babbling stewpot of threatening ethnics. It was the manifest destiny and duty of the denizens of this hellhole to raise themselves out of such wretchedness by their very own bootstraps. With pluck, luck and ruthlessness they might do well in the great race for riches.

19

In his best-selling inspirational boy's books Horatio Alger, Jr, a defrocked minister, showed how the lad that struggles hard against poverty and temptation will inevitably become rich and famous. Excellence, as a virtue, is not mentioned. But his Ragged Dicks and Tattered Toms end their race with plenty of steaks and gold.

However, in the Lower East Side of that period there were plenty of Paddys, Antonios and Hans Gustavs hanging around the mean streets, dead-ended, on the curb of criminality. Their racial elders ran the neighbourhood, the tribal chiefs at present being the Irish, the Italians and the Germans. Politically, the Jews were nowhere (except as the occasional anarchist). At this stage they couldn't even boast of a decent gang. They were racially the lowest of the low in this most densely populated part of New York (700 dwellers to every acre).

Rudyard Kipling, living not far away up the coast during this era, was shocked and intrigued by the screeching squalor he found in the dirty grey tenement canyons of immigrant New York. He thought it worse than the notorious slums of Bombay. But he was impressed and moved by the Jews, noting the little immigrant boys saluting the Stars and Stripes, and the grubby man with greasy curls who was kneeling amid the filth of his one-room rat-trap to bless and then consume two immaculate, ritual, orthodox buns.

Kipling was struck not only by the immaculate food but also by the abundance and importance of feather beds in Jewish immigrant life.

To a family they all seem to sport fine examples. How they have the strength and perseverance to convey them from East to West defeats me. But such attachment to the familial feather bed indicates a sense of values that places comfort and physical well-being as a number one priority. This is something that our Empire Builders, with all their high ideals, could well learn from. For these immigrant Jews are a race that survives and thrives against all odds and flags.

Sophie Kalish (later to be Sophie Tucker, 'The Last of the Red-Hot Mamas') was born in a feather bed during her escape from Russia to America, and in Boston her father sometimes hid under it when he spotted a man of military bearing; the Yoelson family (containing the future Al Jolson) lugged their bed all the way across from Russia too; and, as we have seen, Israel had snuggled in a very acceptable one during their recent American voyage.

And, at present, this multi-coloured quilt was being firmly sat upon by Mrs B as the rickety cart negotiated its way through those teeming, tangled East Side streets—past jams of pushcarts piled with shiny rubbish and kosher snacks, through a constant barrage of strange cries (the most common being 'get-outta-der-way' and 'shuddup'), around conference knots of the orthodox in their familiar long beards, broad hats and trailing black coats.

The journey ended at Monroe St, in the depths of the Lower East Side. Their new home was a cold-water basement flat with no windows.

A little later they moved to a better tenement in a better ghetto: the Italian quarter, titled by fearful outsiders as the 'Spaghetti Zone'—where moustached knife grinders were supposedly sharpening stilettos for assassins; where Black Hand extortionists roamed the streets; where bred the Mafia. The Balines, though, settled nicely into 330 Cherry Street on the third floor of a solid brownstone building dating from the Civil War with a chocolate store on one side and Kennedy's Classic Stables on the other.

We know about the Cherry Street home in some detail because, in the late 1950s, Irving Berlin took a sentimental journey down to the old neighbourhood in the company of a journalist. A childhood situation that sounds most unpleasant to me appeared rosy in retrospect to Berlin. After a dinner which included wild duck and pancake in crabmeat the author of 'Annie Get Your Gun' and 'God Bless America' stood on the pavement looking up lovingly at the dear old slum.

You know, you never miss luxury until you've had it. I never felt poverty because I'd never known anything else. Our family was enormous. There were nine of us in three rooms, and in the summer some of us slept on the

21

fire escape or on the roof. I was a boy with poor parents, but let's be realistic about it: I didn't starve; I wasn't cold or hungry. There was always bread and butter and hot tea. I slept better in that tenement house than I do right now in my nice bed in Beekman Place.

Meanwhile, back in 1892, Moses Baline had to adjust to the laissez-faire life where there was no Little Father or Great Mother, where things were not set in the eternal circle but shot hither and thither madly like an explosion in a fireworks factory. Early on, Moses found out there were no openings for cantors at present. New York was choked with them. But Heaven forbid that he should sink to becoming a member of the working class, the drinking class. He wangled a part-time job as a *shomer,* a meat certifier in a kosher slaughterhouse. He taught Hebrew and the ancient straight and narrow ways to unwilling boys straining to race out into American sunlight. When the work load at Rosh Hashanah and Yom Kippur got too much for the local choir master Moses helped out in his proper calling.

His father had been a cantor. And his father before him and his father before him. Israel, pride of the family, was proving to have a clear, clean soprano voice with a talent for the traditional plangency. He might become a decent wailer; later, he could try the ecstatic songs of the Chasidim. He might make a rabbi, a cantor—the sky's the limit. But for present he must learn the doleful chant of the *schul* and study the Talmud and forget the myriad street sounds floating through the window.

But Israel was a rotten student. His father despaired of him. This boy was always escaping to gang up with goys who called him Izzy. This boy would rather be swimming in the slimy East River (he'd been taught by Irish gang members who'd thrown him in); or listening to embarrassing, excitable Chasidic Jews as they huckstered wares from pushcarts or just plain argued; or swapping Yiddish songs for Neapolitan love slush. A shame for the neighbours! But one of these neighbours had been impressed by Izzy's bravery—when the little black-eyed, black-haired tyke had kept

22

a bunch of Irish bully boys at bay by entertaining them with parodies of the current hit song.

After the ball is over, see her take out her glass eye;
Put her peg leg in the corner, screw up her bottle of dye.
Stick her false teeth in the drawer, hang up her wig in the hall
Then what was left went to bye-byes . . .
After the ball!

Keep 'em laughing and they'll lose their appetite for slugging you. Keep moving, keep talking. Talk! Izzy at eight had mastered the slang rhythms of the street while his mother (God protect her she should have to hear such stuff) had never learned Yankee speech and Moses spoke it in a well-nigh impenetrable accent.

Suddenly, in 1896, Moses died. Mrs Baline became openly what she had always been tacitly: the head of the family. Israel must go out and work.

So, at the age of eight, he left school to hawk newspapers and carry telegrams, and even to sew collars. At night, before supper, he was required to deposit the day's takings into his mother's aproned lap. He was assured of food and lodging no matter what. But just a few blocks from Cherry Street another world flickered enticingly. Free, wild, exciting: the Bowery! Over the years there had been plays, books, songs and reproving articles published about this gay and dangerous twilight zone of saloons, gambling hells and opium joints populated by a gaudy cast of painted women, bounders and rounders, and assorted pork-eaters. Already, during his newspaper hawking, Izzy had peeked into the odd saloon, heard the songs, seen the sights. And liked it.

One night, after dropping the money in the apron and eating the supper, he simply upped and left home and mother. He went on the bum in the Bowery. He was fourteen and it was a shame for the neighbours and for the local Jewry in general.

On the Bowery, garishly and splutteringly lit, was block after block of democracy alive and kicking like there was no tomorrow. At least six saloons and one dance hall for

23

every block, so the reformers claimed. Ladies of the pavement, of many races and colours; brazenly plying their trade under the eagle eyes of their owners. Rickety-rackety music from tavern pianos, German brass bands, strolling glee groups—making for a vital pageant that blew away the choking dust of Hebraic life with its restrictions and reproaches. No more long beards on long faces topped by forbidding skullcaps. But, also, no more safe and snug Cherry Street haven where were the eternities of a glass of hot tea, warm cake and an expansive mother at the altar.

A Jewish boy, well-raised, adrift now in a sea of alcohol! But, bothered or not, Izzy straightaway joined the rogues by becoming a Bowery entertainer. That very first night on the bum he plunged through the swinging doors of Callahan's beer joint and was soon impressing the clientèle with his punchy version of the current 1902 smash weeper, 'The Mansion of Aching Hearts'. He made the 15 cents necessary for a slat bed in a nearby flophouse.

For the next year or so he served the first part of his musical apprenticeship. He bum-busked. First as a duo, leading Blind Sol with one hand while the other hand clutched the tin money cup as they roamed from sawdust dive to penny ike to dives like the Bucket of Blood. Next, as a member of a busker boy gang, skulking the waterfront saloons like MacLear's, sometimes lurking in nearby alleys to pounce on some penny-laden solo singer. Then, branching out solo himself to beg nickels at the Choo-Choo Palace, Flea Bag and Suicide Hall. At Diamond Lottie's place he'd sidle up and give her his little boy grin; he'd break her into a laugh with a Hebrew dialect comedy song so that she'd display the diamond embedded in her front tooth; he could make the hookers water with a ballad about fallen country girls. Sweep up the pennies and on to Steve Brodie's, the ex-pugilist with the blind piano man and blood-soaked sawdust and black tobacco wads as trademarks of his saloon. Brodie was partial to knockabout Irish numbers like 'Throw Him Down, McCloskey', but in the wee hours, when the Tammany Hall politicians emerged from the back room, orders went out for some make-'em-cry stuff like 'The Picture That Is Turned Towards the Wall'. Watch big men cry! Micks with beefsteak faces and no necks, powerful thugs who controlled the politics and crime of New York (both the same thing) from these Bowery saloon back rooms.

Once Izzy got up when it was daylight and headed uptown for Tin Pan Alley, the song-factory street. He wanted to get to the source of his material. He wanted to meet the versatile man who could turn out a comic coon song one week and a tear-jerker the next. He wanted to be in the presence of a complete music machine emblazoned with the gilt-edged name: Harry Von Tilzer. What a resounding name! Izzy penetrated the inner office and directly he saw Von Tilzer he knew that this man was one of the boys who'd gone astray and forsaken the synagogue. But he looked the perfect gentleman in his frock coat and wing collar. A highly respectable industrialist and he appreciated the boy's drive. Sure he could have a job with the Harry Von Tilzer Music Company—he could go out and plug 'Rufus Rastus Johnson Brown'. Go get the copies from the professional department. So Izzy became a song plugger for a while and he enjoyed it, especially when he got to sing from the gallery in Tony Pastor's Music Hall. That was real show business. But there wasn't the quick money you got from Bowery busking and Izzy, now feeling he was a bit of a veteran, decided to return to street level and hit the saloons again. The pennies turned to nickels and dimes. He was a hit with the Irish bosses.

And one night, when he was on his way to Piggy Donovan's hash house, he bumped into Chuck Connors. This bottle-nosed gent was the self-styled Mayor of Chinatown, a magic warren not far from the Bowery, where the food was tasty and the opium out of this world. Connors, very much the big b-hoyo in his fur Derby and short green jacket, told Izzy he was too good for the likes of bums such as Brodie. Told him he could get the boy into a select busker gang on the cushy Chinatown slum circuit. Connors had a swell deal conducting Park Avenue dudes in nightly tours of the red-light districts. He liked the jewboy's way with a song parody but he should avoid wise-guy comedy at the Dead Rabbits club dances because the Plug Uglies—you know, the Five Points toughs with their hats stuffed with metal and leather—were visiting the Connors parish and looking for trouble, especially with uppity Jews. Izzy piped in that he didn't care for private functions like the Dead Rabbits because the orchestra was usually stuffed with flutes and piccolos and led by a professor who demanded written arrangements from busker boys like himself. Izzy said he was an entertainer not a long-hair. Connors said yes, yes, but he didn't have to sell himself so hard. Come along to my place and we'll talk terms over a stack of reds or maybe he preferred whites. Izzy said he'd rather talk over a stack of music-hall songs like the ones Mr Connors delivers so well at Callahan's to the judges and lawyers who know a fine line. Say, you're cute with the words, laughed Connors who was a Britisher and could rattle off lots of clever British songs like 'I Live in Trafalgar Square' and 'If It Wasn't for the 'Ouses in-Between'.

Izzy admired the words to the limey songs but the rhythms were kind of boggy. At Connors's joint that night he delivered some hits by George M. Cohan, the kid currently taking Broadway by storm with his razzamatazza jingo show *Little Johnny Jones.* When Izzy ended with Cohan's 'Yankee Doodle Boy' everybody in the joint applauded the feisty little fellow. Some tarts said they felt proud to be American; a couple of thugs, who specialized in chawing off ears and breaking legs, gave Izzy the nod. And Connors pronounced gravely (he'd had a few belts): 'You know what you are, me boy? You're the Yiddishe Yankee Doodle!'

After an encore, 'Give My Regards to Broadway', Izzy collected his money off the floor and left while the going was good. Broadway success was better than Bowery success and Cohan wasn't much older than himself. Clocks were ticking and Izzy was antsy. But for now it was the trudge to the lodging house for that 15-cent cubbyhole, open at the top—so he wore his pants as pajamas because a pal, a busker, had recently had his underwear stolen after

26

he'd hung them on the cubbyhole wall. You can't trust anybody. You got to lift off into the Cohan world. Was Cohan the mick who liked yids, or had his name originally been Cohen? The name is the mask and the mask is the man.

Izzy went to sleep on a good tip from Connors: next month 'Nigger' Mike Salter was opening a ritzy place in Chinatown. It'd be a prime stopping-off spot for Connors's slumming parties and so the tips'd be great. Izzy should apply fast for a job as a singing waiter. Connors and a judge or two were prepared to recommend him. It was a step up.

The Pelham Café, located at 12 Pell Street in the heart of Chinatown, opened in the spring of 1904. There was a ring of British classiness about the name, Pelham. New York Sunday papers in those days were full of fawning reports of the London Season. The café's front lived up to its name—decorated with ornate iron-trellis work and woven into the iron a sign in careful script informing that the Pelham specialized in Jetter Pure Beers and also served wines and spirits. Inside, in the traditional half-light, the proprietor would explain that no grub was sold and no Chinks were served.

Mike Salter was a Russian Jew so swarthy of hue and simian of build that he was nicknamed 'Nigger Mike'. And pretty soon the Pelham Café was popularly known as Nigger Mike's. Salter had long-established connections with the underworld, politicians and the police, and all these parties were to find his saloon a pleasant lair in which to do business or simply relax. Mike often had to act as honest broker in their ruptions but he also cultivated a reputation as a shady character himself. When he was drunk he would claim to have heisted many a bank and sometimes he would proceed to rob his own till. But when he was sober he could be a pussycat, paying for mobsters' funerals, slipping the widow a pint of rye in church, and letting needy fat girls work in his backroom brothel.

It was at dead of night that Nigger Mike's came alive— swarming with underworld types both flashy and fishy

Some shone with an unnatural glow and some were self-proclaiming dope fiends. Not a few were posing as reprobates. Mike encouraged all this local colour, very good for business and the tours.

For, at weekends, Chuck Connors would lead his slumming parties through the thrilling depths of the Lower East Side. Megaphone clamped to mouth, he'd point out such sights as Chinatown's opium parlours while ignoring the anatomical museums, second-hand clothes' stores, Chinese salvation mission and the dumpy Yiddish Theatre squashed under the elevated railway bridge. The party was speeding to the evening's climax: a few minutes' devilish fun at Nigger Mike's.

Sulky, the barman, slings beer to an army of tray-balancing bow-tied waiters. The more experienced can serve a party of eight with their different drink concoctions while singing the hits and kicking the nickels and never spilling a drop. Hunched at the thickset upright piano is Nick Michaelson, the orchestra. He knows every song-trick from Home and Mother through Coon Song to High-Class Ballad. Cigarette dangles as he pumps calmly, never showing any emotion even when a fight erupts; he's doing his job and it's all jakes so long as he gets paid on time.

Izzy Baline, sixteen, got along well there from the start. He already knew the latest songs, the latest slang, the latest attitude. He was becoming American. The tray-balancing and the nickel-kicking he was to learn from his protector Kutch Kutchinsky, head singing waiter and a brute with a foot like a crate. The boy's progress was watched by Jubal Sweet, one of the professional reprobates hired by Salter. Later, in 1924, Sweet told a reporter for *Liberty Magazine*:

> Like it was yesterday, I remember Oiving Berlin. Looked like a meal or two wouldn't hurt him. Wasn't strong and didn't look like he would get away with a nickel or a dime that one of the other guys claimed . . . This here Kutch sorta took to the kid and seen to it that nobody stuck nothing over on Oiving . . . Now a singing waiter couldn't be stooping over every time a coin hit the floor.

Spoil his song, like—see? No, he'd keep moving around easy, singing all the time, and every time a nickel would drop he'd put his toe on it and kick it or nurse it to a certain spot. When he was done he had all the jack in a pile, see?'

Oiving got to be pretty good at it, only he wasn't so casual like Kutch. Nervous like, and he had a neat flip of the ankle. Like you'd brush a speck offa the table with your fingers.

As a singing waiter Izzy was paid a flat $7 a week. As a nickel-kicker he could make up to $10 a week. Plus a bit of door-opening, he was totalling around $20 and that was OK money. His hours were from 8 P.M. till 6 A.M. or whenever Mike fell off his stool. Word was he was getting to be quite the entertainer and his timing on comedy songs was particularly skilful.

And so, for two years, he sang and he kicked and he slung at the Pelham. Tenderloin life grew to be routine—but there were diversions: like the night Frisco Joe, grabbing the gun from the house icebox, slew Hobnailed Casey because Hobnailed had decked pianist Michaelson for messing up his waltz. Izzy had to step in quick so he led with a comic punch, 'A Woman Is Only a Woman But a Good Cigar Is a Smoke', while Frisco Joe bled to death in the snow outside.

Another diversion was much nicer: Chuck Connors, minus his megaphone, came in one night bowing and scraping to one Prince Louis of Battenburg. The Prince had been tipped off to this saloon by his friend Grand Duke Paul Pavlovitch, the Tsar's uncle. Connors set a bunch of lagers down for the Prince and his party and signalled Izzy to entertain. So Izzy gave them a selection of George M. Cohan songs and the Prince laughed and clapped along strictly on the beat. He said the Grand Duke had been right—this was the genuine American article.

When he was leaving he pulled out a wad of notes and offered Mike a tip. The proprietor bowed and declined, adding it was payment enough just to be in His Highness's presence. The Prince turned and offered Izzy the wad but Izzy followed his boss's example. He said: 'It was my honour to sing to you.' He waved the money away and then skipped to the door to open it.

Wowee, such a gesture! But it got Izzy his first press notice. Herbert Bayard Swope, then a reporter for the *New York World,* was in the Prince's party and he wrote up the incident, singling out the magnanimity of Izzy Baline. Izzy was fixated by the sight of his name in print. But then he got to thinking it didn't look so good next to a resounding name like Battenburg. It looked lumpish.

Late in 1906 Mike Salter was in quite a kerfuffle. Callahan's, that dump round the corner, was drawing the patrons away from the Pelham—and not through their beer, broads and rough trade but through their music. Callahan's had sired a hit song: 'My Mariuccia Take a Steamboat', with words by Georgie Ronklyn, one of their waiters, and music by their resident pianist, Al Piantadosi. Everyone in town was going 'toot toot', making like boat whistles, trying to be stage Italians:

> I can't tel-la you how I feel-a
> Since she's gone away,
> I look-a just-a like de ba-na-na peel,
> Since that very terrible day

The sheet music indicated 'Three big long whistles' just after the *allegretto moderato* and there were more to come. Salter was going through a fragile period on the water wagon and the song was sending him to pink elephant land. To make matters worse the song was published by his one-time pal, Ted Barron, who hob-nobbed with senators and even dedicated songs to them.

Salter put the order out: we can beat Callahan's and their wop song. We'll produce our own house hit. Izzy was so nifty with the parodies—he should write the hit. But keep it clean. Get Nick Michaelson to knock out a tune. Do it quick.

The two employees patched together a similar jingly

30

wop-dialect song, calling their effort 'Marie from Sunny Italy'. Izzy took a few liberties—rhyming 'queen' with 'mandolin' (though it depended how your accent was). Nick's tune, as jumpingly rhythmic as Piantadosi's, raced like a bugle call and had some fine hooks.

A penniless young classical violinist transcribed the song because neither Izzy nor Nick could write music. Then the boss took the manuscript to a decent uptown publisher, Jos. Stern & Co. The firm had been founded in 1894 at the very start of Tin Pan Alley and had amassed lots of best-sellers. The professional manager judged the song to be quite singable and promised to give it the full push—or-chestrations, male quartette, the lot. And what names did the writers go under? Mike went back and asked the boys.

Izzy and Nick thought long and carefully. Izzy remem-bered Von Tilzer and also that an Alleyman had told him that Von's old name had been plain Gumm. Here was a chance to go Broadway, to shrug off the Talmudic traces. He told Nick and Nick said he'd never liked Michaelson anyway and that it had been given to the family by the im-migration officer because the real family name was un-pronounceable.

'Marie from Sunny Italy' was published as 'Words by I. Berlin, Music by M. Nicholson'. German and British, the cologne of class rather than the smell of steerage.

Immediately, Izzy went to town plugging his song. He bugged poor old Joe Stern daily, telling him that 'Marie' was always being encored at the Pelham. Joe replied that the patrons must be very easily pleased. Izzy asked for more free copies, Joe gave him a certain amount but was getting tired of this thrusting tyke. There were plenty of other Stern songs that needed attention and, anyway, 90 per cent of Alley product never clicked. Like many other pop publishers Stern had an arrangement with the garbage man to come round weekly and pick up the stacks of song 'dogs' out the back. 'Marie' soon proved to be a dog; all Izzy earned in royalties was 37 cents. And life at Mike's began to tumble down: the boss took exception to Izzy's mop of jet-black hair, complaining that it shot off into the air arrogantly. Then, one dawn, a drunk-as-a-skunk Mike snuck into the saloon when Izzy was supposed to be on guard duty but, in fact, was snatching a nap. Mike proceeded to steal $25 from his own cash register, and then woke Izzy to tell him he was fired for being asleep on the job while thieves were at work.

Izzy had little trouble getting a new position as a singing waiter. His reputation had spread. Jimmy Kelly's, a better dump than Nigger Mike's, offered him shorter hours and higher wages. Izzy took a clean apartment and spruced up his attire. Jimmy Kelly, although bozo-nosed, was sartorial-minded. He was a retired prize fighter who wore tails at his bar and recited weepy ballads and dirty jokes to those who accepted a free drink from him. His string of elegant singing waiters was adept at satisfying the taste of their boss: with a shift of voice tone and an eyebrow raised ever so archly, a clever waiter could metamorphose 'I Want What I Want When I Want It' (by musical comedy king Victor Herbert) into an awful smutty object.

From his first night it was apparent that Izzy was becoming very clever. Some said he was too much of a good thing and needed squashing. But he soon had an admirer who spotted something special in him. Max Winslow was professional manager of the Harry Von Tilzer Music Company and the two youngsters had first met when Izzy dropped by to 'The House of Hits' for some free 'artist' copies. Max gave him a bundle and told him to get plugging. Later, when Max visited Jimmy Kelly's, he was amused by the way the kid could turn a Von Tilzer corn-belt nostalgia number into a hot-blue parody. Max soon started taking a bunch of Alley boys down to the saloon to see what the little bastard would do to their songs. They usually had a good laugh and threw coins at him. Then Max discovered they lived in the same apartment building and that they both dreamed of moving on up.

Izzy told Max about his songwriting abilities and showed him 'Marie'. Max asked Harry Von Tilzer to try out Izzy at $20 a week. Harry nixed the idea. If he didn't remember the boy as an ex-house plugger he certainly had heard of his reputation as a purveyor of dirty parodies. Why, he'd poked fun at the farm! Von Tilzer was a man with a reputation as well as a wife and a high white collar.

Max shrugged, but Izzy had caught the songwriting bug. He knew that parodies, however clever, were never going to make him any royalties. He hummed a tune to the Kelly pianist and scribbled some lyrics based on the old saying, 'The Best of Friends Must Part'. And the published song was his first solo creation—but the sales were zilch. Still, he was starting to meet other songwriters and to exchange ideas. There was Maurie Abrams, a fellow Russian refugee. A good 'ear' man on the piano, he'd made useful Alley contacts and was published grandly as 'Maurice Abrahams'. Vaudeville acts, especially the animal variety, bought his material by the yard. Later, he was to write some big hits and marry singing star Belle Baker. But 'Queenie, My Own', the Berlin & Abrahams effort, got printed and that was all.

Izzy followed with another solo song, 'She Was a Dear Little Girl', which stage star Marie Cahill interpolated into her show, *The Boys and Betty*. Izzy was thrilled to be heard on stage but disappointed by the sales. Then his old rival Al Piantadosi, at liberty from Callahan's saloon, collaborated with him on 'Just Like a Rose' which withered and died at the House of Harry Von Tilzer. Around this time Izzy met Edgar Leslie, a Connecticut Yankee and fledgling wordsmith who hung out at such Alley commissaries as Lindy's restaurant and Kelly's saloon. Leslie was to achieve success later with his words to such classics as 'For Me and My Gal' and 'Among My Souvenirs'. But in 1908 he was living on his caustic wit, his favourite expression being 'What the hell', expressed drily and without emotion. It was the summary of his life's philosophy—for already he'd entered the school of hard knocks, Tin Pan Alley, armed only with his cunning way with words. He read lots of newspapers and magazines; he even read books. He worshipped Gilbert & Sullivan; his favourite song was Sullivan's 'The Lost Chord'.

But for the time being Leslie had to make do with a

song he put together with Izzy: 'Wait, Wait, Wait'. When they showed it to Max Winslow he agreed to show it to Mr Von Tilzer and the upshot was that the song made $200 in royalties. But just as Izzy thought he was nicely set up with Von Tilzer & Co. what did Max do but resign! He was to become professional manager at a brand-new publishing outfit with a rather daunting, rather educational, name—the Seminary Music Company. Max soon put a stop to that. Within weeks it was simply the Ted Snyder Music Company.* Within months it was 'Inc.'. And within time, if Max's plan went right, Izzy would be working there too.

Max told Izzy to come up and see them sometime when he had a hot number.

The Ted Snyder outfit was run by Snyder alright but it was bank-rolled and eagle-eyed by Henry Waterson (sometimes 'Watterson'), a diamond merchant and a terrifying presence. An older man. Ted Snyder was in his early twenties, a tall, lean, smart cracker with a long nose and a rich, pouty mouth. Raised in Chicago, he'd started his professional life as a bill sticker and then had moved up into free-lunch saloons where his piano playing competed with the patrons' din. When he graduated to night-time performances he found that people seemed to enjoy the little tunes he improvised after he'd run out of current hits. Ted only played by ear but it was a hell of an ear for the styles of the day and he nursed a quiet ambition to get into the song business. He wanted to prove that Dad had been wrong to smash to smithereens the cottage piano his mom had bought him as a child. Eventually, he emigrated to New York and after only a few years and a few semi-hits he was able to wangle the financing for a company he formed with a fellow songwriter. In 1908 along came the wealthy Waterson with a better offer and a buy-out clause.

---

*The Seminary Music Company, however, continued to operate in the same building as Snyder, Inc. till at least 1912. Seminary published some Scott Joplin rags and it's thrilling to imagine Joplin and Berlin, the two Ragtime Kings, crossing each other's paths on that winding, draughty staircase. Perhaps they met and exchanged ideas and raggy phrases. Who knows? Irving knows—but he's not saying.

Ted eagerly responded to the promise of Waterson's pocket book and the name 'Seminary'. Besides, Waterson promised central heating in winter and superior electric fans in summer. All Ted needed now was some money music.

It was a comedy poem that got Izzy into Ted Snyder's and changed his name to Irving . . .

One of Kelly's regulars, a song-and-dance man, told the bar he needed a stop-gap song in a hurry. Currently, he was playing Tony Pastor's theatre and he'd thought of sticking in a topical poem in 'wop dialect' between his heavy ballads. Recently, there'd been a rush of immigrants into the city and this excitable and slightly sinister race seemed a good subject for comedy. Audiences enjoyed letting off steam by laughing at stage antics by stage dagoes. Maybe it stopped people whipping their asses, who knows? Anyway, the needy vaudevillian was steered to Izzy because he was the resident expert on wops.

So Izzy obliged with 'Dorando'. It was a timely song. At the 1908 Olympic Games in London the Americans had scored some triumphs. One was delicious and concerned a funny little Italian marathon runner called Dorando Pietri who'd been disqualified because good-natured British doctors and nurses had helped him across the finishing line. Fair play—after all, the poor beggar was within a few breaths of the line before he collapsed. But the judges made the American boy Johnny Hayes the winner and up went the Stars and Stripes. Hayes was a teen-age shop assistant in a New York department store. The city went wild. The Italians got sullen in their ghettoes. Tin Pan Alley shot off a few songs about the Games in general, like 'Hail to the Boys of the USA'.

But Izzy concentrated on the human angle. His number had a Dorando running in Madison Square Gardens and an Italian barber betting his shop on his fellow countryman. Dorando loses yet again but he explains to the barber that his defeat was due to having been fed Irish stew instead of spaghetti. The song 'Dorando' had a rollicking lilt and plenty of race nonsense. Izzy handed over the recitation to his client and asked for the promised $10. But the song-

and-dance man said he'd changed his mind and was going for a number about a baby on the telephone.

So Izzy thought of Max and the Snyder people. Maybe this was the hot number to slay them with? Well, he'd certainly *tell* them it was the one. On a freezing morning in 1909 he was climbing the winding, draughty staircase for a meeting with the powers that be—a poem in his pocket. His suit was immaculate.

Mr Waterson was waiting in the inner office and he immediately demanded a performance. He liked it, he said, even before Izzy had finished reading the words off the beer mat, but what did he know? he added. So Snyder came in and said he liked it, too, but where was the melody? Izzy said he didn't sing so good but the tune was in his head. He was lying to his teeth. Snyder led him into a cubicle where was swinking a house arranger at a huge upright and a music rack spread with manuscript paper and many pencils. Izzy, rising to the challenge, hummed a rather nervy and lugubrious melody to the arranger who jotted it down without showing any emotion. Snyder told Izzy to see Mr Waterson on his way out. Waterson gave him $25—'as an advance on royalties'. And Izzy had been prepared to sell outright! What was his print name? Izzy had been deliberating on this for ages. There was Washington Irving, the famous writer. There was Henry Irving, the famous actor. There was even Irving Jones, a successful writer of clever coon and rag songs. 'Words & Music by Irving Berlin' sounded perfect.

'Dorando' sold a lot of copies around New York but didn't mean much to the country at large. Still, Ted Snyder was happy and he pigeonholed Irving Berlin as a comedy-dialect guy and he asked for more of the same.

Now, just recently, there'd been a brouhaha over Richard Strauss's opera *Salome,* a long-hair German thing based on Lord Alfred Douglas's English translation of Oscar Wilde's French play. All very involved but the fuss had been caused by the opera's 'Dance of the Seven Veils' in which a voluptuous lady in the corps de ballet gradually removed these veils in a sort of artistic striptease. Clergymen had denounced the dance and the burlesque theatres had adopted it as a staple act. Irving Berlin thought up a 'Salome' switch in the 'Dorando' manner. Instead of making Italians the comic figures, how about Jews?

He put this idea to Edgar Leslie as they were sitting in Lindy's chewing the cud. They were an odd couple, Irving and Edgar. The Jew in the tight city suit with the broad stripes, the Yankee in the thick British tweeds and wool tie. But they both liked pancakes with maple syrup and often over plates of such they'd enthuse about songs, their rhymes and rhythms. Leslie and Irving agreed that the Britishers really knew how to write the comedy to a T. In 'Poor John', a 1906 hit by Leigh and Pether of London, the girl is introduced to the boy's mother who looks her up and down, shakes her head and pronounces, 'Poor John!'. And then in 'Waiting at the Church' the bride receives a note from the groom stating that he can't get away to marry her today: 'My wife won't let me.' You could build a whole vaudeville routine around that number. Clever material, hard to beat. Still, Irving and Leslie thought they'd have a go. And in the tougher American manner. After all, they had bustle and beat and plenty of comic ethnics.

So together they wrote and composed a 'Salome' switch. Sadie Cohen becomes a vaude sensation with her Salome dance but she shocks her kosher boyfriend Mose. He leaps to his feet and yells out: 'Oy, oy, oy, oy—Where is your clothes?' The punch-line goes: 'Oy! Such a sad disgrace—no-one looks you in your face; Sadie Salome, go home!'

The humour was in the tradition of the American stage Jew which had been established by the 1900s through the characterizations of such Jewish comics as Frank Bush, Weber & Fields, and Joe, Lew and Ben Welch (no relation but they all seemed to like this Anglo name). The Jew on stage was portrayed as a money-grubbing, hand-rubbing, hunched old creeper with crepe hair and long gabardine and evil beard. With ears bulging and hooked nose as thick as a Californian banana, old Solomon Moses was not a salubrious sight. All deep city and threat. Solly was only in life for the money. As yet, few American Jews complained.

Indeed, this stereotype wasn't confined to vaudeville and burlesque but was an essential ingredient of the Yiddish Theatre. Its greatest star, David Warfield (born Wohfelt), specialized in such roles.

But since the making of money fuelled the American locomotive this dirty, dark object was an essential element in the advance of the Republic. Nevertheless, Solomon Moses was as attractive as a lump of coal.

However, in 'Sadie Salome, Go Home!' the team of Leslie & Berlin had done away with the old image of the foreign Jew (possibly involved in international money intrigues, too) and replaced him with a ridiculous 'Mose'— a decent mother's boy who is scandalized by Sadie's flesh revelations. Later, much later, Irving Berlin admitted this about the Sadie song: 'As much as anything we did it to see whether we could get away with it.' With a raggedy, racy tune (and a touch of Yiddish melancholy in the minor verse) 'Sadie' sold over 3000 copies—and not only in New York.

Henry Waterson summoned Irving to his inner sanctum and put a proposition. Upon signing this contract Irving would be joining the staff of the Ted Snyder Company, Incorporated. Irving would become a company wordsmith (or *lyricist,* if he so wished). If he signed he'd get a salary of $25 a week, plus royalties. Think about it.

Edgar Leslie said that was a jail sentence. Roam the range, sell to the highest bidder, be an American. Leslie was a confirmed freelance, always would be. But Irving thought hard—and decided to throw in the waiter's towel. Just before his twenty-first birthday he signed on with the Ted Snyder team. He was joining the great brotherhood of the song-manufacturing business. For Irving Berlin this was a move nearer to becoming a real modern American.

But was there still lurking round the circles under his eyes the phantom of Mother Baline, apron held open, lips waiting for the seal of a kiss? And wasn't She imbued with centuries of Hebrew culture that couldn't be casually discarded like a dated straw hat or a guttural name? Traces of Israel Baline would forever remain on Irving Berlin, like buttered bagel on a yacht-club tie.

38

3

Origins of the Alley

Irving Berlin had reason to feel at home and with family in the Alley he was entering. A clutch of blocks centering on 28th Street between 6th and Broadway, Tin Pan Alley sanctuaried such names as M. Witmark & Sons, Shapiro-Bernstein & Co, Jos. Stern & Ed Marks. Izzy's mother could be assured he was in safe company. Why, Mr Von Tilzer was so respectable a married man that philandering songwriters, off for a naughty night with a girlie, would often gain easy entry to the best bedrooms in top hotels by simply registering as 'Mr and Mrs Harry Von Tilzer'.

In under twenty years these publishers of Jewish origin had built a million-dollar industry, an achievement they were justly proud of. They were providers of what we now call a 'leisure service': popular music for all occasions and moods to be fed to the American people everywhere, whether they be in vaudeville theatre, saloon, department store in New York (home and the nerve centre of show business), or whether they be in hick cities, tank towns and distant orifices of that great sprawling goddess of plenty. In the terrifying Deep South, so the Alleymen learned, the natives actually bought songs about Dixie! Not that the writers had ever strayed there, even for research purposes. No sir – an Alleyman stayed in his place in Gotham within sound and smell of old Broadway, and there he invented Dixie songs, or whatever was required, in that relentless song factory that never struck.

A Santa Claus factory. You were interpreting to the

people their dreams (like Freud was doing in another field). Up in the office cubicle in the brownstone building, night or day, you banged out songs in a rarified air above the mainstream culture below. But yet, when you hit (as hit you must, Irving) you were helping mould that very culture. You were contributing.

Researching in the vaudeville theatre you wanted to watch the *audience*, not only the *act*. You needed to scrutinize that phantom public, those mysterious masses, and feel their pulse. There was to be no art for art's sake in this cut-throat business of babies at the telephone, babes on the dance floor, mothers, coons, Dixie and, generally, dog eat dog.

But. We were saying that this new business is a proud one. We have fraternities, we give each other awards. We are like any other business: the ledger-book rules, supreme. And our work has even gone international, making the Old World sing and dance with an almost Hassidic fire-joy. For example, Harry Von Tilzer's 'Under the Anheuser Busch', a waltz hymn to a domestic beer, has clicked in England where it is known as 'Down at the Old Bull & Bush' – but we keep the copyright. A Britisher would knock you down if you told him his pub song was of Alley origin. And by an American Jew. Of course, no red-blooded American of Jewish ancestry would dream of advertising such a fact.

Still, this transmigration of a song is thrilling. It happens even in liturgical circles (which is where most Jewish music is to be found). At many a Jewish festival these days you'll see the men snaking across the floor as they sing their Yiddish version of 'The Marseillaise'. As General Booth of the Salvation Army said: 'Why should the Devil have all the best tunes?'. In our business we have *organized* – by taking a little here, a little there, and pasting it all together as one. Alley music we have put into proper categories; all the song-and-dance models of the American past we have codified: ballad, waltz, march, plantation, coon (rough, comic, refined or serenade). We have dream songs numbered in our warehouses to avoid confusion.

Sheet music is selling like never before. A medium hit sells 600,000 copies while a smasheroo starts at a million and may sail as high as 5 or 6 million. The ledgers show

40

that since 1900 we've pushed over 100 songs into the million-seller bracket. And the public get value for money. In the 1880s (before our remodelling) publishers were charging a dollar a copy. By the nineties it was 40 cents. By 1900 we'd whittled it down to 25 cents. Now we can proudly charge one thin dime.

And you get a nice, big, tall piece of music in two dazzling colours with art as captivating as a comic book, plus rich fruit-cake advertising copy on the back. We have simplified catalogues and complex sales methods. We can supply everybody's needs. We are go-ahead and progressive. We are truly American.

This new business had been made possible by the American Industrial Revolution. Getting up steam at the end of the 1860s (following the unpleasant interruption, the Civil War) this sweating engine had clanked so hard and so efficiently in gobbling up Virgin America that by 1900 the USA was the Number One Industrial Power of the World. An extra-ordinary fervour filled the land. Business became the be-all and the end-all, life's greatest adventure. Any man could – and should – get rich quick. Grab that opportunity and ride. American savvy, know-how, hustle and bustle. The envy of the Old World. The racing figure of Uncle Sam with pointed beard and coat-tails flying – that roaring Yankee trader – had become the archetypal American in the popular mind over there in Europe.

And Irving Berlin's brothers, his forerunners in the new thing called Show Business, had become keenly aware of a mass market hungry for entertainment, a market created by this Industrial Revolution. Into the big cities had been drawn the faceless ones who were to feed the machinery. By night this mass needed refreshment with a bit of tabasco. An escape. For the urban workers had left behind in the countryside their folk music, a relic of the old days when music was a part of work – bringing on the rain, raising the crops, blessing the marriage. The New Urban Folk needed instant entertainment, ready-made, off-the-peg.

But there was more to this new public than ex-ploughboys and European immigrants, the urban proletariat. Show Biz

41

soon discovered that the real money was to be made from the new middle class, a burgeoning polite mass – and a status aspired to by all Americans after assimilation. It was the middle classes who were the patrons of vaudeville, a clean version of the old-time Variety. Now, by 1909, vaudeville was the country's favourite entertainment. It was the middle classes who bought the millions of pianos on which to play the sheet music. It was the middle classes who were abandoning the Victorian ethic of all work and no play, of uplift and improvement, in favour of some fun and games for their own sake. They no longer drank Coca-Cola as a health improver, they drank it as a pleasurable soft drink. They no longer ate exclusively at home and stayed there stolidly every night. Now they were relaxing in restaurants and night clubs. Of course, the middle classes still required refinement: night-time entertainment was gentrified as 'cabaret'. Anything French spelled 'class'.

So here was this out-going, energetic public bursting forth around the turn of the century in search of entertainment. And, in the music field, here were Izzy's brothers stepping into the breach to satisfy that desire. There was nothing conspiratorial or sinister about the predominance of Jews in Tin Pan Alley. The vacuum existed and the Jews, like nature, abhorred it.

They were in the right place at the right time. Between 1881 and 1914 more than 2 million Jews fled from Eastern Europe. Most of them settled in America. During this period the West was enjoying the biggest consumer boom the world has ever known – and the chief beneficiaries were America's big cities. Techniques for servicing the consumers were, as yet, undeveloped. The perennial outsiders stepped in.

They sprayed Puritan America with a joy, an energy, an élan, that had been absent in the upright, stiff-backed Yankee trader. The nineteenth-century businessman had been sure of himself to the point of smugness and inertia. Let the public come to him! The Jewish-American entrepreneur dashed out to meet, greet and possibly hug his potential customers.

Most importantly, the city – the future – was no object

of fear and loathing to the Jews. For centuries they'd been caged in ghettoes, brooding inwardly, trading quietly. They had no ties to the rural life, to the old homestead and swimmin' hole. They had no race memory of a glorious pastoral past, a golden age. They had no homesickness for any Fatherland because they were without country, flagless. So, unlike the other immigrants, they weren't burdened by nostalgia for old folkways. The Jewish way of life, inextricably bound up in religion, was kept under wraps, off limits. If its musical flavour was to exude into mainstream America then it did so surreptitiously, clad in a black mask like a thief in the night.

The young Jews, without long beards and broad hats, entered the promised land with slates wiped clean. They were ready to be assimilated into the mainstream even if this meant becoming chameleons. They would change their names, their accents, they would not know their fathers. They would be flexible, adaptable, bending over backwards or sideways, doing the required gymnastics to suit the winds of change. Even scenting those winds, perhaps. Yes, they would gladly evict their own personal tastes in order to calculate the tastes of the multitude. And always they were on the move, on the up and up. A restless people – and terribly restless for education. More so than any other immigrant group. Reading, writing and calculation were drummed into their children relentlessly. Get it down on paper, then it exists. Get education and therefore get ahead.

By 1910 the Jews, as a whole, had become the most successful ethnic minority in America. They were the envy of many. When they were too visible they became subject (like the Irish and Germans before them) to the growing zenophobia called All-Americanism which was caused by the depression of the early nineties, the closure of the Frontier, the new imperialism, and the intense fear of rural folk for the city slickers. In particular, the waves of immigrants from Eastern Europe were damned as dangerous and corrupting 'hordes'. Jews were banned from private clubs, private schools and universities. The corporate communities of established business – like banking, law, medicine, steel and oil – were closed to them.

So how did they get to be so upwardly mobile? They stepped into marginal trades like clothes manufacturing, jewellery, the fur business, grocery, cigar-making. Some of them ventured into the rogue business of mass entertainment: popular theatre and popular music. In penny arcade peep shows they started inventing the movie business. Alone, as always, they were at least able to be their own bosses. And from the vantage point of street level they would observe the goyim in his many ways and means.

Into this vacuum, where no privilege flew, the Jews brought the right combination of qualities to succeed – in particular, in the industry and art of American popular music. Bright, energetic, prepared to speculate, and not handcuffed by Yankee notions of propriety and modesty, the Jews of Pop were exactly the operators required to respond to the revolution in manners, morals and recreational habits that was marking the new century.

These marginal tradesmen were to display a glittering song shop, a moveable feast rolling along with a trumpet accompaniment that constantly praised the American Way. Their songs were a national anthem of patriotic sales pitches. And when Irving Berlin joined the train in 1909 he was, by chance, going to latch onto a music that was so bouncy and bumptious – so full of chutspah – that the rest of the world was certain this was the very quintessence of the American soul. Ragtime had been developed, like all the other pop music models, in the fusty old nineteenth-century. But it was in the 1910s, if I may anticipate, that ragtime really came into its own, as the sound of the city and as America's first true music.

Irving Berlin and the Alleymen were to be the perfect riders for this prancing, jiggling music – the eternal wanderers on the back of a hot black horse. They directed ragtime, they gave it a mouthpiece. They were encouraging the sleepy giant America to let rip as the new Yankee Doodle Ragtime Kid, the personification of a boyish society. Of course, George M. Cohan – an Irish-American – had invented the cocky strutter but it would be the Jews who would replicate and distribute him. And also, of course, our Alley song salesmen were only releasing those rhythms of joy that beat down in the hearts and souls of their native-born hosts.

We shall discover later that ragtime as music was nurtured in native America, far from New York and the Alley. We shall go back and see how the song models of pop had existed long before the arrival of the new and nervy East European immigrants. We shall see that Irving Berlin, like any other man, invented little – but he seized the right moment and squeezed out the essence of his time. I am not claiming all of early twentieth-century pop for the American Jews.

But, all the same, it was a pretty solid achievement – to permute a ghetto culture into the world of New York show business and, from this moated halfway house, to propagate a slangy, seemingly All-American pop style that would be embraced not only by their native hosts but also by the Old World even as far as Russia. Full circle – Berlin and his colleagues strike back at the sons of Cossacks with sounds that delight and hurt not. What a way to win a war!

We need now to look at America's music before Alley organization and centralization. The raw material for Berlin and his colleagues was already thick on the ground: what these consummate actor-managers did so well was to snatch up and adapt the props, scenery, make-up and myths that had been lying around higgledy-piggledy in the nineteenth century.

Before the Alley organization the American music publishing scene was a lovely mess. The music covers could be gorgeous art works – hand-lithographed, personally signed by the artist; lavender or otherwise scented; shimmering in many colours. The publishers of these beauties were spread out lazily and crazily in every city and almost every town of the vast Republic. Their musical offerings made little commercial sense but they seem today to be a marvel of eclecticism, like a truly free-form radio station serving the community good things whether it wants good things or not.

Somewhere in the stacks of these serendipity publishers were to be found: imported British motto songs, real Swiss yodels, paraphrases of Grand Opera, 'The Pope He Leads a Happy Life', too many songs about George Washington, too many marches of mundane arcaneness like 'The Ocean Telegraph March of 1871', plenty of lively dances including polkas, gallops, lancers and even a few tangos. And somewhere, too (and most interestingly), the truly native vernacular songs like 'I'm the Father of a Little Black Coon' and 'Drill, Ye Tarriers, Drill'. It seemed almost rude that the tinted faces and muddied boots of the latter works should be found in the catalogues of these dear old fogey publishers. But the publishers weren't too bothered – for they were a sleepy lot and, like proprietors of an old country store, they were proud of stocking every kind of item, only they often couldn't exactly lay their hands on the item you wanted right now.

They had hits by default. For example, Lowell Mason's hymn collection sold a half million – but that was over a half century. Some of the more enterprising New York firms sometimes took ads in trade journals:

Firth, Pond & Co.
As specimens of our popular pieces we will mention
THE OLD FOLKS AT HOME
That most beautiful American melody, nearly *Forty Thousand Copies* of which have been sold!
(From: *The Musical World and New York Musical Times*, 1853)

The main money came from such sweet music – especially written for the genteel parlour trade. The musical forms had their origin in Europe but by the 1850s they'd found their glory in America. The country was still a big, hostile and unruly map – a collection of small towns with wide open space in between and the odd flickering beacon of a city – and so Americans were forced to make their music in the safety of hearth and home. At least, those who were middle class or aspiring – the lumpen, those who harboured the seeds of ragtime and jazz, went about their folk ways without buying sheet music or pianos.

But in the decent, middle-class home, that haven shuttering out the sounds of the rude world, was expected to be prominently displayed – a harmonium or a piano. Especially a piano. That triumph of the combined inventiveness of Europe and America. An orchestra in your own home. A solid piece of engineering and a fine hunk of furniture. A gathering place, what with the framed family photos, the flowers and all the knick-knacks. A piano was an imperative item for a fellow that was doing well and elevating himself.

But, of course, a fellow didn't actually play the damn thing. That would be effeminate, like those English fops who smoked cigarettes. In the American home it was the womenfolk who played the piano and mostly the young ones at that, while their brothers were out playing ball or fighting and their fathers were sneaking a game of poker or a quick snort in the saloon.

See those demure young ladies sitting at the big ugly square piano with their backs arched, their arms never swinging, their eyes never turning up (even if the song was inspirational). They must aim at pleasing and not astonishing. In mellifluous virginal tones you will hear them sing to the assembled family and small circle of friends of matters poetic ('Jeannie with the Light Brown Hair'), or comic ('Oh, Susanna') or pathetic ('The Old Folks at Home'). A gamut of emotions, a satisfying show.

These three examples of thoroughly decent songs for home consumption had all been written by Stephen Foster. Carefully crafted, written for the genteel market, published in New York. And yet, after his death in 1864, Foster songs had been slipping inexorably into the folk fund – so that, in years to come, people believed that sad darkies on dripping plantations had really been the true authors of 'The Old Folks at Home', making it up as they wept along, snatching the melody from out of the sky or under the ground. And by the new century everybody claimed that Old Kentucky Home as their very own spiritual abode. The songs had become part of the public's domain.

But when Irving got an Alley office of his own he put up a framed portrait of Stephen Foster. Every songwriter acknowledged a great deal to Foster. He'd blazed the trail – perfecting the song models, forcing the public to laugh and then cry, to dance and then sit quiet; allowing songsmiths to rest in safe Northern cities to write of the cares and joys of the rest of that wild sprawl, especially the moss-smothered Old South in the days before the Unpleasantness.

Foster was America's first fulltime Compleat Songwriter, but he operated in the dark days before show business was properly invented by the East European immigrants. His work and his influences must be discussed if we are to understand the musical setting that Berlin and the Alleymen inherited and streamlined.

Born well-heeled, the son of a Colonel in Pittsburgh, Pennsylvania, Foster was educated at private schools and thoroughly grounded in the music of the European masters by a German pedant. The Foster family was from solid Anglo-Saxon stock and comfortably settled. So Stephen wasn't hell-bent on wiping out a past of oppression or repressive religion. He was quite assimilated into his country. He need wave no Stars & Stripes. Yet, like the Alleymen who were to follow in his footsteps, *hiding behind a mask*. He wrote from the heart of a Negro, yet he knew next to nothing about the race. He wrote in a foreign style, not on the banjo or bones.

He was part of the European tradition that still hung over America like a grim schoolmaster with a thwacking cane. Every schooled musician took up the given European art-song manner but there was a touch of folksiness accepted, especially from the books of Dubliner Tom Moore's transcribed Irish folk songs. Foster's tunes were suitably pentatonic but the lyrics spoken by his dusky primitives were often rather too scrubbed. He was fond of Italianate *appogiaturas* and arpeggiated piano accompaniments. He had studied *lieder* and, indeed, translated several German art songs.

He was, in truth, thoroughly European and thoroughly genteel (he was, at first, frightfully ashamed of his minstrel numbers). He was convinced that his artistic worth lay in his high-class ballads – poetic, pathetic and sentimental – and that these songs would assure him immortality. In this vein of course there was 'Oh, Willie, We Have Missed You' and a heap more about Willie, but the critics dismissed them

48

as trash and the public didn't buy. Then he tried with 'Old Dog Tray', in the Scottish tradition, and, suddenly, the public liked this type of number, even though he himself hated dogs and used to chase the noisy devils with a red-hot poker.

Now, as the professional, he tried firing off on a host of topics, trusting he'd hit somewhere, sometime. The darky gew-gaws he'd left behind – he had progressed to songs of social protest, war, comedy (about shrews, about comely moustaches); he started a series of dreamy ballads that culminated in 'Beautiful Dreamer'. And then there was 'Jeannie with the Light Brown Hair', a work he considered his masterpiece. But the blessed public didn't buy this one! Maybe the publishers hadn't advertized heavily enough? His royalty statements were dreadful. But, at least, he had royalties – Foster was the first songwriter to be given royalties.

The public, the publishers, even his own wife – all were treating him badly. Him – the lonely, misunderstood artist expressing himself through the tragic and comic and black *masks!* Was there no way to fit into democracy without actually lowering yourself into the mess? What a stupid, vulgar people the Americans could be! You filled concert halls with 'Yankee Doodle' played on rows of bottles or bashed out in variations by ten pianists. Not even a real American tune but just the English nursery song, 'Lucy Locket Lost Her Pocket'. General Ulysses Grant, later to be President, told Foster that, even if his songs were brilliant, this soldier couldn't understand them because the only melody he recognized was 'Yankee Doodle'.

Foreign artists, soulmates of Foster, had problems with Americans, too. Charles Dickens, on tour with his readings, found every other man to be a con artist or an ex-President. In polluted Pittsburgh he took tea with a sixteen year-old Foster. But the famous writer was tired and testy. He loathed America, especially its spitting. Stephen learned nothing, remaining star-struck. Tom Moore, compiler of all those beloved Irish song books, was warned not to tour America (if he valued his sanity) by no less than John Howard Paine, lyricist of 'Home Sweet Home'. Paine, a sensitive man, couldn't bear his homeland and eventually landed the job of US consul in Tunis – the further away the better for him. But old Tom couldn't resist the money and anyway his interest in 'native wood notes wild' should have endeared him to this barnyard of honest-to-goodness plain folk. But he hated it, finding few real folks but plenty of pretentious bourgeois waffling of opera. Some nights he was faced by frightening audiences howling as one, without a trace of individuality.

'These Americans are a motley mixture of weak barbarians,' he told Henry Russell, another of the many foreign entertainers criss-crossing the country. An English Jew from Sheerness in Kent, Russell was the first truly modern singer-songwriter: a popular artist with a canny sense of what the public wanted. His job was helped by his genuine love of Americans. He was well trained in the classics and Italian opera but he gave the people his genteel song act instead. At a little portable piano he faced his audiences and boomed out in his deep and refined voice his own clever compositions: 'A Life on the Ocean Wave', and many yearnings for the old village pump, the old family clock, the old spinning wheel. *Old* – an essential ingredient of conservative pop. He milked his audience nightly as they never had been milked: the tears fell like rain when he sang his 'Woodman, Woodman, Spare That Tree!' Yes, and *he* mixed his metaphors too – and they loved him the more because he seemed real and singing straight from the heart.

But he never got carried away in his act. Remaining distanced from his melodramatic material, he stayed cool and kept his sanity. And being Jewish he was always on the outside looking in.

He also sang some nigger minstrel material and the Foster plantation songs were always popular. Foster admired Russell no end. If only he, Foster, had had this Britisher's panache and bravado! But he had always been ambivalent about this song business. He was so upset by reviews condemning his darky material that he asked Ed Christy (of the Christy Minstrels) to leave his name off 'The Old Folks at Home'. And after Christy obliged and the song sold well Foster had the gall to demand his name be printed on the cover. He wrote to Christy that his songs had made 'Ethiopian' minstrels acceptable to 'refined people'. And Ed was rightly furious because he it was who'd been barnstorming in blackface around America sweating these nigger pastiches into the bestsellers they'd eventually become, while this Philadelphia powder puff had stayed safe at home, fearful of the rough touring life and the tough business ways of New York. A 'gentleman of the old school' he called himself! Christy scrawled across the back of Foster's letter of demand: *'Vacillating Skunk'*.

Foster was a hopeless businessman and a rotten husband. The last years of his life are shrouded in mystery. His songs weren't selling certainly, but where did he go at night? There were rumours he'd turned pansy. He lived alone and died a drunk and a bankrupt. He'd been infesting a room on the Bowery. America's first songwriter had not been living The Ordered Life.

Disorderly conduct was to be the pattern for many a lonely songwriter in those Bohemian years before Alley organization. Despite the Foster royalty precedent songwriters still tended to sell their songs outright for a few dollars. Then, as often as not, it was round to the Grip, the Black Rabbit or the Slide to gulp down killing concoctions like brandy sour mash, sherry cobblers, rum and gum. Joe Murphy could be seen most days and nights propping up a bar, teasing the pansies, starting a fight or two. Like so many of the Bohemians he'd originally been a good country boy, but New York city had lured him with its sights and lights and quick money. After a particularly bloody saloon fight he went back to his room and wrote 'A Handful of Earth from My Dear Mother's Grave' and he meant every word and note. He sold it for more drink and the song became quite a success but Joe was felled by the booze and a sexual disease.

There was dear James Thornton, singing waiter and monologist, who often fell off stage due to liquor, who once reported seeing men with crabs' legs and who used to learn a page of a dictionary a day (reciting the page loudly as he stumbled down the sidewalks of New York). He managed to give us the lovely, lilting 'My Sweetheart's the Man in the Moon' and the close harmony favourite, 'When You Were Sweet Sixteen'. But he died broke. Then there was Charles Graham ('Two Little Girls in Blue') who succumbed in Bellevue Hospital's Alcoholics Section near Foster's death spot. Hart Danks ('Silver Threads among the Gold') died in a New York rooming house, leaving a note which read, 'It's hard to die alone.'

By the nineties the business was pulling itself together and even songwriters were becoming more responsible – becoming publishers. Paul Dresser, for example. A prince of ballad writers and a prince of a man, he was truly moved by his own material: when he played 'On the Banks of the Wabash' to his novelist brother, Theodore Dreiser, they both soon had tears streaming down their cheeks. Paul also wrote of country girls who sold their souls for gold in the big city. Again, he cried when he played his latest song about a fallen woman, pumping out the tune on his portable organ in a swell Broadway hotel to a dry Maxie Hoffman who was only there to take down the notes for publication. Resplendent in his high silk hat and frock coat (beaten only by James Thornton's clergyman costume) Dresser, a big man with a big heart, would go forth between songwriting chores and champagne dinners to dispense thousands of dollars to starving songwriters and publishers.

But when he had the audacity to get into publishing he came a cropper. For a few years he floated well but, in 1905, he ran out of money and couldn't publish his new song, 'My Gal Sal'. Tin Pan Alley was now firmly established and none of the Alleymen would help him out. So – broke and broken-hearted, he upped and died. 'I'd warned him earlier to get wise,' said Frank Harding, a pop publisher who'd pioneered the business in the eighties. 'I told him times were changing and the heat was on.'

Harding had seen the writing on the wall, spelling the end of the lazy-river meanderings of the good old days. Publishers, with glinty eyes on the gold, could no longer afford to stretch out their legs in some small country town where bees buzzed louder than their music presses. The new breed of hustler songsters were honey-hiving in roaring New

York where there was no time for altruistic sentiments, but plenty of time for product that reeked of sentimentality.

In the 1880s Harding had issued his due quota of tear-jerkers; he was no stranger to the genteel parlour trade: 'Half of our women customers wanted to be led astray. And the other half wanted to read about it,' he liked to say to comparative strangers in Manhattan bars. And if the stranger bought him a drink he'd expand: 'Of course, we tried out our "fate-worse-than-death" ballads on a quite different crowd. We'd test 'em in the saloons, brothels and variety houses in and around New York. These rounders, roisterers, gangsters and tarts – they were real softies under the shell and cried like babies at songs about babies. But, in heartland America, our sheet sales were always far better than in New York, funnily enough. In fact, New York sales were never good. I guess it was because the denizens, locked in the bowels of the Bowery and such, were never home for a hot dinner and the old slippers, hearth and piano. They were out on the town, living it up. *Ragging* it.'

Harding, the true pioneer, had made a good deal of his money from earthy material: Irish shenanigan songs especially.

The Irish-American trend in pop songs preceded ragtime by a decade and it needs to be examined – because this ethnic spirit was soon to be absorbed, like ragtime and the thrust of the East Europeans, into the Yankee Doodle popular image.

Hearty, rambunctious jig songs were the forte of the immensely successful variety team, Harrigan & Hart. And Harding published their stage songs. But the strong sales only reflected the equally strong impact of the Irish in America. At first there was a good deal of native American prejudice against them: the familiar notice 'No Irish Need Apply' even became a song title.

Escaping from the Great Irish Famine (and the general beastliness of life in the Ireland of the 1840s, the new arrivals brought to America a lustiness for life as a grand hooley with plenty of donnybrooks. Songs reflected this knock-about attitude: 'Down Went McGinty' and 'Throw Him

Down, McCluskey'. Nor must we forget 'Who Threw the Overalls in Mrs Murphy's Chowder?'

Spitting in public had been common enough when Charles Dickens had visited America in the 1840s (he'd noted that they even practised it in decent Washington hotels) but, by the 1880s, with the settling in of the wild Irish, this spitting had gotten quite out of hand. At the popular Harrigan & Hart shows the throwing of spitballs at the boiled white shirts of the dudes in the orchestra stalls (and even at the actors) was punishable by a whack from the bamboo pole of the security thug strolling the aisles. Ned Harrigan, a writer (as well as a comic actor) and, therefore, a wise and reflective man, distanced himself from his rowdy and often violent fans. The New York of the Harrigan & Hart musicals was acknowledged to be the most disorderly city in the western world. Harrigan's main theme in his work was 'tumult and consternation'; he used to say that 'haste and strife' were the two words that best summed up his city of work. In his song 'The Old Bowery Pit', about a theatre, he writes: 'You talk about blood, it was thicker than mud, oh! – you could not see action for smoke.' He shrewdly realized, sensitive man, that this 'knockdown and slapbang' was what the cretins wanted. So, in his nine plays concerning the antics of a para-military group called 'The Mulligan Guards', he wrote much 'melodious rowdyism'. For example: one of the most popular routines involved a German-American dance-hall owner who, by mistake, rents his premises to an Irish social club *and* a Negro social club – on the same night. The blacks take the upper floor; the paddies are at ground level. There's a fearful racket as both races jig and carouse – until, finally, the blacks succeed in collapsing their floor thus enabling the sketch to climax with a thunderstorm of inky bodies hailing onto the wearers of the green.

But by the nineties the thuggishness of the stage Irish had been complemented by a sweet nostalgia expressed in pretty waltz songs. This rough-and-smooth slotted in well with the quaint 'plantation' and threatening 'coon' songs fattening the catalogues of pop publishers at the turn of the century. Ragtime and rowdyism combined to create, finally, the figure of the New American on stage – best exemplified by the swaggering self-confidence and jingoism of George M. Cohan who claimed to have been born on the Fourth of July and proclaimed himself 'The Yankee Doodle Boy'. Reality supported some of Cohan's boasting: America was the greatest industrial nation and was becoming a world power. But matters were far more complex than the showbiz stereotype would have the world believe. Micks, yids, wops, dagoes – all were to be melded into the American 'slicker' by the coming of the First World War. But, in the matter of the Black American, the ghost of the coon had yet to be laid.

Irving Berlin and the Alleymen were to inherit the tail-end of the song-type cycle which had started in the Stephen Foster era. The Alleymen's greatest contribution was in assimilation and organization and it is during the nineties that we have to say goodbye to the genial old-time publishers like Frank Harding. When Ben Harney introduced ragtime to New York vaudeville in 1896 Harding published his songs. But it was the snappier Witmarks who really capitalized on ragtime. There was no stopping them and soon they had taken over the Harney ragtime copyrights. They were in time to reap the benefits of the craze for ragtime and coon songs. We shall deal with this phenomenon (which sprang from the minstrel-show tradition) in the next chapter when we discover Irving Berlin celebrating the last of the red-hot coon myths in 'Alexander's Ragtime Band'. Meanwhile, we will see how Tin Pan Alley, as a work place and work force, was finally established and named.

The energy came not so much from the Witmark brothers (who were long-settled German-Jews of decorum and taste) but from hungry young upstarts from the hinterlands. Coming in on the end of the parlour-song era, the shoestring company boys had their hearts in the Victorian age but their heads in the twentieth century. And the canniest were to catch the ragtime whirlwind.

Charles K. Harris was typical of the new breed in all ways except one: he never really cottoned on to the staying power of syncopation. He took the fatal step of developing

55

personal tastes once he'd graduated from shoestrings to silk cravats. But, it seems, he was the first of the Alleymen.

A German-Jew born in New York State in 1865, he had knocked around a bit as a bell-hop, a pawnbroker and a party banjoist. Settled at last in Milwaukee, Wisconsin, he decided to have a go at the songwriting game. He knew nothing about music technically but soon he'd made up a heap of good songs like 'Creep, Baby, Creep', 'Hello, Central, Hello' and 'Humming Baby to Sleep'. Babies, telephones and coloured crooning were contemporary stuff, even futuristic. Charlie managed to place these efforts with publishers and decent sales were generated – but it was a painfully slow process and Charlie, a modernist, was thoroughly fed up and terribly impatient with these old fogies.

They didn't get hawking like good medicine-show men in the spirit of Barnum. They didn't advertise enough, they left it to Charlie to drum up business. They slept in their clutterbuck offices full of deadly tales of the sea, of hymns and high-class 'thee' and 'thou' epics. Charlie was a tiny fellow but he bounced high when he got excited, his red curls shaking away.

He decided to do away with the old fogey middlemen. He set up shop in Milwaukee, hanging out a sign stating boldly: 'SONGS WRITTEN TO ORDER'. For a maximum fee of $20 he'd manufacture songs for all occasions. The essence of the Alley. Eyes wide open, ears hard-pricking, pencil and paper at the ready (sometimes a shirt cuff could do), Charlie was always on the job. Watching the passing show from his song-smithery, scanning the newspapers for stories, listening for new street catch-phrases, jotting down lines at the theatre. *Studying the copyright laws*. Most important. Old Will Rossiter, the Chicago publisher, had kindly taken time out to give him the lowdown on these copyright laws.

And after hundreds of self-penned, self-published songs Charlie suddenly scored big with 'After the Ball' in 1892 – the year Coca-Cola stopped calling itself a medicinal tonic and concentrated on the pleasure aspect; the year that the Irving Berlin family arrived in New York.

56

'After the Ball' was a three verse sob story of tragic misunderstanding and unrequited love. Thus it was lyrically well within the genteel ballad genre – but the tune was lean and keen in the chorus: an extremely catchy melody, plugged three times. Charlie had fashioned a conscious hit and he marketed it as such. The song was to lay the foundations for popular music as big business. Sigmund Spaeth, the dean of writers on early pop, has written: '(It) was the first song to "sweep the country", the first "smashing, sensational success" of modern times.'

Charlie had originally crafted it for a local amateur minstrel but the idiot forgot the words at the first performance. No more amateurs from now on. He pushed, he scuffled. He got May Irwin, the stentorian comedienne, to include it in her Broadway act. *Click No.I.* He bribed J. Aldrich Libbey, equally stentorian, to slip it into the touring show, *A Trip to Chinatown*. Libbey would get his picture on the sheet cover and a cut of the royalties—that was the bribe, an early version of payola. The show became a national success, much of this due to rural interest in the dopers of Chinatown, but not a little to the haunting quality of 'After the Ball' (the chord sequence matched the earlier waltz, 'Over the Waves'). Then Dick Jose, big-voiced fellow and popular act, carried the ballad up and down the West Coast. And nor would Charlie forget dear Helen Mora, who warbled it in all the leading vaudeville houses of the midwest. A more than respectable sales result from a very respectable song – but sold with all the force of a marauding Hun. Charlie was bouncing with glee.

And now the old fogey publishers came running to him with offers. No dice! He wasn't selling, he'd maybe lease. He was having a hard job keeping up with the national demand for copies, the presses were grinding out 25,000 a week. Within a few years 'Ball' had topped 5 million in sales. But by that time Charlie had moved to very nice offices in New York where he was definitely *Charles K. Harris* with his photo on every piece of sheet music as a guarantee of real quality. In his wing collar, frozen tweed suit and sporting a well-waxed moustache, he set a good example for the many fledgling pop publishers who now flocked to New York, shoestring boys with a dream and a sure-fire hit-song idea. There was Joe Stern and Ed Marks, ex-shop assistants; there was Harry Von Tilzer (born Harry Gumm), an ex-circus man, trailing a string of brothers; and there would be Shapiro, Bernstein & Co.; and Leo Feist, Inc. ('You Can't Go Wrong with a Feist Song'). The new fast boys joined Chas K. – and he, in turn, was joining the established firm of M. Witmark & Sons, established 1886. The House of Witmark certainly wasn't run on the lines of an old fogey country store but, until the arrival of the likes of Chas K., the Witmark boys weren't exactly shooting in a straight pop line.

They really *were* boys. Mere teenagers when they started but already shrewd businessmen, with a real pro performer in the kid Julius. They published full-spectrum music. Maybe they were scared of being vulgar? After all, their papa had risen to lieutenant in the Civil War. When Julius was touring in '*A Trip to Chinatown*' he'd dared to offer to buy 'After the Ball'. Charlie told him where to stick his cheque in no uncertain terms. Charlie hadn't forgotten that only a few years ago he'd presented the Witmark kids with a certain hit in his song 'Where the Sun has Set' and they'd let it rest, leaving him with a paltry 85 cents in royalties. After the clicking of 'Ball' and the setting up of plush offices in New York he had that cheque framed in gold and hung in the reception area (which also featured a splashing fountain). The Witmarks might have a lieutenant as a father but Chas K. had dash.

Anyway, a year after the 'Ball' success what do the Witmarks do but publish a copycat ballad called 'Two Little Girls in Blue', written by that English soak Charles Graham! The Witmarks were besotted by the British. They were always sailing across to sniff out some more Grahams or even a Harry Dacre ('Daisy Bell'). No doubt the British were clever songwriters but they were dozey, too. The Witmarks admitted that the British songmen were too full of old-world charm, courtly grace and French brandy. Very fond of long lunches. But no long-range drive.

Then, of course, the Witmarks went overboard for ragtime and coon songs. They must have felt that some fast catching-up with the times was necessary. Or maybe they just lucked out? Who knows? – it's a funny business. Change is the only eternal. Charlie had never felt comfortable with coon songs. He published a few, wrote some too – but he always felt they were a passing craze and a nasty one. However, by the early 1900s he knew that the game was up as far as his interminable story ballads were concerned. His tearful babies and misunderstood women would have to be altered to suit the demands of these faster and more cynical times. The love song no longer needed a story, it was becoming slicker and more universal. On the stage the Victorian ballad was being travestied: Charlie had noted the success of 'Don't Go in the Lion's Cage Tonight' by 'Baldy' Sloane.

Well, Charlie proved himself à la mode by publishing, in 1909, two songs that were the antithesis of the lugubrious ballads that had brought him fame and fortune. And they were both solid hits: 'I Wonder Who's Kissing Her Now?', a super slick love song; and 'Heaven Will Protect the Working Girl', a parody of Victorian moral bust-heaving. There! He could relax a while. And certainly the ragtime craze had faded away, like all novelties. Of course, during the heat of the craze he'd met some interesting characters, you always did. Like little Irving Jones, a real darky, who wrote some very funny coon songs (better than the average watermelon, razor and chicken numbers), a witty and well-dressed negro with an engaging stammer. What bad luck to be born coloured! And where was Irving now that the craze had passed? Still, you can't afford to be sentimental in this business. You must be up with the times, perhaps even set the standards of the times, you must codify, settling the dust of the day on paper . . .

To that effect Chas K. had written and published a little red guide book called 'How to Write a Popular Song'. He stated categorically that the day of the 'rough coon song' was over:

Styles in songs change as quickly as those in ladies millinery . . . One season coon songs may be all the rage, then suddenly the simple love ballad sets the pace, only

59

to give way in turn to something else that hits the fancy of a public that is always capricious in these matters, whatever it may be in others.

Mr Monroe Rosenfeld chose to disagree about ragtime – and indeed about most everything else. He saw himself as the residing expert on the pop music picture. Chas K. had never got along with him. The antipathy went back a long way: in 1892, as a reviewer of songs for the *New York Herald* he'd bluntly stated that 'After the Ball' had 'absolutely nothing to recommend it'. Chas K. framed the clipping and later placed it next to the Witmark cheque in reception. He despised Rosenfeld as an old hack, and a gimp to boot.

There may have been some professional jealousy involved. They'd both started their hit careers by writing sob songs, Rosenfeld's ballads preceding Chas K. by a few years. But Rosie, as his friends called him (and he had many) could never settle down to just one task – like the making of money. He was always on the move, knocking about the US of A. And, unlike Chas K., he firmly believed that ragtime was much more than a passing fancy. He believed ragtime was here to stay, that it was fundamental in fuelling the motor of American pop. Typical ravings of an egg-head musicologist, jeered Charlie. He hasn't had a hit in years so he writes about the biz instead!

In 1902 Rosie had gone down to St Louis, Missouri, to interview a coloured composer who proudly claimed to be 'The King of Ragtime Writers'. Scott Joplin impressed Rosie considerably: shy but with a studious demeanour and a jaw set in grim determination. An artist. Already his 'Maple Leaf Rag' (1899) had set the form and style for instrumental ragtime, a perfect model. 'This quaint creation,' wrote Rosenfeld in the *St Louis Globe-Democrat* (June 1903), had become a 'byword with musicians and [has] circulated itself throughout the nation in vast numbers'. Joplin played him a new rag called 'The Entertainer' which impressed him: 'It is a jingling work of a very original character, embracing various strains of a retentive character which set the foot in spontaneous action and leave an indelible imprint on the tympanum.'

Quite heady for the newspaper readers and a body blow against the many detractors of ragtime. Rosenfeld didn't deliver this mouthful to Joplin in person. Instead, he replied to 'The Entertainer' by executing a little hopping step which accentuated his gammy leg. 'You look like old Jim Crow,' said Joplin, adding, 'That's what they call "buck jumping" down in the hollow where the jook joint is.'

Then he told Rosenfeld about his dream of writing some grand American work. 'I am toiling upon an opera,' he said in serious tones. Rosenfeld knew that this was no coon-song darky, no opportunist Broadway scuffler-shuffler like Irving Jones and the rest, selling out the race for a mess of dollars. Scott Joplin, he wrote, was a dedicated composer whose ambitions rose even above ragtime. '[He] affirms that it is only a pastime for him to compose syncopated music.'

Rosie thought that perhaps Joplin was soaring out of the ball park. He understood the limits of pop and he himself revelled in its huckster aspects. Most of his life he'd engaged in huckstering his songs and his articles, a man who lived by his wits. Old Frank Harding it was who'd encouraged young Rosie to leave the Ohio sticks and come to New York and learn the tricks of the trade. Rosie had learned how to beg, borrow and steal songs; to place them with several publishers at once and to sometimes reap as much as $500 as an advance. Another trick was to sell the idea outright and then hire a writer to flesh it out with notes and lyrics. He called that 'sub-contracting'. With the rest of the money he'd sail off to the races, to the wine bars, to busty women with pianos in their apartments and a desire to be wooed.

From the middle 1880s Rosie walked with a limp. This was caused by an accident involving one of his famous rubber cheques. After he'd bounced the cheque in a Manhattan bank the police were quickly summoned but Rosie retreated out of a window. Trouble was – he was two storeys up and so he had a nasty fall. The resulting limp he concealed by wearing vast and billowing bell-bottom trousers (in bright checks). He complemented the trousers with wedding-guest jackets and gold-trimmed waistcoats. All this, together with his Saturnine face and silky moustache, made Monroe Rosenfeld a very colourful character in a business that, as we have seen, was growing more and more serious and ledger-minded. Mind you, in his day Rosie had had his fill of hits: 'Johnny Get Your Gun' (with minstrel dance), 'Come Along You Sinners' (a rousing spiritual), 'With All Her Faults I Love Her Still' (Theodore Metz complained that Rosie had stolen his melody but Rosie knew Metz had stolen it from some peasant in Europe), 'Those Wedding Bells Shall Not Ring Out Tonight' and 'Take Back Your Gold'. These last two were big sellers and very much in the Charles K. Harris mould.

Rosie should have followed Harris to the end of the line – and abandoned the street for a publishing office, good steady job, with hot dinners and early to bed. But Rosie, because of fate or his own perverse personality, had a strong touch of the itchy-koo and preferred to stay outside the system, at liberty. By 1909 he was dead broke.

The editor of the *New York Herald*, an old friend, took pity and commissioned him to write a series of articles on the burgeoning song factory now nestled on 28th Street between 6th and Broadway. So one steaming hot afternoon in August there was Rosie hobbling up the stairs of the Harry Von Tilzer Publishing Company in search of copy.

Now, Harry was a character too, but he also knew how to balance the books. He'd started life as Harry Gumm of Indiana with four brothers and an itch to get out of the backwoods and into show business. From selling shoes he'd got into a circus band and then a vaudeville band. He was a good, if illiterate, pianist. Then he got into songwriting and poverty in New York where he shared a cold-water flat with Andrew Sterling. They wrote together by the light of the lamp down in the street. After the usual hard knocks they scored with 'My Old New Hampshire Home' and the like; and in the coon-song era they really struck gold with 'Rufus Rastus Johnson Brown' and 'Alexander (Don't You Love Your Baby No More)?' Whenever a blackface act was called 'Alexander' it was always good for a laugh – something ridiculous about a darky being called such a grandiose name.

Harry was grand these days – if not grandiose – with his

assumed last name of 'Von Tilzer' and his suite of offices. He was quite respectable and always home in time for dinner. Recently, he'd been reading Sigmund Freud and he'd had a brainwave. What about this for a title? 'I Want a Girl Just Like the Girl That Married Dear Old Dad'?! Rosie said it was good and Harry nodded. And what could he do for Rosie? Rosie explained about his commissioned series of articles on the song business. Harry was in a hurry and he wondered why Rosie wasn't still in the game, writing hits. You must keep young – it isn't enough to sport loud check trousers. Rosie pulled out his notepad, wiped his brow with a red silk handkerchief – and then the phone rang. There were more calls until Rosie's face must have looked despondent because Harry suddenly began dictating:

'You need a good title. Look, it's a hot day and the windows are wide open. Listen to the sound of my friends and rivals bashing out their music on bashed-up pianos. It's a helluva racket. It's like a kitchen clatter. You know what I call this area? TIN PAN ALLEY! And you can print that if you give me credit.'

Rosie printed it but he didn't give any credit.

4

Come on and Hear!

The American song scene was thus set. Stephen Foster and his disorderly colleagues had modelled the song styles, while Chas K. Harris and his coordinated brothers had met the market, eyes down on the ledger line. Onto the stage, sure-footed, stepped Irving Berlin. Only a bullet could stop him now. His audience – twentieth-century society – was ready, eager to get out of house and home, to go places and do things. And when, like a fairground barker, Berlin invited everybody to come on and hear Alexander's Ragtime Band who in the world could resist such an exciting and insidious siren? Especially when this rocking ragtime pleasure boat would sail safe in the bosom of that sweet old Swanee River where nostalgia steamed continuously from an ancient soup?

We will now examine how Irving Berlin, an Alley neophyte in 1909, became the Ragtime King by 1912.

We last left him about to start reporting for work at the Ted Snyder Music Company, 112 West 38th St, New York, New York. For $25 a week, plus royalties, he was to provide words, and words alone. No messing about with music at this stage of the game. Ted was the melody man and though he couldn't read or write the little black dots he paid guys to take down the music so skilfully they could score a squashed fly on a manuscript. Irving should forget about 'lyrics' and anything high-flown and stick to the parodies, the cute and clever lines, the jerky patterns of saloon and street. So sometimes his grammar was wrong? Put it down to Siberia, to the immigrant boat, to no schooling. And chalk it up as a possible hit – because that slangy style is how the customers talk.

Irving worked real hard. He was putting words to a song a day, sometimes more. He was even writing copy for the Snyder ads in *Variety*, the new show-biz trade paper. In June, when New York was getting ready for a sweltering summer, he announced in a bold type, half-page ad:

> WEATHER NOTES – Look Out For A Cyclone!
> 'MY WIFE'S GONE TO THE COUNTRY'
> '(HURRAH – HURRAH)'
> Discovered by those 'It' Song Explorers IRVING
> BERLIN, GEO. WHITING and TED SNYDER.

The ad was directed at 'recognized artists' who were encouraged to visit the Snyder office where they could avail themselves of a free demonstration – by Irving Berlin himself in one of the better cubicles. And also the artist could pick up his or her free 'professional copy'. Like most of the songs on which Irving worked in those early days, 'My Wife's Gone to the Country' was packaged for hurling across the footlights of vaudeville – a loud report of quick wit with a sting in the tale, some good one-liners and punch lines.

This comedy song became Berlin's first hit and it was the talk of the trade. Snyder, twenty-eight, and Berlin, twenty-one, were firebrands flaring at the end of the Alley. New kids in town. The New Era was arriving, said the trade papers, and banished were the 'tiresome old ballads and quaint comic songs of the past'. Snyder, the guy with the un-poetical name and a lean and hungry look, bean-pole tall, was reputed to have but one desire: work. On the run always, he kept no regular hours, eating lunch out of his desk drawer, drumming up melodies fast on his office upright, melodies all fired up with a heap of 'staggeration' (according to *Billboard*). And Berlin, the little runt with the smirk and the mop, wasn't far behind Snyder in the hard-work stakes. But who the hell was Geo. Whiting?

The song had hit like a flash flood in summer, but in fact there was much sweat in its making. In 1920 Berlin levelled with *American Magazine* about the rules for writing pops and, in particular, the truth behind this song. One can see how, already, he was dedicated to the crafting of commercial music, careful to obey rules, archly conservative.

One night in a barber shop, I ran into George Whiting, a vaudeville actor, and asked him if he could go to a show with me. 'Sure,' he said, and he added with a laugh, 'My wife's gone to the country.' Bing! *There* I had a common place familiar title line. It was singable, capable of humorous upbuilding, simple, and one that did not seriously offend against the 'sexless' rule; for wives and their offspring of both sexes, as well as their husbands, would be amused by singing it or hearing it sung.

I persuaded Whiting to forget the theatre and to devote the night to developing the line with me into a song. Now the usual and unsuccessful way of handling a line like that is to dash off a jumble of verses about the henpecked husband, all leading up to a chorus running, we'll say, something like this:

> 'My wife's gone to the country,
> She went away last night.
> Oh, I'm so glad! I'm so glad!
> I'm crazy with delight!'

Just wordy, obvious elaboration. No *punch*. All night I sweated to find what I knew was there, and finally I speared the lone word, just a single word, that *made* the song – and a fortune . . .
Listen:

> 'My wife's gone to the country!
> Hurrah, Hurrah!'

'Hurrah!' That lone word gave the whole idea of the song in one quick wallop. It gave the singer a chance to hoot with sheer joy. It *invited* the roomful to join in the hilarious shout. It everlastingly put the catch line over. And I wasn't content until I had used my good thing to the limit. 'She took her children with her – Hurrah! Hurrah!' – and so on.

The idea of audience participation had perhaps been learned from the steamboat-whistle gimmick in Al Piantadosi's 'My

66

Mariuccia'. The invitation to the mob to join in the fun was to find its triumph in 'Alexander's Ragtime Band', of course. Meanwhile, Berlin was learning the controls with which to guide the 'mob' (a favourite word of his) and, by the end of the night, he had a serviceable tune ready for this comedy number. A jumpy two-beat Celtic thing, Snyder liked it enough and put in his two bits by stuffing in some harmony.

Rushed out to catch the summer season, the song caught on at once in vaudeville. The papers were full of vacation news and many were the rotogravures of buxom society belles showing off in Saratoga. Husbands still working in town had a chance to sow wild oats. The song was an amusing way of touching on a sore point: there were millions of faithless husbands in puritan America – so many worms in the bud that conservative estimates reckon that one in ten Americans had syphilis. That very year, 1909, a magic bullet was discovered in 'Salvarson' but this was a well-kept secret with the press. They were more interested in the silly summer season and in this sensational, naughty comedy song. The *Evening Journal* commissioned Irving to write 200 extra verses and Irving obliged at once. God – how he worked! He was worse than Snyder.

And he was much cleverer with the press boys. He loved 'em, they loved him. He was good copy. He told them the song was written in an hour and introduced by the vaudeville acts 'by means of typewritten lyrics and interleaved sheets, pending the making of plates'. At least, that's how the *Billboard* editor printed his comments. In November he gave them some even riper stuff:

A true happening was the inspiration for this song. In July, a New York woman set out for Ocean Grove and on arrival, discovered that her watch and a small fur collar were missing. She thought it had dropped on the soft dining room rug, and so she wired to the maid at home, 'Let me know if you find anything on the dining room rug.' A few days later she got from the maid a letter saying, 'Dear Madam, I was to let you know if I found anything on the dining room rug. This is what I found this morning: three cigarette ends, 36 burnt matches and one pink slipper.'

Good old Irving! A feisty little guy with a blue sense of humour. Yet also a guy whose mood could change in a flash, becoming melancholy and silent. You could see him alone in restaurants where they had music with the meals, and there he was listening intently to the band or the pianist or the singer; you could see him alone in cafés, near a bunch of talkative Broadway weisenheimers. Suddenly, he'd jot down some lines. You could see him sometimes up and down Broadway at the end of the day (when he'd just got up), hurrying along, hugging himself, enjoying being in the noisiest city in the world. Rejoicing in the sound of trolley cars, elevated trains, pneumatic drills, steam hammers, hand organs, fish horns, junkmen yells, hucksters with cowbell attachments, banging elevators, the chap who whistles and the gang that serenades in harmony up the alley, the falling down boarding houses with fighting tenants and red-whiskered boarders choking newcomers while mothers and babies squall in the kitchen and Johnnie plunks the banjo to a song that Irving had a hand in putting together!

After the summer hit with the Wife Song there were changes made: Geo. Whiting lost *his* wife in a divorce action (but she returned to him when he made amends by writing the words to 'My Blue Heaven') and Irving Berlin was allowed to work at his apartment in his own peculiar hours. And he now had himself a hundred-dollar piano, but a rather special one.

It was an old-fashioned carved affair, a typical piece of heavy Victorian furniture. But with an attachment that was coming to be commonplace among the un-schooled songsters of Tin Pan Alley: under the keyboard was a lever which shifted the entire works so that the player could instantly be transposed into any other key while still fingering his favourite. All Irving could play in was F#. All he used was a finger in each hand. All he knew so far was what Ted Snyder had kindly taught him. All night long he laboured at this piano, blackening the bass keys with cigarette burns, packing more and more downy white feathers above, below and behind the strings so as to deaden the noise and thus not disturb the neighbours, and hammering out a tune that he wanted to flourish at Ted.

By the end of 1909 he'd proved he could handle a lot of the song models and wasn't just a wordsmith, a gagster, a parodist. He was becoming an all-round, fully fledged Alleyman. With Ted he'd written 'Do Your Duty, Doctor' (a love-sick coon song), 'Wild Cherry Rag' (a hot-dance number), 'Next to Your Mother, Who Do You Love?' (a comedy love plea), 'If I Thought You Wouldn't Tell' (the 'greatest conversation number'), 'I Wish That You Were My Gal, Molly' (the wooing song that Chuck Connors, King of the Bowery, sang to his rival's 'bundle', and won her over) and, not missing a trick of the season, 'Christmas Time Seems Years and Years Away' (a march song 'you can sing before or after Christmas'). And that's to name but a few.

He'd also scored with two songs written and composed by himself alone at the transposing piano. A Yiddish ragtime novelty called 'Yiddle, on Your Fiddle, Play Some Ragtime' (combining two song types) and a paraphrase of the famous light classical piece, 'Spring Song' which he cheekily called 'That Mesmerizing Mendelssohn Tune' and snuck in some tricksy fills ('Kiss me like you would your mother, one good kiss deserves another'). The ad in *Variety* ordered the trade: 'Get It and Make Your Act Classy.' Classy? Not yet. The sassy, hyper, action boys at Ted Snyder's hadn't yet come up with a real, sturdy, high-class ballad – like 'I Wonder Who's Kissing Her Now?' which Chas K. Harris had published this very year – a number that could bloom into an evergreen and live down the ages and keep you and the children, and the children's children, in the money.

But next year, in 1910, Irving and Snyder stuck to the pop novelties. Perhaps they had a hunch that git-go restlessness was in the air. Perhaps they had noticed a deeper tilt forward as the rushing businessman lanced along the sidewalks; perhaps they had spied that harried female stenographer as she gobbled her snatched lunch at the cafeteria. Perhaps they read the article in the *New York Herald* in which a Dr Shrady, psychiatrist, claimed that:

the subconscious mind takes in all today's multifarious noises and only later reacts. A man wears out, he breaks down. The high blocks of the big cities make noise reverberate. Businessmen are always in a wild rush. Unlike Europe America doesn't break from 12 to 2, business is done between mouthfuls. The Europeans call it 'The American Disease' and we wonder why Americans die young and their widows go off to bask in Pasadena.

Snyder and Irving chose ragtime to express the new fever pitch whistling round the cities. Ragtime, their ragtime, had shed its rustic rural ancestry, was no longer restricted to Negroes and plantations; it wasn't coloured time any more but modern times. It was now the rhythmic reflection of slangy, witty, short-handed modern speech patterns—with dolls and babes and somebody doing it if you don't. Ragtime was going white-face and was standing for all that was up-to-date and peppy. There were still to be found funny darkies peppering the rag songs but these characters were being replaced by the regular city folk, the ones who ought to have known better.

'Oh, That Draggy Rag' that made you want to go to heaven on an Erie train, but 'Stop, Stop, Stop' you order when you didn't really want him/her to stop at all but to keep on satisfying that something by tying yourself right up your lover's side and then frying each kiss in honey, um-um-um-umm; and your attention turns to the magical maker of music as food for love, to the 'Piano Man' who sits on his stool like a king on a throne with the melody just nestling in his fingertips and then oozing out all over the keys so that the girlie-girl feels like kneeling and appealing to her piano man and the whole deal's becoming a sizzle but nothing compared to our dandy old darky 'Alexander and His Clarinet' which he plays outside Miss Eliza's window with so much vim that in the next verse he's played himself into her bedroom where he performs so well that in future she can't sleep a wink, crying out constantly for her lover Alexander and especially for his clarinet.

'Alexander and His Clarinet' died but the vim and vigour lived on in Berlin and Snyder: later that year they took it on stage for their booking in the Shubert revue, *Up and Down Broadway*. They needed some air to test these pop novelties and anyway Irving was a fit-to-be-hog-tied ham. Can you imagine these two Alleymen tricksters clad in billowing white bags and striped blazers and carrying tennis rackets as they try their darnedest to stroll onto the stage like swells and discover a restful garden and, what luck!, a piano?!

Settled on stage the boys fell into their natural street rhythms, giving the mob out there in the gloom a new number about a leader man playing ragtime music grand with a trombone blowin' and dem fiddles goin'. But if that don't get 'em the next one will – a dialect song, not a Yiddish one, but a tale of 'Sweet Italian Love' and how you don't need a moonlight lovey-dovin' because you can make da sweet Italian love in da house or on da roof or even in da cellar and when you kiss your pet it's like spagette . . .

After the show Snyder said that the act went down fine but how long can you keep comedy novelties afloat at today's stormy pace? You need sturdier songs, you need a comprehensive catalogue. So Snyder's next work was 'Roses and Memories', a descriptive instrumental to be played *Andantino con moto*. Irving had a try at an instrumental, too. Early one morning, in one of the Snyder cubicles, he knocked out a lively march with a bugle-call motif in the main strain (the trio) plus a snatch of 'Swanee River'. It had all the other parts and modulations like any decent march or rag classic form.

'Alexander's Ragtime Band' was tried out at Jesse Lasky's Folies Bergere, a lavish cabaret theatre, but nobody paid much attention and management soon dropped it. Snyder didn't bother to print up copies. Irving slipped the manuscript into his desk drawer. He didn't trust it in Snyder's drawer as that was full of lunch remnants, some of which dated back months. Anyway, instrumentals these days were dicey sellers. Take 'The Grizzly Bear' for example: George Botsford, a fine ragtime player and one of the Snyder staff pianists, had come up with a good jumping tune and a voguish title, referring to one of the weird new dances hailing from the outer reaches. Lately, the New York papers had been reporting the popularity of barnyard dance steps involving turkeys and chickens from out of the South; and from the West coast came the Grizzly Bear, whatever that was. Supposedly there *were* steps but nobody seemed to know how to execute them and anyway the dance, like the other animal dances, was really just an excuse to get close to a gorgeous bundle and hug her tight. Any night at a Broadway cabaret or dance hall you could see folks bumping and bouncing and improvising, like they were infected.

'The Grizzly Bear' as a plain instrumental didn't take off. So Snyder got Irving to *describe* the dance, to tell the people what to do to the new restlessness. Irving was so very good at writing *about* a subject, whether it be syncopation or ethnicity, and injecting that subject with his own quirks: in the Grizzly Bear song the man says, 'If they do this dance in heaven, shoot me hon', tonight at seven!', followed by 'You and me is two, I'll make it one when we get through.' Strong meat but A-OK instructions and perfect for vaudeville shouter queens like Sophie Tucker and Mae West. The latter, with her 'special action' breast and thigh-patting movements, won hands down for suggestiveness.

'The Grizzly Bear' song was a bestseller and the first pop to describe the coming craze of dancemania.

Right in the middle of all this frenzied activity Henry Waterson, who had taken a shine to Irving, invited the lad to accompany him on a trip to Britain to see how their local representative Bert Feldman was getting along. They sailed in early October, 1910, on the *Lusitania;* once on board Irving simply couldn't relax but kept pacing the deck and constantly refused quoit games with the ladies. Henry got him interested in betting on how many miles the ship would cover each day. Henry lost a lot of money on that game. Irving wondered how his songs sold in Britain; said he'd like to meet the guys who wrote 'Poor John' and those other witty music-hall jobs, oh, and what about fixing a meeting with the musical-comedy writers that Jerry Kern had mentioned, like Leslie Stuart of 'Floradora' fame? These guys were published in high-priced sheets, loftier than the Snyder 10–cent pops. Henry said the money's in the 10 centers because you can sell in more volume but you got to keep moving with the times.

London, black and sooty and grim and cold, was miles behind the times but charmingly full of old-world manners and Dickensian characters. Bert Feldman, a sporty, no-nonsense bachelor with a dangerous moustache, was told by Waterson and Irving to get ready for the ragtime onslaught. Feldman replied that he was ready, aye, ready and had instigated a sixpenny-edition series with black-and-white covers that was already selling very nicely, thank you. He was betting on ragtime, not to worry. As for his music rivals, Feldman told the New York dynamos to take a look around and watch out for the horse manure.

At Francis, Day & Hunter, in Charing Cross Road, they were led through a rabbit warren of pokey, narrow, windy corridors which led nowhere; in musty cells sat hunched clerks at high desks; on Fridays the songwriters lined up at the side door to sell a few songs about kippers and mothers-in-law. At least Francis, Day & Hunter had a window display. The rest of the London publishers were shrinking violets, ashamed of the game or too darned well-bred. The publishers of the 'drawing room' type songs had placed a gulf between their dignified material and music-hall or pop songs. They were proud of never having window displays, never advertising, and never, ever talking to the newspapers. The British pop publishers still adhered to the system of giving music-hall stars exclusive performance rights to songs, thus killing widespread plugging. What's more, these ruddy stars demanded a cut of the royalties before taking on a new song. It's enough to make me lose what hair I've got left, said Feldman, but at Christmas pantomime time all songs become 'free', anyone can sing them, and that's when we get our big sales. And, by George, do they love the Berlin songs! 'Yiddle, on Your Fiddle, Play Some Ragtime' did very well last Christmas and we were able to give our staff a slap-up dinner with crackers and cigars.

Irving was thrilled to meet D. Eardley-Wilmot and Hermann Löhr in a quaint little Bloomsbury bar where they sipped best sherry. These two gents had just written a superior ballad for Chappell's, a high-priced and fancy firm who published the best of the musical-comedy men (some of whom were Oxford-educated and others were educated 'near Oxford'). Irving was given a copy of the song, 'Little Grey Home in the West', and when he got back to lil' ole New York (very thankful to be safe in the twentieth century again) he had a Snyder pianist run it down and take it to bits. Irving was most impressed and so was Snyder. They got together and wrote a high-class ballad called 'Dreams, Just Dreams', splattering it with lines that sang of 'missives of sweet consolation' and sunbeams in flight and an eery thought about love finding a grave – and rhyming it with crave.

The song was no good but you must keep expanding and Irving was determined to pursue this line and reach the plateau of lasting ballads, permanent fixtures in the catalogue. To this end he played the nighthawk, sitting up alone in his flat, wired on coffee and cigarettes, punching out a new song till way past dawn and then in the morning hurrying into the Snyder office where a staff arranger, slowing him down, would ink the number into literate form and so, finally, Irving could hit the pillows till well into late afternoon.

A cock-eyed life but demons were driving him and sometimes the syntax was screwy when the feelings were right. Yet still that great big block-busting ballad hit deserted him. Would he ever reach the ranks of a song poet like Victor Herbert, whose current smash was 'Ah, Sweet Mystery of Life'? Here was this roly-poly smiley broth of a Dubliner downing oysters by the dozen, having a wonderful time and writing classics with ease! And here was edgy Irving, with matching luggage under his eyes and a wild anarchist look in those black eyes, worry-warting himself so much that meals became a tornado in his stomach. Hard candy helped settle him but another bad habit was formed.

It was, however, a pop novelty that did the trick for Irving in 1911. 'Alexander's Ragtime Band', dusted off and set to words, was to make him America's top songwriter by the end of the year. And by the end of the following year, 1912, over 2 million copies of the song had been sold in America

alone, while in Europe the song was to be credited with
starting the craze for American syncopation. In 1913, when
Irving appeared as an act at London music halls, audiences
believed him to be the one and only King of Ragtime and
assumed that he'd written every single ragtime song ever
dreamed up.

'Alexander' opened up the whole world to Irving Berlin.
And he, in responding to the promise of the word 'ragtime',
was tapping into the mood of the era.

Yet, although the song spoke about ragtime there were but a
few specks of syncopation. Rhythmically, it was still Irving's
failed march instrumental of 1910. As to the music that
was re-discovered in the 1950s and enshrined as 'Classic
Ragtime', with Scott Joplin as its martyred saint, Berlin had
this to say: 'You know, I never did find out what ragtime
was.' The trick, unconsciously played, was in capturing a
nervous restlessness that was in the air, a dancing virus.
'No-one was more flabbergasted than I was at the smashing
hit it made,' he told a reporter in the 1920s.

We must now examine the music and words, before
tracing the song's phenomenal success trail.

The chorus made good use of familiar quotes – a bugle
call and a snatch of 'Swanee River' plus a smeared, repeated
opening phrase. A leftover from the march (which has the
same form as classic ragtime) gave the verse a novel twist
to the ear: it modulated at the end into the subdominant
key, thus setting the chorus onto a fresh path. No popular
song had done this before. Many were to copy. Had Irving's
key-change lever inspired such a shift?

The words bore traces of minstrelsy. The excited singer,
exhorting his honey to hurry (and, oddly, 'let's meander'*),
proclaimed that Alexander's was the 'bestest band what
am', noting that 'the clarinet is a colored pet'. Yet the cover
art-work and most performances depicted Alexander's band
as white-face. The song, therefore, wasn't shackled but
could race free through the new electric world. It was, in

---

* Not so odd when you realize there are few words that rhyme with
'Alexander'.

fact, a clarion-call summons to everybody to come take part in some twentieth-century fun. A similar summons became the anthem of 1950s youth when rock & roll arrived: Bill Haley, the square-dance caller instructing his hon' to get her glad rags on and 'Rock Around the Clock'.*

After he'd got over being flabbergasted, Berlin coolly analysed what he called his 'accidental hit' and suggested

> 'that the lyric, silly though it was, was fundamentally right. Its opening words, emphasised by immediate repetition – 'Come on and here! Come on and hear!' – were an invitation to 'come', to join in, and to 'hear' the singer and his song. And that idea of inviting every receptive auditor within shouting distance to become a part of the happy ruction – an idea pounded in again and again throughout the song in various ways – was the secret of the song's success.

And now the story:

Early in 1911 Berlin had been invited to join the Friar's Club, a charitable show-business fraternity. This was a great honour – and he got an even greater one when he was asked to perform in the fourth annual Frolic of the Friars to be presented to the public at the New Amsterdam Theatre on Sunday night, 29 May. The star-studded bill included his mentor, George M. Cohan. The act that he would be in was called 'The Piano Bugs', a 'travesty' (a take-off) of Jesse Lasky's 'Pianophiends'. A bunch of piano-pounding Alleymen would unite on some hilarious novelty number, to be written – by Irving Berlin.

So he fished out the march manuscript and knocked out some words which he later admitted were 'simply terrible' and 'silly in the matter of common sense'. But they fitted the tune and the show's setting which was the 'olio', or variety bill, portion of a typical minstrel show (George M. Cohan would provide some 'nigger comedy' in his 'Pullman Porter Ball' sketch). 'The Piano Bugs' were led by composer Jean ('Chinatown, My Chinatown') Schwartz at a baby

---

* Interestingly, Max Freedman, who co-wrote this song, was born in 1893, only five years after Irving Berlin.

grand and he had in his command such rag composers as Henry Lodge and George Botsford as well as the highly successful ballad composer Ernest Ball (who went on to write 'When Irish Eyes Are Smiling' and 'Let the Rest of the World Go By'. Doing his best with a finger in each hand was Irving Berlin.

'Alexander's Ragtime Band' was well received by the (mostly industry) audience but it wasn't a riot. And press coverage was overshadowed by the death, on the Monday, of W.S. Gilbert (by drowning). The great lyricist (father of musical comedy) was revered in America and had become a particular hero of Berlin's. However, Max Winslow was determined to hang in there with 'Alexander'. There was something about the demand-call of those words. But nobody else in the Snyder office had much faith in the number, not even Irving. No plugging planned, no advertising, no nothing.

Max reckoned there'd be few stage plugs. Summer was coming in and that meant most of Broadway would be dark. Too hot and sticky for theatre-going. Of course, George M. Cohan would keep his latest show running but that was an exception, that was unstoppable George M. plus his unstoppable public. Most of New York society would be cooling off at fashionable watering places with the press reporting breathlessly on their hats, cravats and such. Already there had been articles about the craze for 'frapped milk with a twist of lemon' as a chaser for champagne cup. The Silly Season was here again and no wars were around to offset it. But, after all, the Silly Season of 1909 had led Snyder to sell a heap of sheets with 'My Wife's Gone to the Country'.

Only one 'Big Summer Show' was being advertised: *The Merry Whirl*, a two-part extravaganza at the Columbia starting 12 June and scheduled to run through the entire long, hot summer. Fat chance. Boasting a company of seventy-six and two star comics (Morton & Moore), *The Merry Whirl* attempted in its ads to appear a real ritzy Broadway show. But it was really only tits and ass set to music. For the Columbia Theatre was a burlesque house, although it did claim to have brought 'distinction' to this lower limb of the theatre art.

The show already had a full score by Leo Edwards but Max was undaunted. He would make 'Alexander' a necessity and notify Aaron Hoffman, the producer, to that effect. Hoffman was 'in meetings' every time Max called round to the theatre but, finally, he trapped him one morning in the subway, forcing a professional copy on the startled producer, inviting him to lunch at Lindy's, and informing the world that Hoffman's hand held a 'certified future smash'.

After lunch, and a good one too, Hoffman decided the number might make a big production set-piece for the finale to Act I, 'The Magic Ring'. Here's the deal: a grandfather clock (comic Morton) comes to life and meets up with an animated snowman (comic Moore) who's just waltzed in off the street. Next we bring on the girls, first in bevies and then in droves, all of them dressed for the summer heat: very lightly. Get the picture? Makes as much sense as a Cohan show and there's little else running against us – only a quick run of mouldy old-timers at the Colonial, songs of the Gay Nineties and all that crap: James and Bonnie Thornton reviving such cadavers as 'When You Were Sweet Sixteen'. At the Columbia show-biz was bang up-to-date.

The show opened well and reviews were good. The *New York Herald* described the plot as best it could, adding that 'the chorus flashed on and off at the slightest provocation in costumes that were pretty, new and fresh-looking, if sometimes a bit too scant'. The reviewer went on to note:

> Of the 8 or 10 musical numbers 'Alexander's Ragtime Band' with the grandfather clock and the snowman was the one that pleased the audience most, and when a Columbia audience are pleased they show it in no uncertain way. They applaud and whistle and decline to let the show go on until they have encores enough. They seemed to be endless for this number.

By the middle of July a phenomenal heat-wave was killing off hundreds of New Yorkers. More theatres closed. But George M. Cohan soldiered on – and so did *The Merry*

Whirl. The *New York Herald* reported that 'the large chorus of young women are determined to keep the theatre open all summer'.

What made the show a survivor was not the extensive electric fans, nor a long bar featuring cooling drink concoctions, nor even the sexy females. It was 'Alexander's Ragtime Band' that made the show the hit of the summer and everyone in the trade was amazed by this phenomenon, unknown in the history of the business.

The Ted Snyder Company was caught unprepared and orders had to be farmed out to rival presses. *The Merry Whirl* had started the rush in New York and environs – but now came demands for copies from other parts of the country. Somehow, simultaneously, the song had caught the mood of the nation and singers who took up the number found an immediate audience. In Chicago vaudeville, Emma Carus (a discovery of Rosie Rosenfeld's from back in the nineties) made the song a hit, shouting strenuously from the depths of her ample bosom. When Emma ordered you to 'Come on and hear' you'd better obey; her audiences immediately fell into line. Snyder's rewarded her by ovalling her picture on the cover of early editions. Also, on the road and in New York, a young fellow called Al Jolson (born Asa Yoelson in Russia) was selling 'Alexander' like the devil to audiences at Lew Dockstader's minstrel show.

By the autumn countless acts, human and animal, were using the song and most of the USA was aware of Alexander and his crazy band and that this crew was telling America to get up, get out and have a good time. And in England, in Europe, and even in Imperial Russia, the song was spread, understood as the anthem of a new and coon-liberated ragtime dance in which everybody and his wife could take part and no special dance clothing had to be worn. Yankee Doodle was conquering peacefully.

Irving himself was at once tickled pink and bemused. It was nice to have a hit but the taste of the mob was so hard to fathom. All that night work trying to score with a high-class ballad and then international fame is gained by way of a novelty song, an accidental! 'The musical sensation of the decade,' barked *Variety* in September, reckoning that the new boy would net $50,000 by year's end. Don't question the mysterious hit-making process, bask in the dollar success.

But Irving's big thrill came when he, a wandering insomniac, found himself one dawn in a sleazy part of town. Standing in front of a beerhall, surveying his line of tarts, was a skinny pimp in a shouting overcoat. As the icy wind blew the creature moved his shoulders like a boxer, swivelled his neck around the celluloid collar, snapped his fingers and clapped his hands alternately, while singing in an eery, light tenor: 'Come on and hear! Come on and hear! I got the best tarts in the land!' Irving, fascinated, hung around until he saw himself in danger of becoming a potential customer. He went home very happy and slept like a baby.

In that same September he was booked as a headliner at Hammerstein's vaudeville theatre. In tails that almost dusted the stage he did a sixteen-minute act, introducing some of his latest offerings – a 'wop', a 'yid' and a 'coon' song – and also a fizzy thing called 'That Mysterious Rag'. The man from *Variety* wrote that the newcomer had a 'dandy style in delivering a song'. Everyone agreed with *Variety* that Irving Berlin was the 'instigator of the present craze for ragtime songs'. Everyone agreed with the Hammerstein placard that claimed Irving Berlin was the Ragtime King.

And yet Alexander, a jovial, pop-eyed conductor of African origin, was also fixed in the public mind as the very essence of hot rhythm. The mythical coon, the fantasy, the man who really wasn't there – he simply wouldn't go away. Minstrelsy's great black paws were messing up the progressiveness of the twentieth century.

Like a hovering ghost this bogeyman spoiled what should have been a triumphant party for Irving. At the end of 1911, with the Ted Snyder Company's coffers swollen with ragtime money, Henry Waterson invited Irving to come aboard as a partner (albeit, a minority shareholder). From now and henceforth the company was to be known as 'Waterson, Berlin & Snyder'. There would be a grand party to celebrate; the press would be invited.

Henry looked marvellous. He wore his broad-brimmed

hat and his string tie and he conducted the party like a minstrel interlocutor supreme. At the appropriate moment, and when everybody's glasses were charged with real French champagne, Henry made a little speech about Irving. Then he cracked this one directly at the Ragtime King: 'You know, Irvy, there's a story circulating on Broadway – that the reason you can turn out so much golden ragtime is because you got your own special piccaninny tucked away in a closet!'

Everybody laughed like hell. Even Irving smiled wanly. But inside he was churning. What an unjust crack! He'd worked up his ragtime himself – by mixing skillfully from the ingredients at hand. He was a concoctor, almost an inventor. He wasn't stealing anything from anybody. He knew what real coloured people were like. He knew that these days they preferred to be called 'Negroes', that there was a brotherhood of fine, upstanding New York Negroes right now creating operas and poetry and that not a few of them held college degrees and could score music and quote Voltaire. He knew that there was a Negro music company called Gotham-Attucks and that they were in need of a hit. He knew all this but he was still smiling and holding on to his champagne.

But, surely, as song salesmen, the assembled company understood that Alexander only existed in the minds of himself and Harry Von Tilzer and the white coon vaudeville act from which Harry had borrowed the pretentious name? Surely these people here knew that all of us were dragging on the nigger-minstrel tradition which dates back donkey's years to when an itinerant army of Jumping Jim Crows had got together to rattle the bones, bang the tambourine and plunk the banjo into a major industry that, incidentally, did wonders for the sales of wigs, swallow-tail coats and boot polish?

Why America and the world were so obsessed with the spectre of whites as blacks was a matter for historians and not for Alleymen. But one thing was quite clear (and Irving would have shouted it out loud at Henry's party if he'd been that way inclined): the all-dancing, all-laughing, all-excited, chickened-out, watermelon-gorged Negro was

81

actually a marionette whose strings were wound tightly round the fingers of the songsmiths of America. And all Irving was doing was serving the public to the best of his abilities. The sooner this dancing coon could be eliminated the better!

I like to believe Irving was thinking these good things at Henry's party.

5

The Strange Myth of the Hot Coon

Unfortunately, the myth of the black prisoner in the closet persisted long after Henry's party. It wasn't only Irving Berlin who was accused of ripping off the heart and soul of the American black. Many other white songwriters and performers were to be condemned. Generations of well-meaning and guilt-ridden historians, journalists, musicians and plain members of the public, have credited ragtime, jazz, rock & roll, and anything soaked in syncopation as the contribution – and the only one – of the Afro-American. All God's children got rhythm – who could ask for anything more?

Black Americans were to ask for much more. And as the nineteenth century turned into the twentieth they were to ask for it within the formalities of the white master: in books, poems, paintings, and art music; in business and the patent and copyright offices. They were to prove that they were men, albeit tinted. But in popular entertainment, in informalities, they were to find it well nigh impossible to smash the mould that cast them as the ever-loving, red-hot coon. They made some progress after the 1860s, they actually appeared on stage, they eventually made it to Broadway – but they still were wearing the mask and playing the fool as Sambo, Rastus, Jim Crow and Zip Coon. They never really got the hang of organization. They never got gung-ho in a team. But maybe the Big Lie was too big to destroy – and who would pay money to watch a blackman who acted just like you and me?

83

It has been the Big Lie that blacks are born with a monopoly on the Big Beat. This injustice, starting in the eighteenth century, lasted well into the Age of Rock – Mick Jagger's strutting and shouting shows that the white nigger-minstrel tradition is still alive. Historians, explaining the popularity of the minstrel show (from the 1850s until the late 1890s it was America's favourite entertainment and its only theatrical contribution), claim that the black mask was an attempt to satisfy a variety of cultural needs within the instant USA (a country founded on theories and rules). These needs included: All-American folk heroes speaking the plain truth in dialect (as opposed to the high-falutin' European culture of the East Coast elite); licensed Fools who, from behind the blackface mask, could satirize the topics of the day whether they be immigration, women's rights, redskin uprisings, or crazes for phrenology and electricity.

Perhaps the minstrels satisfied these needs. But couldn't Daniel Boone or Davy Crockett have played the American hero, straight or comic, as well as Sambo? I believe that Sambo, the blackface mask, was chosen as the figure of fun and fear because (a) he looked different, (b) ignorance as myth portrayed him as the ultimate in libertine fantasy, (c) in creating Sambo the American people were able to cartoon away the basic contradiction of their civilization: that, in this land of the free, there were certain citizens who would never be treated as such.

But looks played the biggest part in the popularity of Sambo. Minstrelsy had a morbid fascination for the physical details of the Negro – from his woolly hair, wide and flat nose and quivering nostrils, thick lips and vast cave mouth, down to his huge feet with prehensile toes. The sheet-music cover artists grew skilled at depicting this monster from the Deep South. The women were cast as fat earth mammies or dusky desirable maidens. The women definitely got a better deal in the myth. Sometimes a black girl was actually elevated into romanticism, on a plane with white maidens. For example, Edwin Christy (who founded an early and highly successful minstrel troupe) wrote a song in 1853 called 'She's Black but That's No Matter'.

My Dinah, dear me, she's beautiful quite,
As a star that shines calmly, at close of the night.
A voice like a Siren, a foot like a Fay –
She's just such a gal you don't meet every day . . .
VOICE (spoken): BUT SHE'S BLACK!

The blinded lover goes on for verse after verse, singing the praises of his girl. But the voice keeps interrupting: 'BUT SHE'S BLACK!'

The voice in the song was facing reality. Miscegenation was a crime in many states and a horror in the South. And yet there must have been much clandestine coupling between black and white because it was estimated that, by the early 1900s, over a third of America's Negroes were mulattoes (mixed blood) and, within this category, were mathematical gradings like quadroon and octoroon. The real, dark darky, the black-as-night African of the popular songs and myths, was the Invisible Man as far as the outside world was concerned. And the real music of the black American was never exposed to the average white American. Inside the Afro-American church, the camp meetings, the jook joints and honky tonks, was growing and thriving a musical culture that truly could be said to have black characteristics and African retentions. But few outsiders ventured into real black America and so the 'pop coon' was a stage invention and was to become such an established convention that by the end of the nineteenth century blacks were joining whites in creating songs to support the myth of the hot coon.

Let us look at the history of the stage Sambo in a little more detail because he was to become a staple character in pop songs right up until the 1970s, e.g. 'Bad, Bad Leroy Brown'. He lurked in some of Berlin's hotter numbers. He was never a true impersonation of the Negro, any more than a man in a bowler hat sipping tea and shouting tally ho (or wearing a cloth cap and muffler and speaking in a Beatle accent) is your real Englishman. Unhappily, he first appeared as a song subject in late-eighteenth century London when the Age of Reason was giving way to the Age of Romance and tales of primitive, natural South Sea savages were filtering into the stuffy, over-civilized drawing-rooms of the rich and bored.

In a spate of polite novelty songs he was pictured as pathetic and long-suffering as a slave but a tiresome buffoon as a freedman. Thus Mungo in breeches and periwig should be kicked about indiscriminately. Here, right at the start, we have the two essential stereotypes: the pure and under a magnolia tree in the moonlight; and Zip Coon, the smart-assed city slicker in sausage-skintight pants, swallow-tail blue coat with padded shoulders, and everything else in But – in his childish bounce and stamp and shout and smile there was a freedom that everyone envied and desired.

In America, where matters were complicated by the presence of real blackamoors as cogs (or clogs) in the economy, the two basic characters were soon established by white American entertainers: Jim Crow, the servile, slow-witted old shuffler who'd be far better off back on the plantation where, after a hard day's slaving, he could blubber nonsense songs as he lay sprawled and stuffed with baked possum under a magnolia tree in the moonlight; and Zip Coon, the smart-assed city slicker in sausage-skin-tight pants, swallow-tail blue coat with padded shoulders, and everything else in the line of the latest high fashion, living at no fixed abode but living definitely for the fun of the fleeting moment (and probably off the earnings of a comely octoroon).*

---

* This must not become a history of blackface minstrelsy but, in passing, it might be worth telling the story of two Jim Crows as an example of irony. Thomas Rice, the 'Daddy of Minstrelsy', was an actor at liberty in Louisville, Kentucky, in 1828. Not a salubrious city but full of amusing Negroes. Rice, mooching round the stables, was so intrigued by the peculiar song and dance of a crippled black groom that he borrowed the entire spectacle for his stage act (including the cripple's ragged outfit). 'Jump Jim Crow' was an immediate success with audiences and, by the late 1830s, Rice had not only played Jim in New York but also in London. Other 'Ethiopian Delineators' copied him and, eventually, troupes formed and these became the first American minstrel shows. But 'Jim Crow' burst the bonds of mere entertainment: by the 1890s the word had become pejorative, standing for all that was shuffling, deadbeat and backward about the Southern Negro. The segregationalist statutes passed by the Southern States at this time (in retaliation for the sudden appearance of Zip Coon, carpetbagger freedman sent by the North as the scourge of the South) were called 'Jim Crow Laws'.

Caged within the minstrel show, which had settled into its classic format by the 1850s, our stage Sambos (active Zip and passive Jim) were soon institutionalized as conventions: golliwogs for the purveying of polite family entertainment. Eastern good taste, based on Old World models, had smothered the raw-onion belches of the native American bushland. The real people of colour were again left waiting in the wings.

This move towards gentility in the portrayal of blacks is reflected in the names of the minstrel companies. They were 'Sable Harmonizers', 'Nightingale Serenaders', 'Aeolians' and even 'Opera Troupes'. Publicity pictures showed that, out of character, the minstrels were sober, even sombre, citizens and all without a trace of Negro blood. Newspapers were asked to please make this clear.

After the Civil War, with minstrelsy now America's most popular entertainment, the business went big. M.B. Leavitt coined the word 'Gigantean' to describe his shows, while the Barlow Brothers were content with 'Mammoth' and 'Magnificent'. Colonel Jack Haverly came up with 'Mastadon' and his big bass drum was posted with the boast: 'Forty Minstrels – Count 'Em! Forty!'

This harmless moveable fête was perfect for whole families who could attend a performance without fear of meeting any real darkies or other improprieties. On stage the shining black moon faces formed a decorative half-circle background to such star turns as dancing turkeys, singing cats, and the Eight Foot Giant from China. Nowhere was

---

But who was the real Jim Crow? Not a cowed dog at all, nor a comic cripple. An early American success story: born in 1754 in South America his freed black parents had been captured and brought as slaves to New York. There they had led a slave uprising which ended with their both being burned alive as punishment. Their son escaped and, as Jim Crow, became a popular New York street busker well known for his fiddling and his Yambo Yam dance. He made enough money to eventually settle down in Virginia with his white wife and a passel of slaves. He died peaceful and portly in 1809.

But this Jim Crow didn't fit neatly into what the public wanted of Negroes so his story was forgotten. It appears, however, on neutral territory in Harry Reynold's book, *Minstrel Memories*, published in Britain in 1928.

there the danger of even an echo of the real black bogeyman. Blackface had become commonplace: everyone's uncle blacked up at parties or picnics or office functions. Edwin Booth, the famous thespian, had once done a Sambo act in a courthouse; P.T. Barnum, standing in for an inebriated minstrel, blacked up to sing 'Such a Gittin' Upstairs'; Alley publisher Julius Witmark started show life in blackface; one of the Rockefellers joined the world of burnt cork and boot polish for a while. Like dressing up for a costume party, minstrelsy was a great way to get out of yourself – but it was only a temporary escape from the serious business of real life.

In the full-time professional minstrel scene there were yodelling minstrels, Negro Dutchmen, coal-black Hebrews, Irish-American Ethiopians (like Jerry Cohan, father of the great George M.) and assorted blackface female impersonators and bagpipers. In Britain the movement away from minstrel similarity to real Negroes had started much earlier. There had been precious few examples to study – most blacks were the servants of the rich and so it was in the salons of the rich that such entertainers as Charles Dibdin gained first renown. E.W. Mackney and J. Cave took their blackamoor acts into the wider world of the early music halls where Great Men like William Gladstone and Robert Peel were sometimes moved to tears by the sooty image of a universal sufferer, resembling nothing more frightening than a chimney sweep with an exotic brogue. Even William Thackeray, a seasoned Irishman, was held prisoner by the artistic refinements of Albion minstrelsy:

> I heard recently a minstrel with an ultra-negro complex sing a negro ballad that I confess moistened these spectacles in a most unexpected manner . . . I have gazed at hundreds of tragedy queens expiring on the stage in appropriate blank verse and I never wanted to wipe them . . . and behold a vagabond with corked face sings a little song, strikes a wild note which sets the heart thrilling with happy pity.

Of course, there was a sizeable number of people who felt that the Americans were better at depicting Negroes. After all, they had plenty of them at home to study. Within a few months of the debut of the Virginia Minstrels (the first minstrel show proper) in New York, 1843, the American troupe was showing off its noisy new act to excited Liverpudlians and, later, to the Royals themselves. One of the Americans, Dick Pelham, liked his reception so much that he settled in England. E.P. Christy, the future impresario of minstrelsy, stayed on long after the end of the tour, enjoying great success in Dublin and Blackpool.

But by the 1870s the British delineators had established troupes and theatres and halls and a polished refinement that led their spokesmen to claim that minstrelsy had been brought to its hightest state of perfection by the British. Their dancing was better (based on the Lancashire clog dance), their songs less morbid and lugubrious than the childish Americans, their vocalizing less guttural (especially on the lower notes). They had exported their own brand of nigger minstrelsy all over the Empire; in India the Ethiopians of Albion were especially loved by the natives and many a tense moment between the races had been settled by a song and dance. There is no record, however, of what the Ethiopians of Ethiopia thought of the Ethiopians of Albion.

The headquarters of British minstrelsy was St James's Hall in Piccadilly. To this Mecca flocked the faithful and their wives and families; from remote counties journeyed clergymen in search of vicarious thrills from little black Sambo. But more and more the shows whitewashed the negroid: bills might hold classical vocalists fluttering of larks and sweethearts, or earnest gentlemen in frock coats exhorting the congregation to push a little harder up the stream of life.

Philip Lee, son of a Dorset clergyman, had grown tired of the enervating uprightness of local minstrelsy. At the same time he had, through reading novels and studying sheet music, become intoxicated by the vision of dashing frontiersmen and prancing Negroes, neither of whom ever stopped for tea. When his father offered him a chance to visit the source of his insobriety he kissed the hem of the old man's surplice.

In New York, ostensibly on his father's estate business, he wangled an introduction to the Manhattan Minstrels, a fraternal organization of wealthy New York businessmen. The members, tickled by the boy's naive talk of cowboys, Indians and 'buck niggers', decided to hold a dinner in his honour at their minstrel headquarters, the Gramercy Park Hotel. Little did Philip Lee know that he was to be yet another victim of the Manhattan Minstrels' infamous 'Green Englishman Bean Feast' ritual. In other words, these captains of American industry were about to indulge in practical jokery of a most violent nature (but typical of that age and country).

Young Lee didn't demur when, upon entering the banquet room, he was blindfolded. He hardly uttered a sound when he was forced to walk the gauntlet to get whacked on the bottom by gleeful members. He did express surprise when he was scissored in the neck by massive thighs and kicked in the face by hobnailed boots. He expressed dismay when made to crawl the length of a table spread with many layers of buttered asparagus. At the end, unmasked and awarded many slaps on the back and grips of the hand, his only words were: 'But where are the *real* blackamoors?'

Where indeed?

The real black man had entered the minstrel game proper a few years before this 'Famously Funny Lee Dinner' (as it came to be called in minstrel legend). Just after the Civil War, trailing Emancipation Day, 'all-coloured' troupes emerged to offer All-America a nostalgia trip backwards to the good old days of peace and plenty, of blue blood and lemonade, of hot possum and happy niggers, stabled and statued in the Old South.

For Sambo had survived the war intact and Mr Interlocutor was still the Massa, still the Bossman: blacks were required to continue to play the character invented by their masters, indeed to puff out the caricature; white men would continue to run the successful shows, to rule the minstrel industry. So – both culturally and economically the New Negro, the Freedman, was really only exchanging one form of bondage for another (just as he was to exchange plantation for ghetto).

In the entrepreneurial stakes (winners must be slick-witted, close-fisted, groin-kicking, money-grabbers) the freedmen were to prove poor runners. They simply weren't yet the managerial sorts. In the precision-drilled, tight-assed, ensemble performance required by late Victorian minstrelsy, they were considered raggle-taggles. Slavery, of course, had tied them to the nursery, denying them the vital school of the rough-and-tumble market place, denying them the right to assemble, organize, to take part in the Great American Race. Peculiar and characteristic race talents – a lope or amble melting into a dance; a turn of phrase, a tone of voice soaring into a song – which had been retained and nurtured in an isolated environment, were to be only gradually revealed and absorbed by the world at large because of the imposed straitjacket and iron mask of the requirements of the dominant race. The dancing, prancing Afro-American, whooping and hollering and getting responses from a liberated white soul, was to be a subdominant chord (but, like that chord, subtly insidious) until the call of rock & roll, until tambourine gospel became secularized.

But now, after these generalizations, back into the minstrel fray – to see how blacks fared in show business, in dealing with Sambo, coon song and Tin Pan Alley. In this all-white game the Negro had to obey the boss's rules or perish.

At first, in the sweet air of Emancipation, it seemed that negritude might be an advantage. Now, blurted out the publicity, audiences can see the genuine, bona-fide darky plucked fresh and wriggling from cottonfield, cornfield, canebrake and barnyard, framed in the limelight to perform his native African dances and songs naturally – no need for woolly wigs – and spontaneously – no need for musical education. These ex-slaves are raw slices of reality, children of natural impulse playing out their recent history. Come see the Southern life of overseers and bloodhounds tempered by mammies crooning in the moonlight. A never-never land which should have been left virginal.

91

What a tremendous opportunity for blacks to join American Entertainment! Soon after the Civil War there sprang up black troupes, usually calling themselves 'Georgia Minstrels' (though mostly Northern outfits) to distinguish themselves from the white 'Nigger Minstrels'. Some reviewers were amazed to discover that the complexions of real Negroes ranged from Black African through Brown Mulatto to Fair Octoroon. A few black minstrels were so white they were made to black up. The antics of these Georgia Minstrels generally demonstrated that the authentic black could 'act the nigger' as well as the whites. That was the key test. The minstrel-show convention had to be continued because it pulled the country together.

The first fully professional Georgia Minstrels were actually from Georgia. Claiming '15 Genuine Ex-Slaves' performing 'Pure Plantation Melodies & Songs of the Sunny South', the outfit had been assembled by W. H. Lee, a white. Finding audience reaction in Georgia to be lukewarm (too close for comfort, perhaps) Lee sold off his troupe to Sam Hague, a Yorkshireman with years of music-hall experience and a dedication to the Lancashire clog dance. Expanding the troup to twenty-six he painstakingly taught his boys the official clog, togged them out in bright plantation costumes (complete with rags and patches) and then shipped them to Britain to tour as 'Hague's Slave Troupe of Georgia Minstrels'.

Meanwhile, a black entrepreneur had entered the business. Charles 'Barney' Hicks of Indiana started his own Georgia Minstrels – all black and none from Georgia. Hicks pushed the aspect of slavery days and high jinks on the old plantation. He was a tough guy and he was determined to pop to the top, tint notwithstanding. He would play the bastard as well as the whites. The best black talent came to Hicks because he promised good money and a life above the scuffle round the chittlin circuit offered by the other black managers.

Hicks had plans for a dream. When the dream didn't pan out in America he took his boys to Europe where word was good on Negroes. He was received with much graciousness and it was most refreshing. The Germans especially were enchanted by the scenes of plantation life and delighted by the interpretation of Stephen Foster songs. In England Barney Hicks met up with a despondent Sam Hague. Sam was having trouble keeping his black troupe afloat. It seemed that British audiences found the real thing in colour too crude for refined local minstrelsy. There were no calls from St James's Hall.

Hague and Hicks joined forces, integrating their troupe for a change of visuals and adding a touch of decorum. But still no success. Eventually, they sold their Georgia Minstrels to Charles Callendar, an American saloon keeper. Hague declared himself finished with coloured or integrated shows. Instead he went the British way with a blanched show of impeccable taste and he had the nerve to carry coals to Newcastle by taking his troupe to America. Actually, they went down very well and were much copied by the Americans: only the two end minstrels were in blackface (burnt champagne cork, claimed Hague) – the rest sat stiffly in full evening dress with gold-braid accessories and sang classy ballads and operatic stuff that was close to Grand. The timing of the ensemble work and the clipped accents were given high marks by minstrel critics.

But Charles Callendar, with his new property, returned the Georgia Minstrels to the old plantation routine, beating all twenty-seven of his black impresario competitors in box-office returns. However, in 1878, with minstrelsy become big business and conglomerating fit to burst, his coloured boys were taken over by the mighty Colonel Jack Haverly, the man with the Mastadon Minstrels. The Colonel swelled his Georgians up to 100 'all genuine' coloureds, cut the minstrel show to the bone and concentrated on showing his 'natural children of bondage' in scenes of plantation life which were 'truthful to nature'.

More gobbling continued when the Frohman Brothers bought the troupe and made the spectacle even bigger and more 'documentary': in the plantation scene were real logs, real moss, real swamp water. They carried their olfactory props and their cast around the country in a special railway car upon which was painted an announcement: 'AFRICA'. The African angle was popular in the early 1890s because it promised Victorian America entertainment with the bonus of educational value.

Barney Hicks was not interested in this African route. As an American entrepreneur he didn't see the jungle path leading him into the mainline of show business. Hicks was a man in a hurry, very angry and with a sense that time was running out. After his own minstrel troupe fell apart (a combination of bad management and social conditions) he managed troupes for white owners. Then he had another try with his own show. But, once again, it was like wall-banging – the same horrid circuit grind: the dime shows, the tank towns and the frequent threat of the noose.

Finally, in a desperate and brave move, he stole a black troupe from their white boss. Then he sailed them off round the world where they performed before crowned heads and chieftains, too. He took Uncle Tom to faraway places where Uncle Sam had never been. And in Australia and New Zealand the Barney Hicks minstrels were adored as would anybody be adored who had travelled that far. When he died in 1902 he was still in harness – entertaining the natives of Java.

Billy Kersands had started his career as one of Barney Hick's 'Georgia Slave Brothers' just after the Civil War. He was in a Hicks & Hague show in Britain, showing off his beautiful and graceful soft-shoe shuffle called 'The Essence of Old Virginny'. Sam Hague said he noticed a lot of Lancashire clog in the step. Billy kept smiling his gargantuan smile as he rasped the sand to the 6/8 rhythm of 'Swanee River'.

After the Hicks & Hague débâcle he returned to America in search of regular wages. He got them with 'Haverly's Genuine Coloured Minstrels'. In 1882 the troupe, under the new name, returned to Britain with Billy as chief comic, and a chorus sprinkled with some mighty pretty octoroons. Sixty-five Negroes on stage and well-drilled for a change! The British were most impressed with the precision. And Billy, with his big head and big nose and mouth so big he could juggle billiard balls inside it, was like a Dixie parallel to the sooty, gormless North Country comic idiot. He was always getting the worst of it and hollering like a prune-fed

cow. He gave a command performance for Queen Victoria
and made her smile when he said that, if his mouth was any
wider, he'd have to move his ears.

By the 1890s Billy Kersands was known as 'The Shining
Star of Black Minstrelsy' and the race saying went that a
show without Billy was like a circus without an elephant.
So, like Barney Hicks, he decided to run his own business.
He was soon floundering, playing the tank towns, the tent
shows, the toilets, etc. The chitlin circuit always went
round and round and never up like an arrow. And yet he
enjoyed himself. Everyone felt sorry for laughing Billy.
Even when he made fun of his big black head, nose and
mouth. Even when he thundered out his tale of an old
Uncle Tom moaning about his daughter's elopement with a
store porter:

> De chile dat I bore,
> Should tink ob me no more
> Den to run away wid a big black coon.

Lord, how even the poorest of the poor blacks would roar
with laughter! Dame Fortune may not have smiled upon
them but Billy's plight was worse. And Billy never hit the
main event, never got to play Broadway, never forgot
Queen Victoria's smile.

In that Haverly minstrel show in the Britain of 1882 were
other race brothers who got the royal seal of approval and
stayed in the pleasant isles and prospered. The Bohee
Brothers, for example, made such an impression with their
duelling banjo act (which they performed in velvet coats,
knee breeches and jockey caps) that a local banjo maker
invited them to endorse his product. In the ads they posed
in formal wear and in the copy they stated that their life's
aim was to raise the banjo out of common minstrelsy and
into the concert hall and salon.

But the banjo in Britain had its uses. An effective way to
win a girl in a boat was with a banjo (far more portable
than a small organ and far more fun than a guitar – easier
to play, too). Most young men about town wanted to learn
the banjo and the Bohee Brothers answered the need by

opening up a 'Banjo Academy' in the West End. The Prince of Wales was one of their pupils.

James Bland had been another star artist of the Haverly minstrel show. In white tie and tails and singing to the accompaniment of a banjo on his knee, Bland introduced the British to his own compositions such as 'Oh, Dem Golden Slippers' and 'Carry Me Back to Old Virginny'. He was acclaimed as 'The Sable Singer of Sincere Songs' and the natural successor to the mantle of Stephen Foster. His lovely barbershop harmony number, 'In the Evening by the Moonlight' evoked ringing banjos, singing darkies and old folk rocking contentedly on the porch – a golden-framed picture of the Old South so loved and missed, especially by those who had never known the place.

James Bland had never known the place either. A middle-class black born in New York, Bland's father was an examiner in the US patent office (the first black to work in this position) and young James had studied music theory at Howard University. To the dismay of his respectable parents James took up minstrelsy after seeing white minstrel George Primrose do his act in a Washington theatre. The boy dropped out of college to become a 'refined comedian' at local society parties, strumming his patented five-string banjo and singing his mellifluous darky songs.

The Haverly gig in London was a godsend. He loved the city, he loved the cut and thrust of conversations among equals of his profession in pub and tea shop and late supper room. He performed for the nobility and lesser swells at parties in Belgravia and Mayfair. He gave his notice to the Haverly show people. *They* could sail back to the land of oppression and oppossum, *he* was staying on in Britain with his friendly hosts.

He wrote songs about London life and a fair lass called Polly. He was offered good billing at high-class music halls: 'James Bland – The Idol of the Halls'. Standing rigid in his Lord Fauntleroy suit with his patented banjo on his knee and his foot on a Chippendale replica, he was a picture of good taste. His name was down for a theatrical club. If he'd had sons, he might well have considered sending them to a prep school in Sussex.

However, this heady atmosphere proved too rich for Bland. He was soon finding himself unable to balance books, food and drink. He was often late for his engagements and forgetful of lyrics. England was kind to him, setting his behaviour down to eccentricity. America could care less. When Bland returned to his native land in the nineties he expected to take up his position as the new Stephen Foster. But pop fashion had passed him by. Tough coon songs were followed by white city ragtime. Nobody wanted the Bland echoes of banjos across the cottonfields. Nobody wanted a dissolute black minstrel in a stained velvet suit.

James Bland died penniless in Philadelphia in 1911, the year of Alexander and his Ragtime Band. He was out of place and out of time.

From the viewpoint of his fellow middle-class blacks the field of entertainment, even of polite minstrelsy, was not a wise area in which to seek elevation. Minstrelsy smacked of a past worth forgetting. It was Africa and noisy slaves. Well-to-do blacks – and there were quite a number – would rather remember brothers like Ben Banneker who, in 1781, had made the first American clock; and inventors of countless practical objects like the folding cabinet bed, the trouser support and a certain type of airship.

Since early in the nineteenth century quiet circles of rich blacks existed in East Coast cities, keeping low profiles and avoiding any kind of public display. They owned livery stables, furniture stores and even plantations. After the Civil War they could claim insurance companies, banks and savings and loan associations. White mobs had a habit of burning down such businesses when the mood took them.

In the nineties this mood grew more frequent. The carpetbagger 'uppity niggers' of Reconstruction were followed by an influx of field Negroes from the South into the big cities of the North. In New York's 7th Avenue a black tenderloin developed: backwoods boys in vulgar outfits lounged on corners asking for trouble; dudes with wide hatbands and flowered waistcoats trod bouncily in pursuit of the earnings of their yellow women tarts.

The wealthy blacks were horrified and said so in their

own newspapers. But, to the world at large, they kept a silence, closing themselves off in brownstone houses where they could live an inconspicuous life. White servants attended them there and, on occasion, their carriages would take them to discreet parties at other well-appointed black homes or to bridge games at their private clubs. Their sons mostly went to black universities like Howard, a few went to Yale and Harvard, and one or two even attended Oxford and Cambridge.

In the nineties the mob developed a way of dealing with blacks who got out of line. Lynching reached a peak of 235 victims in 1892, the year of Charlie Harris's 'After the Ball', the year the Baline family arrived in New York. Next year, at the Chicago World's Fair, the world was shown America as a civilized nation that respected classical culture – and, anyway, the majority of the lynchings had been in the South and the rural South at that. Twenty-eight million people viewed American industrial achievements in neo-classical structures made of plaster of Paris, Ohio. Sousa's band supplied the music to this celebration of progress, just the right stuff for gaining world popularity. On 25 August 'Coloured American Day' was celebrated: black opera singers and string players demonstrated their classical skills; Paul Lawrence Dunbar, the 'ebony poet', read extracts from his work.

But spoiling these achievements was the Dahomian Village. Imported West Africans sat around their wooden huts all day long, drumming and chanting and whittling. Whilst the general public and a few musicologists may have found this attraction educational and even amusing, the Negro middle class and intelligentsia found the Village an embarrassment. The howls and bangs of these 'savages' had as much to do with Afro-Americans as had spears and woad to do with the Prince of Wales.

Dunbar visited the Village, accompanied by his 'brothers', James Weldon Johnson, a college graduate and attorney, and Will Marion Cook who had studied music in Berlin and at Oberlin. They all agreed that the spectacle was fascinating but also crude and totally irrelevant to their current position. This sort of display would have been better confined to the Midway area of doubtful pleasures like Little Egypt and her hootchy coochy dance. A private booth bought one a demonstration of the dance, with plenty of hip-grinding and bottom-bumping. The 'bombershay' (or 'bum-bershay') was another such dance of questionable morality and origin. White writers claimed that all these lewd steps were from the Negroes. Much more acceptable was the cakewalk strutting done by the stately black Dora Dean over at Sam T. Jack's Opera House. *The Creole Show* girls were, of course, light-skinned and much more in keeping with the progressive spirit of the time.

The three educated black men never got to see some of the other fringe benefits at the Chicago Fair of 1893. This was a pity because, on this fringe, was American popular music in the raw: from out of the South and Midwest had gathered wandering entertainers of many hues and cultures; they were here to make a few bucks and swap a few songs and tricks. It became apparent at the Fair that this entertainment underground was cooking a special musical style that was later called 'ragtime'. The new sound was particularly apparent when played on the piano for, on this earnest Victorian machine, one could see and hear the clash of the old with the new as the left hand marched along in strict time the right hand broke up the beat, falling sometimes in front, sometimes in back, like a lurching drunkard having a good time. A ragtime in jig-time. Somewhere in the clangour of this fun fair and its outlying brothels and sawdust saloons was a rather serious young black Texan called Scott Joplin, breaking up the new songs with his version of the syncopated piano style, sometimes introducing his own quilt of rag-tune medleys. Somewhere else was black 'Plunk' Henry of Mississippi who just recently had given up the banjo and transferred his nonstop syncopations to the piano. The banjo may have been the first instrument to emit ragtime but Plunk knew that the piano got a songster better locations with better money.

And somewhere else at the Fair was a red-haired youth from Kentucky who was making the folks roar with his tall tales of Southern city life, tales usually concerning nefarious Sambos being chased by cops. The boy accompanied his crude little act with some jagged piano playing far less refined than the Scott Joplin style. And yet, off stage, he could speak quite nicely and appeared to be educated. A strayed white boy slumming at the Fair?

Ben Harney had picked up his tricks from the Other America, that bush underworld spurned by respectable middle-class America, white or black. Since there was no field recording in those crucial years when the raw material of American pop music was cooking we shall never know exactly how the mixture sounded. From the published evidence of sheet music we know that there was as much of Europe in the mixture as of Africa – for harmony and pianos and German marches (all ingredients of ragtime) were not native to Africa. But what of the rhythms, the nonstop syncopations that could make good girls go bad and boys like Ben Harney tarnish the family name? The skipped heartbeat of syncopation is common to many folk songs and dances, especially those of Eastern Europe and Latin America. Whether this beat originally came from Africa we simply don't know.

The point for the nineteenth and twentieth centuries is that the dominant culture – the world in print – chose the image of the American Negro, the racy 'nigger', as its potent anti-hero, a convenient receptacle for the dumping of a repressed hedonism. The world could have chosen the folk culture of Serbo-Croatians. But the Afro-Americans had the right look and build and promise of violent sex. Their visibility in the cities was also increasing. Sambo was coming close to home, the wraith was fleshing out. Late minstrelsy, a family entertainment, reflected little of this change. Audiences of the 1890s were ready for a zippier coon of formidable ambivalence: the new big bully Sambo would be both a sexual superman and a threatening ethnic. Exciting rhythms from exotic sources would ripple through his big bad body.

While the black middle class was quietly building up businesses certain white observers were bringing back lively tales of high times in the low life of the Other America, especially Black Bohemia. One of the most colourful descriptions came from Charles Dickens who viewed America with fascination and loathing. While visiting New York in 1842 he demanded an evening tour of the Five Points, a hell-hole of festering slums relieved by serrated rows of dance halls, saloons and knocking shops which grimaced round Paradise Square. Everybody knew about this filthy centre of sin and fun, everybody was embarrassed by it. Dickens's hosts tried to dissuade him from such a tour, suggesting a night at the opera instead. But the great writer insisted, even stamping his foot.

The visit to the Five Points (an area which later produced Al Capone) resulted in some dripping purple copy: 'All that is loathsome, drooping, and decayed is here,' he shivered. The high point of the tour was a visit to Almack's, a black-owned dance hall and bawdy house. Dickens was particularly taken with the dancing of a black boy. Swinging left and right while beating time with his feet he performed 'the single shuffle, double shuffle, cut and cross cut' while 'snapping his fingers' and 'rolling his eyes' and 'dancing with two left legs, two right legs, two wooden legs, two wire legs, two spring legs – all sorts of legs and no legs – what is this to him?' As a finale the boy leapt up onto the bar and in a piping arrogant voice demanded a strong drink. Dickens treated him but then found himself having to treat the rather menacing Negro band which had surrounded the tourist.

The dancing boy later came to fame as 'Master Juba': winning prizes as a flash dancer in New York, getting praise indeed as a star act in Pell's Ethiopian Serenaders during their London visit of 1848. The *Theatrical Times* considered him to be 'far above the common mountebanks who give imitations of American and Negro characters'. Soon he was the darling of society parties, chauffeured from drawing-room to drawing-room by liveried flunkeys driving white horses, while he kicked back on the cushions in his red velvet and black beret. Soon he was rather overdoing things and so he died in London at the age of twenty-seven.

The sensational high-speed dance that Master Juba (real name William Henry Lane) had become famous for was nothing more than a shuffled version of the Irish jig – age-old steps from a benighted island next door, but dazzling black magic when performed by a shiny Negro from a wild and dangerous continent of free spirits.

Thanks to Dickens's publicity Almack's, the Five Points dump, became so famous that the owner changed the name to Dickens's Place and hired a bigger band and more octoroons from New Orleans. A New York writer, George Foster, went researching there and came back with a lurid description of the band. He seems to have been at once attracted and disgusted:

> You may imagine that the music at Dickens' Place is of no ordinary kind. You cannot, however, imagine *what* it is. You cannot see the red-hot knitting needles spurted out by that red-faced trumpeter, who looks precisely as if he were blowing glass . . . Nor can you perceive the frightful mechanical contortions of the bass drummer as he sweats and deals his blows on every side, in violation of the laws of rhythm, like a man beating a baulky mule and showering his blows upon the unfortunate animal, now on this side, now on that.

What was this bizarre rhythm? Was it African? If so, which coast and which tribe? Or was this rhythm simply the result of an untutored and perhaps drunken drummer banging in a way typical of cultures untouched by pedants? Could this band, in other words, just as easily have been a band of Eskimos, Red Indians, or aborigines? At least we know what song they were tearing up. George Foster tells us it was 'Cooney in Der Holler', a variation of the slave hit, 'Possum up a Gum Tree', and this, in turn, was a variation of an old Celtic reel.

But, further afield, there was lurking in the bushland of the Other America a rocking and a rolling that was genuinely wild and untrammelled and often in direct communication with God. This rhythm music of the spirit was not confined to any race or culture. It only atrophied when it met with civilization. A few bold researchers, even some minstrels, went searching for this spirit sound, probing the forbidden parts of America.

In the South they could thrill to the wail of slave laments and complaints – those blue devils again! – with their eery squashed melody. On a Mississippi levée they could watch black roustabouts as, with shoulders shaking and bottoms twisting, they negotiated a cotton bale down a recalcitrant plank. And while the men worked their womenfolk stood around shouting encouragement (and the supper menu) with a boom-chicka-boom beat accompanied by a slapping of thighs. 'Patting Juba' was what they called this action and the researchers took note.

So far, so black. But there were white folks mixed up in this dance of life and if only you moved further away from the norm you'd find a wondrous celebration . . .

At twilight a researcher could, if he so wished, view the tongues of flame licking the sky down at the piney woods valley camp meeting. He could feel the very ground shudder to the hosannas of saved souls. Up, up go these souls to batter the good news on the very gates of Heaven. A little bolder, and the researcher is actually down inside the camp meeting, enclosed in the big tent, the inner tent, the happening tent. Now he is caught in the swell of a squishy black-and-white humanity – and the noise! And the *people!* Yet pretty soon he is as one with the congregation, a group welded together by the mesmeric hollering of the sermonizer who pours on the holy spirit till all are fully awakened. Then get ready, people, for a shaking and a falling and a rolling around in the dust! Get ready for a beatific ecstasy. Eat dust and reach for the sky! And now the preacher man is joined by the yelping and yodelling of his deacon sidekicks, and now by the drum thumps and foot stamps and frenzied singing of the congregation. In a little while the great noise has magically turned into a great music. There's dancing to follow and after that a deep sleep and in the morning will be the knowledge that God's purpose has been worked out through the spontaneous combustion of music and dance. Alleluia!

'This has been going on for a week,' says the white revivalist in the crumpled linen suit. 'You should have been here last night. It was the Negro brethren again. You see, they always seem to drown out the white folks when they get carried away into the bosom of Abraham. But after my sermon, all whipped up, they can't calm down and must needs form a ring. And with coats off and collars awry they rotate in a circle, clapping their hands and sliding their feet and bobbing their bodies like redskins on the warpath. Sometimes they whirl like dervishes. But the worst of it all is – they garble our hymns in a most absurd and heathenish manner.'

When a reverend of their own race, an elder from the African Methodist Episcopal Church, told them to desist they resorted to rocking their bodies and rolling their eyes. Instead of the hymn they sang some field ditty:

> Devil to the left of me,
> Devil to the right!
> But Jesus will protect you if you rock all night!

Then the coloured reverend, most irate, stepped inside the crazed circle to remonstrate with the jet-black ringleader. But the ringleader said that his band of brothers had recently formed their own church of God the Dancer and that their spirit dictates that they must *do what they have to do* in order to be in touch with Jesus and therefore you form a ring and look there's a ring over there and another one up yonder. There's no stopping the spirit of the People . . .

The white revivalist offers the researcher tea in his tent and a chat with the black reverend about the problems of keeping congregations strictly in line. But the researcher bids farewell for he needs some sleep and the prospects of getting any at all appear slim while the members of the church of God the Dancer are around. They have decided to praise the Lord all night long.

The researcher has been entertained in a timeless zone, in the whirlpool of the everlasting moment, within reach of the solution to the Great Mystery. But now a riptide tears him away and plonks him back in the straight canal of the nineteenth century.

Left unexplored were some Afro-American cultural treasures. Behind the closed doors of the black evangelical churches were celebrated services in which natural instinct triumphed over unnatural science. Surrounding a sermon of high rhetoric, in which it was proved that the moon is cheese and the earth is oblong, was a swaying choir awesomely dipping and soaring and breaking the European rules but using those Western scales and harmonies as a mattress to bounce souls into a heaven of transcendentalism. A word normally using one plain note would be awarded a decor- ation of several glorious notes and this glittering prize would then speed off up into an African blue sky: 'Jee-hee-hee- eee-eee-zuzzzzzz!'

Behind other closed doors was a Third world celebrating the here and now and certain parts and functions of the body. In jook joint, gin mill, tub jar and hell house – whose furnishings were often no more than two planks and a barrel and whose menus specialized in fried squirrel and bull's balls – was ground out blues and boogie-woogie, that endless wail and endless lope that just keeps rolling around like the solar system is reputed to do. Inside these wretched dumps (especially frowned upon by the black middle class and clergy) danced singles, couples, sometimes whole groups, making groin movements that were variously known as the 'funky butt', the 'snakey hip' and the 'fess mess'. 'Shake that thing' and this'll lead to 'jassin' and, hopefully, 'It's tight like that.'

As far as mainline America was concerned this Afro- American subculture of the sacred and the profane (holding the body in common) was invisible and thus was left to go about its business until well into the twentieth century. For Irving Berlin and Ragtime America such naked carryings- on were not suited to the needs of the dominant culture. Boogie, blues and gospel would have to remain on the shelf – or in the bush – until the times were right, until America was ready.

In our search for the roots of the myth of the Hot Coon we now join not researchers but adventurers in search of clandestine sex. These adventurers were not all fulltime debauchers. Many were bank managers, mayors, police chiefs and other pillars of society. Their money financed a flourishing Victorian underworld of red light and tenderloin districts where satisfaction could be bought from one set of

105

hot coons while another provided the musical accompaniment. In luxurious, if ostentatious, surroundings the white pleasure-seeker picked his black sex partner while a piano 'professor' entertained. Light classics were *de rigueur* at the start of the night's business, blues when there wasn't much doing or the pianist had run out of current pops to play, and syncopated jig-time piano when the couples were dancing their prelude to copulation. Nonstop syncopation seemed the right spice to heat up the customers' blood.

The needs of the debauchers spawned jig-time piano into ragtime. But before ragtime surfaced as a term in popular culture there came the rage of the Coon Song and the Coon Shouter. Like ragtime piano this rage had its musical origins in the establishments of the debauchers – the House of Lords, the Purple Palace, Madam Clam's. Every city had its sporting houses. The Castle, in St Louis, Missouri, seems to have been a remarkable source of songs that later were fished out of the underworld and gutted for consumption in the new world of New York's pop-song industry. 'Ta-ra-ra-bom-deray', 'A Hot Time in the Old Town Tonight', 'The Bully Song' and 'Frankie and Johnny' are all reputed to have been picked up by canny white customers while enjoying adventures at Babe Connors's 'Castle'.

Babe was a big black woman with a taste for gold. She had gold chandeliers in the lobby, gold fixtures in the bathrooms and lots of gold in her teeth. But the nameplate on the front door of her three-storey white house was of gleaming brass and so was the knocker. Old customers – mayors and senators and so forth – had advised her to keep up a decent front. By day she paraded round town in an open carriage with liveried white coachmen. By night she waited to greet her gentlemen as they processed through her door with their fraternal cry of 'Let's storm the Castle!'

When the customers weren't busy with the best Louisiana creoles money could buy they relaxed to the songs of the Castle's star singer – Mama Lou, a huge tree-trunk of a Southern mammy in a calico dress and a head bandana. She shouted her songs in no uncertain terms: there'll be 'A Hot Time in the Old Town' because Mama Lou had found another woman in bed with her man and Mama Lou will be administering some whippings. 'Ta-ra-ra-bom-deray!' was trumpeted—and at the word all the dancing Creole belles lifted their skirts to show off the fact that they wore no underwear. When Paderewski, the famous pianist, visited the Castle he was entranced by this number – musically – and he persuaded Blind Tom, the resident 'professor', to show him how to play the song and the style.

And so the routine of this sporting life might have chuga-lugged along underground for years – winked at, frowned at and occasionally stamped upon. The black servants of this entertainment world would never see the light of day, never see Broadway and the gold in Tin Pan Alley. They would strut their stuff, sing and play their music, always tailoring strictly for the desires of the customers. The white adventurer-customer would stagger home humming a jig-time tune learned at the Castle, later tell the words to the boys at the office, never tell the wife. And in a little while the wife would be playing on the parlour upright a blanched version of 'Hot Time' and 'Ta-ra-ra-bom-deray'. . . .

We will now examine how some aspects of this Black Bohemia were allowed to creep into overground popular music in the 1890s – first the coon song and then ragtime – because American Negroes were making themselves known as more than passive field hands and servants. Social change was to affect the Sambo image established by minstrelsy. But, once again, this image was to be just another crazy mirror distortion of the real Negro, just another stereotype. To show the real Negro would have meant showing the complexity and contradictions of multitudes – and this would have been too much for a new country in search of instant myths for the satisfaction of a society in which the individual counted as nothing except as a vote or a sucker, but in which types, teams, races, blocs, pressure groups, Rotary Clubs and Sigma Chis counted for everything.

First, the lull before the storm of coon songs: in 1891 Willis Woodward, an old-fashioned publisher of New York, put out 'Ta-ra-ra-bom-deray' and let it lay. Harry Sayers, publicist for a burlesque show tour, had taken it from Mama Lou and presented a washed-down version to Mr Woodward, dear soul. But he was no hustler and there was no angle and that was that. The song later became a hit in London when Lottie Collins kicked up her legs and showed her drawers and gave the thing some point. It's all timing and push and organization and knowing the market. Or is it just luck?

In 1894 Woodward chanced upon a very early and quintessential example of a coon song: 'The Possumla Dance'. One Irving Jones had come into the office with this novelty. A studious-looking Negro in stiff collar, pinned tie and sturdy black overcoat, Irving Jones was certainly no street-corner loafer. Word was he had a dynamite stage personality in black vaudeville. In person he was shy and sensitive. He had an engaging stammer.

Yet the song he offered was a violent piece, a parody of the courtly 'Pas Ma La' performed at the Quadroon Balls of New Orleans and, lately, at the Chicago Fair. Jones thought it a clever gag to switch the ball setting to a rough Negro dance hall. Woodward recognized the story as similar to the Irish shenanigan genre but much nastier: when a 'big bully coon' invades the coloured hop there's much 'cutting and shooting'. However, Jones's piano accompaniment was full of delightful syncopations and the staff arranger had quite a task trying to score this odd ragged metre but eventually he corralled the elusive thing.

Poor old Woodward's timing was wrong again! There were very small sales of 'The Possumla Dance'. Irving Jones slipped back into the anonymity of black vaudeville but he kept writing his coon songs. Next year, 1896, the storm broke – coon songs, cakewalking and ragtime became the rage of the USA and then of the world.

Let us look now at the new visibility of the American Negro for it was this visible threat that was to demolish the pastoral idyll of Arcadian Old Black Joe and replace him with a new Zip Coon of vicious criminality or else sexual virtuosity.

In 1865, at the time of Emancipation, there were 4 million Negroes in America. By 1910 there were over 10 million. A migration to the cities, especially northern cities, had begun. New York's black population increased 50 per cent during this period. The hope was, among the enlightened, that coloured Americans would now find their place in society by hard work, thrift and industry. But they must fit in and they must not threaten the status quo. This was the Age of Accommodation and its spokesman was Booker T. Washington, a Southern mulatto who advocated self-improvement through manual labour and domestic work and begged his people to stay down South where they belonged.

The New South, after the 'affirmative action' excesses of Reconstruction when blacks were thrust into political power to spite the defeated Confederacy, dug in by passing a bunch of segregation laws which were dubbed 'Jim Crow' in honour of 'Daddy' Rice's minstrel stereotype. At the Atlanta Exposition of 1895 Booker T. Washington reassured the assembled cotton kings that segregation was the right way for the achievement of mutual progress. It was a fine speech of high rhetoric boomed through a splendid row of gleaming teeth inside a wide and winning smile. 'Thirty years ago,' he said, 'Negroes had only a few quilts and pumpkins and chickens – gathered from miscellaneous sources.' How the masters laughed at the minstrel joke! Then the great and sensible leader held up an outstretched hand and pronounced that black and white should be separate socially *but* – and then he slowly balled his hand into an impressive fist – *but* together economically the two races would be a mighty force. And everyone agreed that Booker T. meant that his people would work hard at being Pullman porters, maids, janitors, field hands, etc. Power would be left in the hands of the white masters. Everything in apple-pie order.

But yet the race violence kept burning all through the Gay Nineties and well into the twentieth century. In the South, in states with those mellifluous Dixie names beloved of songwriters, the killing was often of a sexual nature because the crime was reputedly sexual. It was all fantasy, save for, perhaps, that a Negro had smiled back at a Southern maiden. Nevertheless, the victim wasn't just hung or burned alive – frequently his genitals were cut off. In Mississippi a husband and wife, accused of sexual orgies, were slowly bored to death by a monster corkscrew operated in turn by volunteers from the righteous white mob. In Atlanta fresh Negro fingers were displayed in butcher-shop windows. The North, in Chicago and New York, was content to race riot without dismemberment.

The actions of this fearful period of race hatred (from 1890 to 1910 approximately) were matched – encouraged, even – by words of prejudice from higher sources than street or field. From a St Louis bible house came *The Negro a Beast* (1902); in 1907 was published *The Negro, a Menace to American Civilization*. Social scientist Frederick Hoffman wrote that the Negro was an anthropological freak and would soon die out. In *The American Negro* (1901) Hannibal Thomas made a swingeing attack on all black Americans. This 'unassimilated ward of western civilization' is a 'creature of impulse' who 'lives for his passions' and is 'dominated by emotional sensations'. He is a 'frisky, frothy creature of over-flowing frivolity in speech and action', a 'puerile gossip, obsessed with dress, colours, hair, and personal likes and dislikes', full of 'eager, voluble, incessant chatter'. But, worst of all, he possesses 'an imperious sexual impulse, which, aroused at the slightest incentive, sweeps aside all restraints in the pursuit of sexual gratification'.

This sounds like one of my school reports, and one that I would be quite proud of. The scary thing about Hannibal Thomas is that he was an American Negro. His criticisms would be compliments to a well-off middle-class youth with artistic leanings and a yen for the bohemian life. But to aspiring American blacks of that striving straight period his book was poison.

Nor could the Negro expect support from political and artistic leaders. President Teddy Roosevelt, after dining Booker T. Washington, wrote to a friend: 'As a race and in the mass, they are altogether inferior to whites.' President Woodrow Wilson, in 1912, introduced segregation for all civil-service workers, right down to separate cafeterias and separate lavatories. Henry James, the only American writer to be called Master (so refined that he spent most of his time abroad), spoke for America's aesthetes when he

110

expressed his disgust at the gangs of 'tatterdemalion darkies' lounging around the railway station at Washington DC.

Thus, from all sides, came hatred, loathing, fear, disgust. But it was disgust, claimed Ray Stannard Baker in his pioneering sociological study of 1908 (*Following the Colour Line*) that was the 'main cause of negrophobia'. This disgust was caused by the Negro's 'body odour, flat nose, thick lips, slobber in the voice, unnatural hair, animalism of body contour'. These were the features pounced upon by the nastiest of the coon songs. Ragtime was to point up the nicer features of the myth—rhythm, jollity, a nonstop syncopated party.

In 1895, the year of Booker T.'s mollifying speech at the Atlanta Exposition, 'The Bully Song' was introduced on Broadway and was a resounding hit. What Irving Jones had described a year before – the threat of the criminal black – now became a hot pop hero through the performance of a matronly white woman called May Irwin. A tough cookie, she'd fought her way up from rough-and-ready Variety to the relative classiness of the Broadway musical show. For her new farrago, *The Widow Jones*, she wanted a tickler song novelty.

Charles Trevathan, a sportswriter and night bird, was travelling with Miss Irwin on the Chicago train and for a diversion he sang her a hilarious knockabout story about a murderous coon. 'Needs some polishing but it's a runner for the show, Charlie. Where'd you get the number, you're no writer? Same place you got that cough?' The sportsman admitted he'd taken it down on his shirt cuff at Babe Connors's place in St Louis. 'The girls dance on a mirror and they wear no drawers, see.'

On stage and dressed up and polished 'The Bully Song' was a knockout as shouted by May Irwin. Though the tune was harmless enough the story was lethal. It concerned a 'Tennessee nigger' sniffing around the levée in search of a 'red-eyed river roustabout' who's got the nerve to claim he's the 'New Bully' of the town. This dude is going 'round among de niggers, a-layin' their bodies down', i.e. knifing them to death when possible.

In search of his rival our Tennessee hero seizes his 'trusty

111

blade' (a razor) and gatecrashes the party of Parson Jones. He delivers a speech to the effect that he will 'carve dat nigger's bones' while listening to his groans. Then he offs on his search and eventually the rival bully is cornered and slashed to death by the original bully. A proclamation is broadcast: 'When you see me coming, hoist your window high. When you see me going hang your head an' cry.'

A tall tale from the Negro underworld. Audiences at *The Widow Jones* could plainly see Miss Irwin's detachment from the action: she sang as an actress, she sang without blacking up. She was no minstrel from a pastoral setting. She was a modern woman shouting about savagery near at hand, here in the big city. She was like a street news vendor announcing the latest bloodthirsty edition of the *Police Gazette*.

In February 1896 the new myth of the hot urban coon was set in locomotion by the added accompaniment of ragtime music. Of course, as we've seen, it was Irving Jones who first offered the new package to Broadway – but his timing was off and his colour was wrong. The new offering was made by a sassy kid from Kentucky, a white boy from out of the West who'd been in Chicago and several unmentionables and had paid his dues: Ben Harney.

Now he was erupting nightly at Keith's Theatre in New York with his very own compositions – darky shenanigan tales – fired off by a scatter-gun piano style, drummed along by a curious stick dance, sung like a Negro. But he wore no blackface and his hair was very red.

This is the way his act went: he'd race on stage, bent forward and his full evening dress would have been all correct except that he wore a battered straw hat and he carried a bamboo cane. The hat he'd push to a rakish angle and the cane he'd twirl. After a grin he'd deliver this patter: 'Folks, I'm Ben Harney from Louisville and I'm announcing a new epoch in Ethiopian minstrelsy. Old Black Joe may roll in his grave but I'm giving you the real thing in RAGTIME and I mean RAGTIME!'

Then he'd swish up his tails and settle at the piano bench. While his right hand pulsed out a crush collision of demented notes, his left hand made the bamboo prod in strict tempo. At the same time his feet executed a funny little tap dance. In the orchestra pit below the pianist leader had the job of supplying a rigid *oompah oompah* bass support to the woolly-bully syncopations of Harney's stabbing fingers. After a short while the audience would realize that the boy was actually playing a high-trot version of an old static Baptist hymn. Next he struck up a jaunty vamp and suddenly, from the audience, a coloured boy started hollering some incomprehensible ditty.

This was Strap Hill and he was Harney's boy, his servant, his stooge. Or was he his sidekick, his shadow, his friend? Some folks had seen them consorting together, eating and visiting and such. It was certainly an odd and dangerous relationship.

As soon as Strap Hill had finished his gibberish Harney took up the burden of the 'song'. His voice seemed badly mutilated, scratched and hoarse, as if he'd dragged the larynx across gravel just before showtime. But he made more sense than Strap because he had the remnants of a fine Southern gentleman's accent, and he pointed up the lyrics of his bleeding story-song by dropping into plain talking at certain stages of the comic drama. This eccentric style was utterly removed from the singers of the day, those operatic warblers so admired and imitated by bathtub performers. Harney's sing-talk originated in another part of the tavern: he was breathlessly telling the boys some colourful anecdote. He was a storyteller, using the vernacular – something new in American entertainment because he wasn't playing the coon. And he wasn't playing the normal stilted European-style piano accompaniment – he was playing ragtime. And no two performances were exactly the same. He was spontaneous, he improvised, he moved with the spirits (and sometimes the wines). Yes, he loved the sauce but his ever-watchful, ever-loving wife, a Kentucky babe, was usually waiting in the wings to watch his drinking after he'd whirled off-stage to a high-stepping march.

And now Strap Hill, alone in a pool of limelight, went into an imitation of his master's step. The cunning and crafty boy making fun of the high-falutin' white dude. Body bent way, way back, and elbows out and wagging, legs kicking

113

high, this parody dance was recognized by minstrel show aficionados as a new and quirky version of 'Walking for That Cake', a popular minstrel routine. But when Strap did the cakewalk it became impossibly droll and rustic and quaint.

The topper to the act came suddenly: Mr Ben, proud and upright in a tail coat and shiny silk hat, suddenly reappeared and took over Strap's comic dance. And Strap immediately fell in line behind his master, becoming a shadow-slave. It was awful cute – touching, too. A sort of history lesson.

Harney was a big success at Keith's Theatre. He was soon booked into other vaudeville houses. Word was spreading about his cakewalk, his stick dance and his queer piano playing. 'Ragtime, sir,' expostulated Harney to these ignorant people. 'That's ragtime!' Strap had vanished, but then he'd seen it all before, hadn't he? Or had he? It was all very mixed up, all very Anglo-Irish, Afro-American stew. But Ben Harney was spicing the stew and he was in there first. And when May Irwin started calling herself a Coon Shouter, he started calling himself the Inventor of Ragtime. And so he was – he was sitting on top of the burning bush.

He sang of bush life. Black bush life. And while most of the real blacks in show business were still putting on the swallow-tail coats of minstrelsy, Ben Harney was rag-dragging the rustic past of American popular music into an urban future. Most importantly, he had two terrific songs in his repertoire (he was now in vaudeville, a refined family entertainment). These songs – self-written, he assured everybody – were 'Mr Johnson, Turn Me Loose' and 'You've been a Good Old Wagon but You've Done Broke Down'. They were both unblushingly stained in comic darky life: clandestine comings and goings and lots of illicit doings. This was Bully-land again – with niggers and crap games and chickens and cops. And worn-out floozies who'd been reduced to sex receptacles and were likened to broken-down wagons.

The Harney songs were expressed in dialect as thick as Mark Twain or Joel Chandler Harris and appeared to be

114

THE STRANGE MYTH OF THE HOT COON

authentic. Harney had a clever trick of sticking in extra syllables here and there – so that 'Oh, Mr Johnson, Turn Me Loose' became 'Ogah Migah-hister Jorrah-wonson, Turrah-wurn Me Loose . . .'. Rather like a schoolboy's lingo, like the word-fun of Lewis Carroll and Edward Lear.

Perhaps it was for this nonsense value that the morally fastidious Tony Pastor booked the Harney act for his New Fourteenth Street Theatre. Normally he would never allow doubtful material into his pristine house. An immaculately dressed Italian-American, Pastor it was who had first used the dainty French word 'vaudeville' to describe the refined, decent—almost *scrubbed*—variety acts that he presented at his theatre.

Only a few years back, it seemed, 'Variety' was synonymous with disreputable places into which no respectable married man would dream of taking his family (though he himself would attend every now and then). At old-time variety shows there were dirty songs sung by dirty old men and these songs were danced to by fat women in dirty old drawers. There were overflowing spittoons, there was muck on the seats and one afternoon in Duluth, after the matinée, a full set of false teeth was found deeply imbedded in a frankfurter sausage.

Tony Pastor's vaudeville put paid to those good old days. He featured class acts like Lillian Russell, the society songbird. He had the best performers from the best London music halls. He employed impeccably mannered (if slightly effeminate) male attendants. He even kept a little chapel to the left of the foyer. Smoking was prohibited, perfume was sprayed down the aisles at intermission, no coloured people were allowed to attend and, at evening performances, audiences were expected to wear full evening dress. Should there be a hint of impropriety from stage or auditorium in the presence of Mr Pastor then his moustache, waxed to aggressive points, would wiggle and he'd disappear. One of the stronger male attendants would remove the offending party and Mr Pastor would return, having exchanged his normal black wig for a ferocious red thing.

But Ben Harney passed the rigid test. This ragtime was sporty, energetic, and thoroughly – *bully* (in the new sense of the word: a crack, bravo, alright noise of American triumph). After all, these comic songs were only about coloureds being knocked about in a sporting life officially unknown to the Pastor audience. The men – some of them – smirked knowingly while their womenfolk thrilled to Harney's bully-bashing from the comfort and safety of deep red plush.

'Ogah Migah-Wigger-Higger Hister Jorrah-Worrah Woompah-Johnson-Tuurrrn Me-Hee Loose!' Can't Harney sit still for a second, can't he sing the song the same way twice? It was well nigh impossible for the arranger to transcribe Harney's ragtime. The wife would try to cool him down but then the Negro boy would up and tell Ben some ribald story and they'd both fall about the office, laughing like hyenas. But Mr Frank Harding, the publisher, had said to get the song down on paper as best as possible and not to worry unduly because the song was a gamble, even though the act seemed like a hit. Trouble was – people liked to do things to ragtime – to jiggle about and shout 'bully' and generally carry on – but nobody knew how to play it. At least not in New York. And that's where it mattered because that was where the hits were fabricated.

How to nail down this new craze? How to corner the market? The Witmark brothers, meanwhile, had been delving into the Ben Harney copyright situation. They were keener and hungrier and pushier than old Frank Harding.

They'd learned that Harney had written a 'Ragtime Instructor' and they were anxious to get their hands on this. Sounded perfect for the general public (and, in particular, the women because they, of course, were still very much the main purchasers of sheet music). Already they'd asked Harney where this instruction book was but the wretched man was evasive. Already they'd agreed to publish his other song 'You've Been a Good Old Wagon' but research had just turned up the fact that the song was already in print and had been for a year: published by some hick in the sticks – a certain Bruner Greenup in Louisville, Kentucky.

So the Witmarks, mighty important publishers even if

they did resemble kids, took time out to make Frank Harding an offer he couldn't refuse: for a good consideration they'd take over the 'Mr Johnson' copyright. Frank didn't mind – this whole popular song game was getting to be too serious a race for him. He was feeling thoroughly lymphatic, tired and old in the literal, and not endearing, sense. Harrigan & Hart had been sluggards compared to this crazed Harney and his raging coon! And as for Charlie Harris and these tearing Witmarks – such punks! All scarcely out of their teens. What a business!

Brother Isadore was despatched into the depths of the country in order to verify certain facts. He entrained with a sharp lawyer: for no sooner had Witmark's published 'Mr Johnson' than a rude note arrived from some small potato Indiana publisher claiming this was an infringement on their copyright.

The bad news about Louisville, Kentucky, was that it was an ugly, grimy, smoky city surrounded by flat, scorched earth. There were no bookstores and few music stores. The food was extremely sludgy. The good news was that investigation proved that Harney was the genuine owner and writer of his ragtime songs. Johnny Biller, musical director of Macauley's Theatre, assured Isadore (and his lawyer) that he himself had transcribed 'Mr Johnson' from Harney's own performance. Then Harry Green, a staff pianist whom Biller had had to fire for personal reasons, had stolen the song and palmed it off as his own work to an Indiana publisher.

Mind you, added Biller, Ben most likely first heard 'Mr Johnson' in one of the local darktown jook joints. Patched it up, smoothed it out – like he did with his 'Good Old Wagon' ditty. It's a cunning song that knows its author. Isadore and the lawyer exchanged glances. Anyway, continued Biller, the coloured boys had lots of versions of the 'Wagon' song, all unprintable. Of course, they got the tune from the white hill folk who've been jigging to that thing for donkey's years. Came from some Irish bog, no doubt.

Biller remembered having to take down these two Harney patchwork songs in a foul-smelling Negro barrelhouse one sticky afternoon. Ben was a queer fish: he really loved the Negro life, yet he came from a respectable and old Kentucky family with college presidents, a judge and a newspaper publisher in the background. A well-connected family. His father, a prominent civil engineer, was mortified when young Ben suddenly took up the wayfaring life. Good money had been spent on sending Ben to private school, to military academy – and then in mid-term he takes off to become an itinerant saloon entertainer, consorting with the pimps and whores and easy riders of that low life on the other side of the tracks. What's the attraction? Me, I'll go for hot meals and a warm bed and a home that's paid for.

Isadore assured Biller that Ben Harney was about to become a major attraction in New York. Biller expectorated and told the dudes where they could find Bruner Greenup, the original publisher of 'The Wagon'. Isadore replied stiffly that the House of Witmark had already written and made an appointment.

Big 'B' Greenup had his feet on his desk and a straw hat stuck way back on his head. He offered the two slickers spiked lemonade but they declined. He quickly surmised that they meant business. He told them they could have the rights to 'Wagon' and even the printing plates – for *free*. As for 'Mr Johnson' – why, he'd turned that joker down late last year even though Ben had done a hell of a job trying to sell him on it. 'Wagon', you see, had never sold a darn, and the company had worked up a swell Ethiopian cover with artwork by Zimmerman of Cincinatti – you guys must know of him 'cause you're in the business. Greenup hastened to add that he only dabbled in this music publishing. Stores, all kinds of stores (but practical) were his family's line and had been for years. Ben should've stuck to a proper trade instead of hanging around with jiggers and such. The lawyer got the papers signed and Isadore bid Greenup and Louisville farewell.

They were both relieved to get back to New York and away from these friendly (but slightly scary) country people.

'You've been a Good Old Wagon but You've Done Broke Down' – *Written, Composed and Introduced By Ben*

118

The first ethnic hit (1909)—an item that Tin Pan Alley termed a "Yid Song." High Culture meets Low Culture: the song was inspired by Richard Strauss's opera *Salome* which was based on Lord Alfred Douglas's English translation of Oscar Wilde's French play.

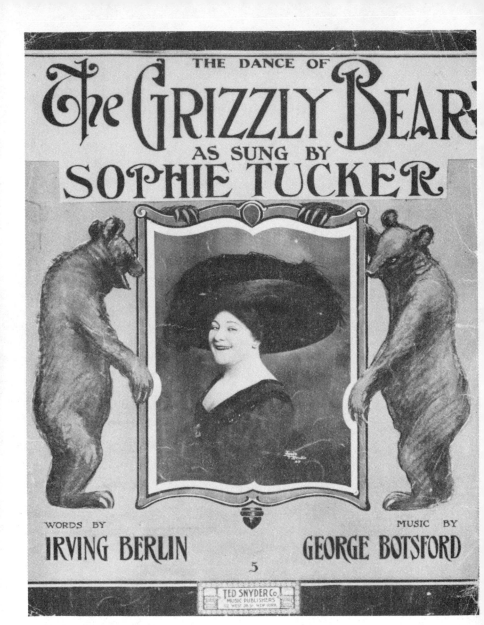

Sophie Tucker, Russian-born like Irving, had made her name as a "Coon Shouter." Now, with this hot dance invitation, she helped launch an era of animal dancing (which was eventually cleaned up by Mr. & Mrs. Vernon Castle). A far cry from the Russian ballet.

Irving looking cat-pleased with himself and inscrutable. He and Ted Snyder performed this "Wop Song" (a trade term) in the Shubert revue. Both
songsters carried tennis rackets and wore striped blazers as they strolled
onto the garden stage set. This, then, was Broadway in 1910.

The real big smash that established Irving as "The Ragtime King," 1911. Note that the band is white and un-raffish, and that the cover artist had a spelling problem.

The first effort: "Berlin" and "Nicholson" were both invented names. This was in keeping with the spirit of the U.S.A.—an invented nation. "Marie" earned Izzy exactly 37 cents in royalties.

May 29, 1911: Irving and his mentor, George M. Cohan, at The Friar's Frolic, taking a breather during afternoon rehearsals. At the evening show Irving introduced "Alexander's Ragtime Band," a new kind of minstrel song—no cork required.

The Hedges Brothers & Jacobson, the most vivacious ragtime act to hit Britain in the Great American Invasion of 1912. But when ragtime faded tragedy struck the brothers: Freddie Hedges gassed himself to death at the seaside in 1920; Elven Hedges was deported and died bankrupt in Paris in 1931. Meanwhile Jesse Jacobson, the tall pianist, had wisely retired from this crazy business and was living at Shakespeare House in Leicester Square (not the quietest of areas, it must be said).

In 1914 Mr. & Mrs. Vernon Castle were the highest paid act in vaudeville. Imagine—a man who danced with his wife! "The modern dances properly danced are *not* vulgar," they wrote in their best-selling book. Ragtime roughness of the Tucker variety was soon smoothed into the Castle's svelte Fox-Trot.

The Whiz Kid at home and actually stationary, 1915. Every object most tasteful. A complete Shakespeare lurks somewhere. Will the promised ragtime opera ever appear? Sounds of the street are walls away in such a ritzy atmosphere where the air is ever still.

Lieutenant James Reese Europe (formerly Jim) leading his
Hellfighters Band into "The Army Blues" by special order of his
General. France, 1918. "Jazz" was killing ragtime and Jim
Europe was finding it hard to create the crude and nasty sound
required by the new "jazz" fans. Back in 1914 when he'd worked
with the refined Castles he'd opined: "It takes a lot of training to
develop a sense of time and delicate harmony." But the new
America preferred chaos—and still does.

*Harney. Original Introducer to the Stage of the Now
Popular 'Rag Time' in Ethiopian Songs.*

There sat his song in bold print and with his picture on the
cover. The smell of the paper was as delicious as ham and
eggs. Ben Harney was jubilant: the inventor had been recognized. He had a plentful supply of rag songs for the future.
Next year he produced, at last, the promised 'Ragtime
Instructor'. And then he went off to reap his just rewards
– touring around America, over to Britain, to France, to
the South Pacific. Somewhere deep in the heart of the Far
East he discovered a lotusland and he settled there for a
while. He needed a breather and the wine and the natives
were fine. Strap liked the atmosphere, too. He and Strap
could be like those characters in his songs – the lazybones
who like nothing better than to sleep all day under the palm
tree's shade.

But maybe Harney knew that he couldn't control a craze.
That ragtime and coon songs and cakewalking had come
from *the people* and were being claimed back by them. No
amount of copyrighting and inventor boasting could stop
the ragtime flood. By the turn of the century this coon
ragtime had become an international habit. Even chauvin-
istic French composers were writing of 'darky dreams' and
'frolics' and general cavorting. In America every band,
orchestra, string serenader group and glee club had some
ragtime in its repertoire. The mighty Sousa featured a cakewalk at all his concerts. He always made a point of bowing
to popularity. In 1899 the situation was ably described in a
song by the team of Gene Jefferson and Robert Roberts:

> Syncopation is in every song,
> Clocks and watches are running wrong.
> Cakewalk music it fills the air –
> You can't escape it 'cause it's everywhere.
> (From 'I'm Certainly Living the Ragtime Life')

It is tempting to state here that the ragtime life described in
this song mirrored the new America of big city, skyscraper,
motor car, telephone and all the hustle, bustle, jerk and
rattle of modern society. It is tempting – but not true. Early

119

ragtime adumbrated the wrath to come in the twentieth century. It was Irving Berlin and his colleagues who were to grab that right moment in the 1910s – in the Second Coming of Ragtime – and to propagate World Ragtime (or the World Turned Upside Down).

Early ragtime – the decade that followed 1896 – was to produce well over a thousand ragtime songs but, in the main, they stuck to the darky lines cartooned by May Irwin and Ben Harney. They were a development of the minstrel tradition – perhaps 'hang-up' is a more appropriate word. Even so, the coon-song craze was not entirely confined to violence. There was a philosophical number called 'I Wants to Live While I'm Living Cos I'se Agoin' to Be a Long Time Dead' from Washington, DC. The House of Witmark did very well with a 'plantation slumber song' called 'Mammy's Little Pumpkin-Coloured Coons' with Julius Witmark on the cover looking civilized and restrained. 'Melinda's Wedding Day', another of their quiet coon songs, was described as a 'Gentle Coon Deviation'.

And on the whole these peaceful songs *were* only deviations from the din of the ragtime battleground where knives and razors slashed incessantly and Sambos fell, only to be replaced by replicas, in a white nightmare. Witmark's didn't corner the market on coon songs but they had the fattest catalogue and they published the song that hit the hardest, both financially and socially: 'All Coons Look Alike to Me' (1896).

The title itself was slur enough without having to hear all the verses and choruses. In fact, the title was all that the world was to remember – an affirmation of a general understanding: they all look the same, you can't tell one from the other. Pure bigotry sold as musical fun. Who wrote this libel? Where were the black writers who might counter such a horror?

Ernest Hogan, a Negro, claimed the copyright. And his success gave his brothers an opportunity to join white Americans as fully fledged opportunists carrying on the myth of the hot coon. Who can blame them for wanting a slice of American pie? And who in white America wanted to know

that 'All Coons Look Alike to Me' was not anti-black at all
but an ironic song of great cleverness?

Let us take a closer look at these black Daniels in the
lion's den of early ragtime.

Ernest Hogan, in 1896, was the highest paid black in
vaudeville. He'd certainly paid his dues on the way up. Born
Reuben Crowder in Kentucky he'd started in the business
as a crowd 'piccaninny' in the touring tent-show version of
Uncle Tom's Cabin. He dreaded crossing into Dixie, the
home of the show. The legacy of the North's victory was
welcoming signs saying, 'Nigger Read and Run – and if You
Cain't Read You Better Run Anyway'. And the *Uncle Tom*
railroad car getting peppered with bullets as it passed
through Southern towns. And horsemen lassooing the black
minstrels and dragging them down main street so that their
swallow tail coats got torn to shreds. But still they grinned
and shuffled and beat the tambourine in the big parade.
You gotta keep grinning, said Hogan. And then you gotta
make them grin too, so's they'll forget to kill you. You gotta
play the game if you're gonna get ahead. And he made an
attempt to join them by changing his name to Ernest Hogan,
a sturdy Irish-American sound. But there was no changing
his colour, that was the rub. Irving Berlin and fellow Jews
had fought race battles too, but the odds weren't quite the
same.

Still, Ernest Hogan was determined to have a stab at the
main chance. He was by all accounts a very funny man (on
stage only – off stage he was a nervous wreck) and a marvellous dancer. By the middle nineties he was billing himself
as 'the Unbleached American' and he was something of a
star up North. One time in Chicago he was visiting the
red-light district (how he loved that sporting life!) and he
happened upon a black saloon entertainer who had a cute
little number. 'All Pimps Look Alike to Me' sang the dude
and these were the last words his woman had thrown at
him. The dude sounded like he meant every word of that
clever, folksy slice of life.

Hogan borrowed the chorus, added a verse to set up the
situation, and when he was next in New York he performed
it to Isadore Witmark, throwing in a cakewalk finale for

121

good measure. Isadore was doing well with the Harney ragtime and he took on the Hogan comedy song. He did some polishing and added another verse. He got Max Hoffman, the house arranger (and erstwhile first violin with the Minnesota Symphony), to arrange it for full orchestra and add a special syncopated chorus. He put a rubber-lipped coon cartoon on the cover.

The song immediately took off, selling over a million copies and becoming the anthem of coonery. Race fights were started by the mere whistling of the opening bars by a white. In 1900, four years later, the song was still causing trouble: it was the test piece at the Ragtime Piano-Playing World Championship held in New York. Duke Travers, a black, was tipped to win but he refused to acknowledge the test piece. He claimed he'd never heard the song and that he never would. So the white boy, Mike Bernard, won and that was OK with Mike because he claimed he'd never heard Duke Travers play ragtime and that anyway he, Mike Bernard, had learned his ragtime from Ben Harney. Mike had been the orchestra pit pianist supporting Harney's flying right hand at Tony Pastor's theatre.

Anyway, poor Ernest Hogan was to spend a lot of time apologizing for his song. At the end of his life he took the line that the 'coons' referred to weren't Negroes at all but were *raccoons.* 'We Negroes have been called every name under the sun, so I added another. The 'coon, you see, is a very smart animal.' But it was no use – Hogan knew he'd kicked himself and his race into that ancient spiral of self-destruction.

Little Irving Jones escaped the wrath of his brothers in higher places. None of his songs were as successful as 'All Coons'. After 'The Possumla Dance' of 1894 he wrote and wrote coon songs, becoming the most prolific of all coon song writers. 'All Birds Look Like Chickens to Me' parodied Hogan's hit; 'The Black Four Hundred' jeered at the pretentions of that very black middle class which would never have allowed him into their homes; 'If They'd Only Fought with Razors in the War' suggested that if the US Army had copied darky battle techniques the Spanish-American War would have ended quickly; 'The Ragtime Millionaire' proposed a seeming absurdity; 'St Patrick's Day Is a Bad Day for Coons' joined two ethnic genres together for some pop fun.

Irving Jones placed his songs with many New York publishers – with Kerry Mills, Leo Feist, Marks & Stern, even Paul Dresser and Chas K. Harris. But, though none really clicked with the general public, many of his coon songs were popular among black vaudeville audiences, especially in the South. Here they were absorbed into the programmes of black songsters to show up later in altered versions on race records of the 1920s (as Paul Oliver has shown in his masterful book, *Songsters & Saints*).

The Jones songs were acceptable to blacks (not yet sophisticated away into white sensibility) because they were seen as caricatures of a world that they recognized. When a black audience was sealed within its own theatre, away from the jeers of the master race, the 'in' humour of Irving Jones could be safely enjoyed. He was one of their own, he was reminding them of the comic foibles of *some* of the less fortunate of their race.

Thus the coon song, like most pop songs, could not be seen in isolation. It could not stand on its own like a work of art. The effect of the coon song depended on the situation. On who was singing what and to whom and where. For example: Leslie Stuart's rippling songs talked of 'niggers' and 'coons' but they were always treated with gentle romance. Who could object to 'Lily of Laguna'? A fantasy dreamed up on a wet afternoon in his native England. A feather sailing near his overcoat and galoshes.

But go to New York and the song-manufacturing business and we'll find little time for romance and fantasy. There, at the same period as 'Lily of Laguna' and 'Little Dolly Daydream', we find Andrew Sterling, seasoned lyricist, coming up with a racist nightmare: a white man is hired by a 'kinky woolly head' to dig a hole. When a crowd of appreciative blacks surround the sweating white his employer boasts: 'I've Got a White Man Working for Me'. In the next verse the irate digger grabs his employer and throws him down the hole. Then he turns on the crowd and proceeds to throw them all down 'to smother in the dusky gloom below'. When he's finished he covers up the hole and declares, 'Remember, coons, I'm far above you.'

And so it dragged on, this tiresome obsession. And often the tunes were good, very good indeed, peppered with syncopation, brimming over with gaiety. Into this ubiquitous coonery of the late nineties came Ben Harney, returned fit and tanned from the South Seas, but quite out of touch with the racy current pop scene. He seemed to have gone rather spiritual, offering Witmark's a strange testament to ragtime as the music of the universe: 'Cakewalk in the Sky'. Dutifully they published it but sales were dismal. Timing, timing, timing! Harney was out of step with the shrill times.

But Isadore still had a soft spot for Ben and in 1899 he ordered that the *Witmark Monthly*, the house magazine, interview their very own 'inventor of ragtime'. Harney expressed his shock and disgust at the 'multifarious commercialization of the ragtime'. And he came clean on his 'invention': he admitted he was not responsible. No single person, black or white, was responsible. The origins of ragtime, he claimed, lay not in American or Afro-American life and times but in lands and islands south of the border. The Spanish touch was the Tabasco that fired ragtime and this tingler long-preceded American ragtime. He said he'd been touring lately through Cuba, Argentina and Brazil and there he'd been staggered to witness the tango, the habanera, the maxixe and other syncopated dignities that lent a transcendental, noble element to dance music. 'I tell you – these tangos will burn you up, forcing you to look heavenwards and forget the mud of Dixie!' He said the Latins were getting syncopation right, had been for years, and that their bands, the Mexican ones, had already penetrated Texas and Louisiana. So watch out America!

The Witmarks published an edited version of Harney's outburst. They ceased to invite him into the inner office for coffee and cake; he had fallen into undesirable company, always escorted by swarthy gypsy types and Negroes who looked much too African. When he started haranguing the female stenographers with tales of how the Caribbean was the real cauldron of ragtime and a good-time for one and all—why, then the Witmarks issued a dictum that, from henceforth, Ben Harney & Company were not to darken their doors again.

The coon-song craze, for all its opprobriousness did at least offer some light: the opportunity for blacks to abandon the archaic minstrel-show format and to mount the stages of white theatres, eventually reaching Broadway with their own musical shows. Sambo stereotypes would still have to be observed but this new development in the myth of the hot coon was to be an important part of a Black Renaissance (which included poetry, novels, art music and painting) that lasted till around 1912. It was a false dawn – to be followed by another in the twenties and another in the sixties – but the chance to be seen and heard in the flesh, minus the swallow coats, was something special for the perennial nobodies of America.

The great white hope of the new black show business was the team of Bert Williams and George Walker. After years of knocking around as Mastodon Minstrels, as San Francisco 'Dahomians' in animal skins, as medicine-show entertainers, they 'arrived' in the autumn of 1896, hard on the heels of the ragtime of Harney and the coon hit of Hogan. They were acclaimed in New York by those in the know as the number one coloured attraction in vaudeville. Billing themselves as 'Two Real Coons' (thus cleverly having it both ways with the races) they presented a sparkling double act of music, comedy and dancing that raised the ancient twin blackface characters to real artistry.

Bert Williams played Jim Crow: slow of wit and foot, defeated and hopeless. George Walker played Zip Coon: cunning and high-stepping, uppity and confident.

When shambling Bert, mouth fixed in an upside-down U, recited his ragtime song 'Oh, I Don't Know, You Ain't So Wahm' like a wounded storefront preacher, everybody could safely laugh and relax – even Booker T. and Dixie senators – but afterwards life rolled along in the same old way. Bert wasn't rocking the boat, no sir. He removed the black make-up and went home to his Voltaire or his Zola, or his Twain.

When dapper George, in his tight-fitting suit and high silk

hat and spats and gloves and monocle, stepped out with his very own snazzy cakewalk he dazzled the ladies on both sides of the colour line. Soon he was being invited off the stage and into the homes of the highest in New York society: he would teach them how to cakewalk, such a quaint new sensation. Taking tea with the nobs he might whirl his malacca cane expertly, might smile his expansive smile, showing off his splendid teeth. He might be admired as a prize specimen. And he was a tiger on their rug.

Next year, 1897, 'Two Real Coons' were going great guns all round New York: Hammerstein's, Tony Pastor's, Koster & Bial's – real big-time. They had a white manager and a tag as 'The Celebrated Delineators of Darky Characters'. Bert had a new song that summed up most of the comic myth items. 'The Coon's Trade Mark: a Watermelon, Razor, Chicken and a Coon'. Had he sold his soul to the white devil for this mess of gumbo? Egbert Williams was no soul brother in the first place.

He was from the Caribbean island of Antigua, a property of the British Empire. His grandfather had been Danish consul there; his mother was quadroon. He'd been to Stanford University, the Ivy League of California. He was a bookworm, an introvert, a superior person. It had taken much study in order to imitate the speech patterns and curious gait of the Afro-American. He was proud of his achievement as a delineator of darky life. He was a rank outsider who'd conquered the idiom. He was on the verge of becoming a star.

In the first place he'd been no soul brother. But in the present place . . . He knew from bitter experience on the road – when the dixie hicks, offended by Walker's smart outfit, had made them undress and climb into sacks and hop out of town – that Egbert Austin Williams, a British subject, could be the best-educated, best-speaking, best-smelling man in America and he'd still be *just another nigger!*

Mr Will Marion Cook was born with very little black blood in him – but enough to show. Musically, however, he'd had the best of everything. At Oberlin Conservatory he'd studied violin and at the National Conservatory of Music in

New York he'd studied under Dvorak. In Berlin he'd been under violin maestro Josef Joachim. But now he was out from under – he was on top and ready to show the world that he was a very special person. He had cultivated a wax moustache and was extremely careful sartorially.

Unfortunately, he also had a short temper and an arrogant manner. He did not suffer fools gladly and in his way were a lot of fools of many colours. He was a man in a great hurry to make great music but there seemed nowhere to go except down that old Dixie trail to the melon patch. For too many doors had been slammed in his face by the guardians of legitimate art music. Too many slaps and slights had caused him to reject anything to do with the music of white America.

But, on the other hand, too much monotonous tom-tomming and cramped, stunted scales had turned him off the music of Africa—that Dahomian village band at the Chicago Fair had been excrutiating! What to do in such a quandary?

Though the line of heredity in American Negro art was dim and thin, Cook believed it to be the only line worth pursuing and therefore he determined to study the coon songs of Ernest Hogan and Irving Jones assiduously. Next he turned his attentions to Williams & Walker for, as performers, they seemed perfect vessels for his bubbling black art.

He decided he would star them in a musical work, an opera even, which would trademark the true invention of his race: *Clorindy, or the Origin of the Cakewalk*. In just one night, fortified with beer, whiskey and raw porterhouse steak, Cook and Paul Lawrence Dunbar (the published black poet) wrote the entire score. Late the following morning Cook was playing through 'my most Negroid song' on the family piano. It was not exactly the normal material for opera or even art song but it was current: 'Who Dat Say Chicken in Dis Crowd?'. Suddenly, in burst his mother, tears streaming. 'Oh, Will! Will! I've sent you all over the world to study and become a great musician, and you return such a nigger!'

His brothers in the business understood, though. They

127

too felt that this was breakthrough time and the main chance must be seized as it passed on the musical merry-go-round. Cook took his plans and his score to them and blazed away. The main regular meeting place for the brothers was in Bert Williams's rackety old top-floor apartment on 53rd St. Here was discussed progress, self-reliance, organization, acco- modation, plus new songs and new skits.

Among the gathered vaudevillians was, first off, Bob Cole. A veteran of black show business, he'd been in the *Creole Show* and the Black Patti Troubadours (for which he'd written skits such as 'At Jolly Coon-ey Island'). Currently, he was touring with *A Trip to Coontown*, the very first show to be totally made, owned and operated by Negroes.

Bob, a bucolic sport from Georgia, had done pretty well for a fellow who'd started his career as a saloon singer. But he was awed to meet the Johnson brothers at Bert's gatherings. These two had loads of degrees. James Weldon Johnson had been to Atlanta University and stayed the course (Bob had put in an appearance for a short time) and gone on to Columbia. He'd also passed the Florida bar and spoke fluent Spanish.*

J. Rosamond Johnson had studied at the New England Conservatory of Music and was almost as well-educated as Will Marion Cook. When Bob Cole expressed his pleasure at being in such heady company Cook mocked his Southern accent. Bert quickly called the meeting to order and enquired about the whereabouts of Ernest Hogan. It was suggested that he was carousing in the tenderloin on race-track winnings, as was his wont.

Then George Walker, in skin-tight grey morning suit, gave an uplifting speech about aims and ambitions, and left. Bert told Cook that the team would play in this *Clorindy* if there was proper, not imagined, financing. And if Williams & Walker weren't too booked at the time. And

---

* James Weldon Johnson went on to become a poet, translator, school principal, novelist, US Consul to Nicaragua, a founder of the National Association for the Advancement of Colored People, and the co-author of *Lift Every Voice and Sing*, a choral work which became known as the 'Negro National Anthem'.

now it was time for a session of their special poker game, Smut, in which the loser of a hand was penalized by having to smear soot on his face.

Cook, armed with Bert's blessing, set off in a mad rush. He got an appointment at Witmark's, ragtime's fountain of finance. For two whole hours he was kept waiting. Finally, Isadore appeared and was brusque: 'Go ahead! What's you got?'

Will was forty minutes into the score when Isadore started off back into his private office. Will, staggered, stopped the performance. Isadore, without turning, said, 'You boys are crazy if you believe any Broadway audience is going to listen to Negroes singing Negro opera.' Will shouted, 'Mr Witmark, sir – if you can get me a production I'll give you all the royalties as well as the publication rights!' Isadore slammed the office door.

But just as Cook was storming out of the House of Witmark he was apprehended by the professional manager: 'Mr Isadore thinks you may have the right stuff for success. He will try to secure a production. Royalty contracts will be drawn up for your signature'. Cook left huffily. He later sent Paul Lawrence Dunbar round for the signing of contracts. Paul was softly spoken and full of charm.

Hustling with as much dignity as he could maintain, Cook eventually persuaded Ed Rice of the Casino Roof Garden to take a chance. This would mean a Negro show right there on Broadway, the Great White Way! Ed said that *Clorindy* would be stitched into his new cabaret, *Summer Nights*, opening in July (1898). There was no question of presenting any Negro opera. *Clorindy* must be a fast-paced sketch with plenty of hokum and cakewalking. Witmark's held their presses until they'd heard what the word was on the show. 'It'd better make me laugh,' said Ed. When he caught Will conducting the theatre orchestra and chorus during rehearsals he exploded: 'No nigger can conduct my orchestra on Broadway.' But John Braham, the English conductor, sitting in the dark of the stalls, ordered: 'Now, now, Ed! Go back to your little cubby-hole and shut up – this boy's got genius!'

But Cook hadn't got his stars, Williams & Walker,

because they were out on tour. Instead, he was given Ernest Hogan and a supporting cast of forty brothers and sisters. Swearing off any drinking or gambling or good times, Hogan concentrated on the business at hand. Somewhere in this mess was a show and Hogan set to – cutting and polishing, throwing out most of Dunbar's wordy dialogue, highlighting the funniest coon songs and the liveliest dance numbers. Black or white or Chinese, this was Show Biz.

On opening night, out in the Roof Garden under the stars, *Clorindy* played to a thin house. Then the big show downstairs finished and its audience milled about, shooting the breeze. When they heard from up above that heavenly Negro chorus and the pulsing rhythms they rushed the elevators.

They laughed with 'Who Dat Say Chicken in Dis Crowd?', they thrilled to 'The Hottest Coon in Dixie', they gave a twenty-minute standing ovation to 'Darktown Is Out To-night'.

Cook's study of the Negro vernacular idiom had, it appeared, the chance of paying off. 'I was so delirious,' he wrote later, 'that I drank a glass of water, thought it wine and got gloriously drunk.' What a heady time! Such an opportunity! 'Negroes were at last on Broadway, and there to stay. Gone was the uff-dah of the minstrel! Gone was the Massa Linkum stuff! We were artists and we were going a long, long way. We had the world on a string tied to a runnin' red-geared wagon on a down-hill pull. Nothing could stop us, and nothing did for a decade'.

Witmark's took a hard look at the show and an even harder look at the sheet-music sales. *Clorindy* was a fine old mess, a mélange of droll plantation hoofing and ensemble singing and not always in unison. Still, it was fun and it ran a whole season. A novelty, said Witmark's.

But of all the songs published only 'Darktown is out Tonight' was moving significant copies. And this at the height of the coon-song craze! Maybe the blacks hadn't got the knack? Anyway, royalty statements were duly mailed. Then one fine day there appears at the House of Witmark an angry Negro with a fierce moustache and a snappy white lawyer in tow. Will Marion Cook has the nerve to dispute his royalty statement, accusing the figures of 'not being commensurate with the success of my play'.

The Witmark brothers couldn't believe such effrontery. They offered the lawyer their accounting books for his perusal. The lawyer expressed satisfaction. Then Isadore, glowing, turned to Cook and levelled: 'You are a clever man. You have great possibilities as a writer. And you will make money for a publisher some day . . . But you will never publish another number with this house as long as you live.'

In September of 1898 Williams & Walker were free to take over from Ernest Hogan when *Clorindy* was sent out on a short Eastern tour. Lots more dancers were added and the cakewalk aspect was stressed. All told, there were sixty performers plus Will Marion Cook conducting his 'Ragtime Orchestra' and throwing the score in the air if he heard too many goofs. But soon the steam and novelty ran out of *Clorindy* and the show was disbanded.

Meanwhile, Ernest Hogan had returned to the rabbit-warren cosiness of the Black Patti Troubadours, playing for his own folk. But trouble pursued him: in New Orleans he talked back to a white stage official who'd laughed in his face when he'd tried to cash his perfectly legitimate cheque. Hogan had thrown a punch. All hell broke loose. To escape the lynch mob he was smuggled out of town and out of the country – touring Hawaii, Australia, New Zealand, anywhere to get himself together again. In 1900 he returned to star in Cook and Dunbar's second operetta, *Jes Lak White Folks* and things were looking up. But one August night he got embroiled in a big New York race riot. He'd met up with George Walker and they were going to have a night on the tenderloin, sowing the wild oats (Bert Williams had wisely returned to hearth and home). The white mob, seeking revenge on a black cop killer, forced Walker to hide out in a cellar all night. Hogan wasn't so lucky: he was so badly beaten up he had to retire from *Jes Lak White Folks*. Bert Williams said not a word, became very withdrawn.

More discussions were held by those at the forefront of Negro stage progress to see what could be done to keep black show-business momentum rolling and the white bosses happy. At the Marshall Hotel on West Fifty Third Street, surrounded by Maryland fried chicken, creole sauces and Pullman porters, the brothers met and argued and planned for the future. George Walker, dressed to the nines and incandescent with ambition and jewellery, usually chaired the meetings. His aim was to play before the most refined and educated white people in America, to show that the black performer could do better than beat the tambourine and rattle the bones. Already he'd made inroads into white society by openly dating a string of white show girls and even a few wives. Bert didn't say a thing. Then he asked how Ernest Hogan was doing. That Irish stage name didn't help Hogan one bit. 'What we need,' said James Weldon Johnson, rising to the occasion, 'is to clean up the caricature. Already my brother Rosamund, in his act with Bob Cole, has substituted "boys" for "coons" in "All Coons Look Alike to Me". Together we are, all three of us, working towards a realization of the importance of the American Negro's cultural background and his creative folk art, and we are speculating on the superstructure of conscious art that might be raised upon them.'

By 1903 Bob Cole and the Johnson Brothers had gone some way towards establishing a place for artistic and non-offensive Negro songs in white musical comedies: 'The Maiden with the Dreamy Eyes', 'Under the Bamboo Tree', and 'Congo Love Song' were among the successes which led the team to be dubbed 'Those Ebony Offenbachs'. They now went a big step further by publishing a suite of six songs showing the 'Evolution of Ragtime' from the African jungle ('Voice of the Savage') through plantation days ('Essence of the Jug') to the sophisticated present day ('Sounds of the Times'). The *Ladies Home Journal* saw fit to reprint some of the songs – so artistic progress had been made towards the genteel trade. And two Broadway musical extravaganzas presented the work as 'pleasing novelties'. The selling point, of course, was the climax: a big singing and dancing cakewalk demonstration. And after that the "Evolution of Ragtime" faded away leaving pleasant memories. But was it art? Or was it just a refinement of the old minstrel show?

Williams & Walker stuck to the old ways, to travelling in the boxcar of mainline show business. Gradually they might creep forward to the Pullman cars (if only George would go easy on the white girls). In 1903 they made a great advance when their show *In Dahomey* played on the Broadway stage as a real honest-to-God black musical. This was a genuine First. The book was by Jesse Shipp; the music was by Cook and Dunbar. The story concerned a crooked African colonization scheme. The hopes and ideals were high. 'My partner, Mr Williams,' said George Walker to the press, 'is the first man that I know of in our race to delineate a darky in a perfectly natural way.'

Apart from that, *In Dahomey* was really no more than a rollicking good vaudeville farce with plenty of opportunities for singing and dancing. Not more than five minutes of plot was allowed to go by before somebody burst into a number. And though Will Marion Cook got the composer credit, the most popular songs were written by others: 'My Dahomian Queen' and others were written by J. Leubrie Hill; 'I'm a Jonah Man', one of Bert Williams's best loved songs, was written by Alex Rogers – and Harry Von Tilzer, an unreconstructed white man who'd written numerous coon songs, contributed 'I Wants to be an Actress Lady'.

The show went over to London where it became a great success because royalty decided to lend approval. King Edward VII commanded a performance as fitting entertainment for the birthday of the Prince of Wales. After that everybody who was anybody went to *In Dahomey* at the Shaftesbury Theatre. Williams and Walker were fêted by dukes and earls. George said the Queen had asked for his photograph; Bert was content to dine and converse with lesser artistocracy. When the show toured Britain Bert took the opportunity of joining a masonic lodge where no colour line was drawn. After much time and study he was made a member of the International Masons in Edinburgh. Of course, he knew that back in America he'd be relegated to the Negro branch.

But back in America there were grand plans to be pushed

133

through. George grew radiant with ambition. He drummed up the mass of money needed to stage *In Abyssinia*, a 'totally African' spectacular, right down to live jungle animals. Reviews and business were good. He got Bert involved ·in the Frogs, a charitable fraternity for Negro professionals organized on the lines of the Friars (from which blacks were barred). All the other stage brothers joined – Cole & Johnson, Alex Rogers, Jesse Shipp, Jim Europe and R. C. McPherson. These latter two were real do-ers in an organization of distinguished-looking gentlemen who were the pride of Harlem and the black community in general. Europe became musical director for Cole & Johnson productions, touring black America with their show *The Shoo Fly Regiment*, a story of industrial education and the Negro soldier. In 1908, tired out from one-night stands in the roughest and most dismal parts of the country, he settled in New York. Seeing that there was a crying need for a central booking agency for black dance-band musicians, Europe formed the Clef Club (in 1910). Previously the brothers had given out cards or hawked themselves around Broadway or hung out in cafés and saloons. Now the buyers could come to the Clef Club and see the lavish shows and concerts. In May 1910, for example, there was the *First Musical Mélânge and Dancefest*, featuring an orchestra of 100 musicians using ten pianos. Joe Jordan, recently the conductor at the black-operated Pekin Theatre in Chicago, conducted his stately number 'That Teasing Rag'; Ford Dabney, a Washingtonian with experience as official court musician for the President of Haiti, supplied arrangements; Henry Creamer, of the Gotham-Attucks Music Company, competed with Kid Farrell for the 'eccentric dance glove championship'.

As a result of such showcases the burgeoning dance-band business came to Jim Europe when they needed a touch of the coloured mystique for the fancy white society affairs. Europe sent his men out to work in tuxedos and took care of the contracts.

R. C. McPherson (who wrote songs under the pseudonym of Cecil Mack) was the doer who, in 1905, started the first black music-publishing company. Gotham-Attucks, 'The

House of Melody', was located at 50 West 29th St, and took its second name from the first Negro to be killed in the Revolutionary War. McPherson had realized that the real money in music lay in publishing and he was determined to grab a slice of fast-growing Tin Pan Alley. The brothers gathered round loyally. A few got involved financially. 'Nobody', which Bert Williams talked into popularity, was Gotham-Attuck's first hit. There followed a string of comedy successes like 'If He Comes In, I'm Going Out', and 'You're in the Right Church but the Wrong Pew'. Clever hot writers like Chris Smith and Jim Burris did business with Gotham-Attucks. But, by 1911, with Tin Pan Alley gearing up for the ragtime song-and-dance mania and competition becoming cut-throat, the lone black music company found itself in dire straits. Black writers no longer felt a loyalty – the white companies paid bigger advances and better royalties. Smith and Burris could go over to, say, a man like Ed Marks, and tap and rap their way into ready cash. And somehow the ragtime life no longer seemed solely concerned with prancing Negroes. Ragtime had burst out of the narrow confines of the minstrel reserve and was now for modern times, for everybody to do. There was no longer that white fascination for black folkways. Irving Berlin had been instrumental in taking syncopation out of the plantation and into the city.

The waning of interest in Negro life was also made clear by the fate of all-black musicals. The appeal of Cole and Johnson's *Shoo Fly Regiment* was restricted to black audiences. It ended up playing Southern tank towns in black-belt ghettos. *Bandana Land* didn't suffer the same fate but there was no doubt that the novelty had worn off as far as the general public was concerned. And blacks with ambition to move up the social and financial scale found these ethnic entertainments too narrow, too aromatic of minstrelsy, too down-home, too darned embarrassing. Rising blacks wanted to be viewed as Americans, not as comic types, not as descendants of Africans; they wanted to be in the swim of current events.

By 1912 the Second Coming of Ragtime, in its guise of dancemania, was making fortunes for those Tin Pan

Alleymen clever or lucky enough to be in tune with their times. And the Black Renaissance was over, a false dawn. Had the general public ever really been interested in true depictions of black life? But equally, perhaps, had they been shown black life in all its complexity? Sambo rears his grinning face. And Negroes in show business would have to take a step back into the shade once again.

Some of the most notable artists who had shone in the brief period were dead: Ernest Hogan, Bob Cole, George Walker – all killed by syphilis. And Scott Joplin, obsessed with his mission to raise ragtime into concert hall and opera stage, was a pathetic wreck of syphilitic rot. The dark pleasures of black Bohemia had snuffed out the light of their artistic dreams.

In 1913, with America still dancing mad, Bert Williams moved into a fine four-storey brownstone house in Harlem. He loved to sit in the parlour where, in carpet slippers and smoking jacket, he could bury his nose in Voltaire, Zola, Oscar Wilde. Sometimes, and good times they were, when he was into Aristotle, he'd take off and, flying above the chaos, he'd look down on the error of Man and Man's disruption of Nature's Order.

Bert's house had everything in order: books, pipes, chinaware on the walls, and trousers. Trousers in their presses, trousers with neat creases down the sides. *Trousers.* If dear departed George and the other well-meaning brothers of his ilk had truly followed their African obsessions they should have run about without any trousers on. And that would never do. The logic of black purity inevitably leads to such problems of negritude.

As Bert had once told the press, it was 'inconvenient' being a Negro in America. But that was as far as he'd go with the press. Nobody in America wanted to know about complexity, diversity, subtlety or shade. In America one was lumped in with all the other Negroes. But he, Egbert Williams, would always at heart remain a West Indian and a subject of His Royal Majesty. Playing the shuffling darky would always be a professional act for him, an act he'd spent years perfecting. And now at last he was free to play

136

in mainline show business, to join the ranks of Al Jolson and W. C. Fields and Sophie Tucker.

In 1910 he'd become a vaudeville single and a star of the Ziegfeld Follies. Next year he was partnering the white comedian Leon Errol. Now he was Bert Williams, a *particular individual*, instead of just another Jim Crow. *Particular* – he was also becoming particular about whom he employed. His West Indian chauffeur was fine but the rest of the brothers who used to be in his employ . . . he'd let them go. It had all happened after George died. He became tired of charity, conscience, of loyalty to the brothers. He didn't feel like being a Negro any more—this face and body were mask and suit. He felt like being a free spirit who happened to work as an actor, and who happened to have to put on blackface as part of his job. At home he put on the carpet slippers and pulled out the books, settling into a granite-and-marble world of past achievements and glories, of eternal verities, of professional disciplines, of peace of mind gained by knowledge and reflection in the vale of tranquillity.

But now his thoughtful silence was being vandalized by shrieks and shouts and foot stomping from nearby. Some church or other. Round and round and round goes the call and response, growing louder and more frenzied all the while. Round and round and round – like a dog chasing its tail, like the history of the poor wretches who'd been dragged to America in chains. Round and round and round – getting nowhere fast with backs slouched and feet dragging across a floor with no bounce, and whose walls have no echo. Round and round and round – and often bumping into others and hurting them or themselves, and then bellowing in an agony that sometimes raised itself into a kind of malformed art. Oh, the waste! Oh, the pity of it all! And who was he to sit in judgement, wearing carpet slippers? He was, at bottom, a Nowhere person too, in a Nowhereland that wants to be everywhere at once.

'What a country! Forever bright and noisy and yet forever lost in the silence of a deep black night.' And having completed this thought the great comedian went to bed.

137

6

Everybody's Doing it now

While Bert Williams was sleeping off his musings on society, Irving Berlin was sitting up at his piano trying to divine what the crowd would buy next. It was 1913 and it was June but he was determined to resist writing about honeymoons, spooning or crooning. He had progressed beyond such clichés. But though he had written a serious (and a hit) ballad in 'When I Lost You' he was still tagged as a specialist in novelty songs. Of course, he hadn't helped his reputation by recently creating 'Rum Tum Tiddle' and 'Snooky Ookums'. The 'Ki-Yi Yodeling Dog' had been buried quickly, thanks to meagre sales.

His apartment was furnished tastefully if a trifle conservatively. Plush curtains, solid period furniture, quiet paintings. Nothing modern. Not for him the mad-dog modern art of cubism, expressionism, fauvism or futurism, that had caused such a furore at the Armory exhibition. Not for him any poems with no rhyme and books with no plot. The complete Shakespeare set that he'd bought on the London trip sat with authority against the wall in an Early American bookcase. Hard to tear up a leather-bound book, easier to pulp loads of failed pop songs. Shakespeare was permanence while, in the whirling world outside, 'Everybody's Doing it now'. What had he wrought? The world and his wife had gone dancing mad, turkey trotting, bunny hugging, balling the jack. It had all begun so quietly back in 1910 with 'The Grizzly Bear' of George Botsford and then he, Irving, had put words to the rag, telling the people what to do.

138

Still, now that the Alley was firmly in control of pop
music and dances he'd have to look to his laurels because
there were plenty of ambitious Alleymen hard at his heels,
panting with dance songs they hoped would sell. All around
him in the Alley they were slaving away: re-working the
old steamboat theme ('Sailing Down the Chesapeake Bay'
by his erstwhile writing partner George Botsford), reflecting
the popularity of the auto ('He'd Have to Get Under—Get
Out and Get Under to Fix Up His Automobile' by Edgar
Leslie and Maurie Abrahams, his pals and rivals), and
cooling the folks down with ballads like 'The Trail of the
Lonesome Pine' and 'If I Had My Way'. Then there were
oddities to contend with, too: 'El Choclo', a 'real Argent-
inian tango', and 'The Memphis Blues' a bit of Negro folk
life.

Would these songs become movements, would these
sounds become styles? For the moment Irving was playing
it safe: he was concocting a song which quoted from almost
every ragtime hit he'd written to date. 'They've Got Me
Doin' It Now' was ready by dawn.

Around lunchtime he'd taxi the number down to
Waterson, Berlin & Snyder. Always a queue at the office
these days. Acts wanting the latest Berlin rag from the
'House of Novelty', (as Ted liked to call the company). All
kinds of acts from trick cyclists to performing elephants.
Variety reported last week that 'Robinson's Ragtime Elephants' are a knockout attraction – standing on their front feet
in the finale, shaking to a Berlin rag. An act called 'The
Ragtime Chinese Laundry' is going great guns with the
Berlin 'Ragtime Soldier Man'. 'The Medley Boys' (who
bill themselves as 'Not the Best but as Good as the Rest'!)
have been pestering for a flash finale so we might give
them 'They've Got Me Doin' It Now'—it's a throwaway
number anyway.

When Irving arrived at the office with the new song he
was immediately pinned down by a voluptuous lady juggler
with flashing eyes who crooned that he'd written more hits
than anyone in the whole world and . . . 'And more failures,
too,' he replied soberly and hurried up the winding staircase
to his private room where waited his 'confidential secretary'.

Cliff Hess was schooled in the dots and squiggles and he also had the patience of Job. His boss was in perpetual motion, pacing and smoking, with ideas pouring out all at once, and the stated aim to knock off four or even five songs a week, and the unstated aim to forget the circumstances of Dorothy's death but to cherish her memory. And to keep working, working all the while because work was the only ethic. 'Ethic' was a word you didn't wave in front of the other Alleymen. Stay tough with the boys, pretending you have a girlie for every day of the week and don't give a damn for them. Talk tough and write sweet when needed. He told the *Billboard* interviewer just the other day: 'I don't write church lyrics on the side, have no passion for flowers, and never read Shakespeare in the original Greek.' But, off the record, he was fondest and proudest of his ballad 'When I Lost You'. Roses and stuff like that had played a big part in that number. So had Dorothy.

Financially, he'd proved his romantic worth with that ballad. *Billboard's* Top Ten best-selling sheet-music list showed 'When I Lost You' up there, together with his usual novelties 'The Old Maid's Ball' and 'Snooky Ookums'. Some smart-alec critic had written that he'd 'committed an unpardonable breach of grammar by putting "happily" at the end of a line' in 'Snooky Ookums'. Then the guy goes on to boast that he knows that 'ookum' is from the redskin word meaning 'dear' and that 'snooky' is from the Sanscrit word meaning 'honey'. Who cares?

Cliff Hess sat by Irving and quietly took down the music to the new number as the composer fingered it out on the upright.

Look! The facts of interest to Waterson, Berlin & Snyder are these: *Billboard* Top Ten lists are gleaned from 312 music retailers and 5 and 10 cent stores around the country; all types of songs are required at all times of day to satisfy the demands of 5000 vaudeville theatres taking in over $100 million a year. Musically, it's ragtime they want right now, despite the odd hit ballad. And ragtime has spread abroad, raging in Europe and tickling aristocrats and even eggheads in Britain.

Cliff Hess, having finished his transcription, reminded

140

Irving that Bert Feldman, the British publisher, had an appointment for 3 p.m.

The Britishers had been hitting town of late, seeking material for local consumption, dealing in a very gentlemanly way. Last week the office had been graced with the presence of David Day of Francis, Day & Hunter. Mr Day had said that ragtime is forcing British writers to pay more attention to melody as opposed to lyrics. 'The swinging lilt and cross-rhythms of the rag-time are much in demand – as for example in "Waiting for the Robert E. Lee", your enormous success.' Irving hadn't bothered to correct him. Everyone assumed he'd written every ragtime song. Fred Day rattled on: 'Of course, the Lee item took time to catch on because our people wondered why there should be such a fuss made about this Lee person, why darkies were waiting so long at the docks for his arrival and so forth . . .' There were people to see and songs to complete or give birth to. Irving excused himself. 'Sir,' said Mr Day, trying to make a graceful exit, 'Your Alexander and his Band are top sellers in my country but it was an effort, a strenuous effort, to achieve this. My friend Bert Feldman can tell you that story – for he is the lucky publisher . . .'

No one at Snyder's could make out the British, even Irving was flummoxed. Why should Fred Day visit Snyder's when he knew darn well that Snyder's have an exclusive deal with Feldman? Could Day be visiting in admiration? Maybe that's why the Britishers lag so far behind in this business. Now Bert Feldman, he was different, he was more American in his hurry and dash and business acumen. Feldman had cornered the market in American ragtime, signing up $15 million worth of our hits. He'd gotten the rights to such catalogues as Remick, Witmark, Chas K. Harris, Shapiro-Bernstein, Jos Stern – and Waterson, Berlin & Snyder. And where was Fred Day? Probably smiling and bowing and tipping his hat and asking directions from nasty New Yorkers . . .

Bert Feldman, beautifully turned-out, arrived on the dot for his three o'clock appointment. But he had to wait till six. He was, though, excused from waiting in the queue. Bert was offered coffee and strudel and told that Mr Berlin was behind in his meetings but would soon catch up. 'He sees two or three hundred people a week – or is it a day? – anyway, it's a heap,' said the female stenographer as she led Bert into Max Winslow's office. Bert's time wasn't wasted. Within half an hour he'd settled a big contract with Max. After only ten minutes with Henry Waterson he'd made an arrangement for import-export. And before drinks time he was up in Irving's office regarding that doleful face.

Like so many people behave in the presence of the awesome, Bert blathered on regardless. Irving listened carefully, silently. So far, Bert said, his company had sold over 500,000 copies of 'Alexander'. 'Funny thing – the early performers couldn't ring the cash registers, and it was the brass bands and acrobatic acts that did the trick in convincing the public.' Irving leaned forward, ignoring the telephone's jangle. 'I've brought a clipping from *The Times* for your perusal. I think it will amuse you.' Irving needed that.

'Mr Berlin . . . We're all looking forward to your appearance at the Hippodrome in July,' said Bert, soldiering on. Irving was perusing the article: 'RAG-TIME'. He didn't see his name but he did see the words 'unpleasant', 'misdirected', 'vulgar'. Bert tried to say lightly: 'This'll be your first trip to our fair city since before the explosion of "Alexander".' Irving shook his head but didn't expand on the matter. Bert said: 'A thousand pounds a week – that's a lot to pay for any artist – of course, you deserve every penny – but even so, that's a lot of money even for mad Albert de Courville.'

'Tell me,' said Irving, breaking his silence, 'Is this de Courville guy really the illegitimate son of the King?'

Later that night (or it may have been early morning) Irving was stuck for inspiration so he turned for relaxation to the article in *The Times* of London. It was dated 8 February, 1913 and it was in the 'Music' department. That's nice, to be in 'Music'. The anonymous writer appeared to approve of ragtime but there was dubious stuff about its origins: 'Rag-Time music has been popular in the United States for about 25 years, and started probably as a debased imitation

142

of the genuine negro song.' What the hell was that? This was news to Irving. Where did these guys get their facts from? Still, he never claimed to know what ragtime was – he just went ahead and wrote it. There's some negativism here: the writer says ragtime's the music of 'the hustler and the feverishly active speculator'. That's bothersome. But later, the piece turns good: 'Here, perhaps, for those who have ears to hear, are the seeds from which a national art may ultimately spring.' Elevation! The challenge of writing a grand opera or an operetta or something of longevity. He'd show them, one of these days, when he'd got the time.

'Tempus Fugit' – that's what it says on the Early American grandfather clock by the piano. Time, you arch-thief! What a race of time, of ragtime, since Henry's party when they'd celebrated the new partnership and the story of the picca-ninny in the closet had come up! His time could be measured in many ways but the most profitable would be in the amount of song product. A stream of ragtime and more ragtime: 'That Mysterious Rag', 'The Ragtime Mocking Bird', 'At the Devil's Ball', 'The Ragtime Jockey Man', 'When the Midnight Choo Choo Leaves for Alabam'. And the Dixie theme (with but a smidgeon of duskiness) had been continued with 'I Want to Be in Dixie' and 'Down in Chattanooga' but he, himself, had never been below the Mason-Dixon line. Nor had many of his colleagues who wrote of Dixie heaven. They sat in their cubicles and wrote of the Old South without ever having to slosh about in the mush itself. And the world, even Southerners, bought the songs. But you couldn't sell them everything – 'Alexander's Bagpipe Band' was left to roam around the bottomlands, hitless in Swanee.

E. Ray Goetz had helped Irving on the bagpipe number. Ray was a good egg and he had a terrific sister. Dorothy was nineteen when Irving met her. He demonstrated 'Every-body's Doing It Now' to her, murmuring in his plaintive and halting style. She responded by shaking and yelling, 'It's a bear!' and the whole song fizzed. 'See that trombone bursting apart,' murmured Irving and Dorothy did a series of oddball dance steps, who knows where they'd come from. She went naturally with the beat, she knew what people wanted. She was the crowd but she wore a golden halo.

There was nothing to be said about her to the press and public, except the legal facts. The engagement was announced and Mother Baline was appeased. So Dorothy wasn't Jewish – but was anybody counting the ham sandwiches consumed by Mother Baline in the lovely house bought for her by her son? Irving Berlin was in love. He was no longer alone. He didn't have to spend so much unearthly time high in his apartment.

Early in 1912 he and Dorothy were married in Buffalo. Then they left the big freeze for the warmth of Havana, Cuba. There was a typhoid epidemic at the time. Five months after the wedding, in the luxurious Riverside Drive apartment where every object had been specially picked for her pleasure, amidst hurrying interior decorators and helpless doctors, she died of that Cuban typhoid.

Ray Goetz came to the rescue of a dazed Irving Berlin. He stopped him dashing off silly songs and he carted him off to Europe on a therapeutic tour. Sometime in August they visited London; sometime or other they climbed the Eiffel Tower. Sometime, somewhere, Irving poured out his feelings about his dead wife into a mould that produced 'When I Lost You' – a slow, mournful ballad full of thick, rich, flowing chords. Much reference to Nature. Nothing about ragtime. Very private, very personal. And yet offered to the public for the usual price. Result: a smash hit, his first ballad success!

Then he disappeared for a while.

Where he went to, nobody knows. Perhaps he took time out to go rambling round Dancing America. 'Alexander's Ragtime Band' had been a timely publication, appearing at the start of an extraordinary and spontaneous mass movement – Dancemania – that embraced wriggling, hobbling, wobbling, shivering, quivering, backing the lady, hugging her tight, bumping your bottoms with all of your might. No longer did the gentleman encompass his partner's tiny hand as a symbol of protection. Now each partner laced fingers,

144

moving within the lacing. And that was about all that was fixed. In Dancing America the ragtime spirit told choreography to go to the dogs, and many other animals. Mature Americans were behaving like beasts in a flurry of animal dances that came and went like scares on a Ghost Train. There flashed: the grizzly bear, turkey trot, bunny hug, chicken scratch, buzzard lope, monkey glide, and kangaroo hop.

'Everybody's Doing It Now' had rightly noted the new movement—those ragtime couples swaying from the hip, freed from the corsetry of Victorian decorum and the dictatorship of Only One Way, they were throwing their shoulders in the air and shouting 'It's a bear!' just like Dorothy. There was neck-holding and lingering physical contact. There was nothing left of the graceful teamwork seen in the nineteenth century ballroom. In those days phalanxes of buttoned-up dancers had advanced and receded with clockwork regularity, dance cards were marked and fans sent messages of love. Much air circulated between the dancers.

The cakewalk – once so daring and rip-roaring – could now be seen, in the perspective of the ragtime anarchy, as a proper team dance in the tradition of decent old-style ballroom dancing. The animal dances were excuses for public love-making and it was hard to police the new dark dance halls. Back in ordered times there were licensed dancemasters in command to lay down the law in bright ballrooms – proper deportment to preserve a graceful carriage, delicate negotiation on the floor in order to avoid close contact or actual bumping. Most importantly: the elimination of all thoughts of self.

But from 1911 the dancemasters of America were in disarray, fighting a rearguard action against the march of democracy and a host of incomprehensible immigrants. Nowadays, all that was left of the old sergeant-major dance master was a pathetic wretch hired by the dance-hall owner to shout into a megaphone: 'Next dance, pul-lease!', 'None of that here!', 'We will now give the refreshments a short rest!' All over the land had mushroomed dance halls, as opposed to the light and airy and well-organized ballrooms, with brassy bands and easy on the violins. In the typical dance hall the gloaming was lit in glitter sprays from a central rotating cut-glass ball hanging from on high. The new world created was an alternative to hearth and home. Here, ordinary folk from many walks of life and countries of origin could be transformed into whirling dervishes or latin lovers. Girls, many from good families, were seen to become shaking Jezebels, leaping up onto tables and calling for more ragtime and faster. This, of course, was the beginning of the end. And the irony was that these seemingly new animal steps were only the old dances of Afro-Americans of the poorer classes altered by belated frontiersmen from out of the West – who ought to have known better. One can see the black middle class shaking its collective head in dismay.

All white America was dancing at all times of day – breakfast dances, lunch dances, tea dances, supper dances, dinner dances and dancing all night and in between. Dancing not only in dance halls but in once-decorous ballrooms, and also in drawing-rooms, hotels, golf clubs and in Central Park. On Park Avenue, in high society, Miss Elsie de Wolfe was pouring tea as Mrs Irene Castle, happily married, tried to teach a civilized version of the Texas Tommy. The lore of the barnyard must not be allowed to conquer!

Meanwhile, the forces of puritanical repression had begun to attack. Since the rise of the city and the wash of East European immigration, Anglo-Saxon nativists looked back with nostalgia on a clean, clear past that was close to nature. The farm symbolized the old morality, the good old ways, the upright English of the Bible. The city symbolized immorality, strange new folkways and aliens. The imminent chaos must be stopped. Social-reform campaigners sought to outlaw the demon drink, the red-light districts, the opium dens, the white-slave traffic, the Italian and Jewish gangs thriving in New York. Fair enough – but the campaigners also lumped in the new energetic dancing with these other evils.

In 1910 *Harper's Weekly* asked 'Where is Your Daughter

This Afternoon?', going on to suggest she might well be turkey-trotting her morals away at an afternoon tea dance in a hotel. That same year a watch was started on public dance halls by Mrs Israels and her New York Commission on Amusements and Vacation Resources for Working Girls. The commission found that 'reckless and uncontrolled dances' were performed, leading into 'an opportunity for license and debauch'. A young woman in New Jersey was sent to prison for dancing the turkey trot one afternoon in 1911. Fifteen young women were sacked from a noted magazine after the editor caught them animal dancing during the lunch break. In 1912 pressure was put on the mayor of New York to censor 'racy' songs, especially those fooling around with the various meanings of the word 'It'. The mayor, sensitive to such issues, said he'd look into it, the matter. Waterson, Berlin & Snyder were made a prime subject for investigation. Their speciality was racy comedy songs.

Whether or not he had taken a trip round ragtime America, Irving Berlin was back from leave by the time of the Snyder investigation and ready to answer any charges of immorality. Was there a moral chasm between 'When I Lost You' and 'Do It Again'? Both were by Berlin but the first was a hit and the second was not a hit – *there* was the vital difference so let's not worry about morals in the marketplace. Let's get on with the job.

Irving, loveless, was even keener than before on the job of satisfying American taste. He was now the Compleat Alleyman. The craze for dancing had instructed him that, henceforth, his songs must have a pulse and must be adaptable to any, and all, new steps. 'When I Lost You' could be waltzed one minute and bunny-hugged the next. American pop and America was on the move and would never again stand still. Irving must needs be in the vanguard . . .

Tempus Fugit. 'They are not long, the days of wine and roses . . .' No time for the leather-bound books. Down below his apartment there was an army of Alleymen following fast the trends of ragtime and dancemania and also producing the odd ballad. Tin Pan Alley was enjoying

147

its most prosperous time and Irving Berlin had many rivals seeking his crown. On the eve of his visit to Britain let us look at his competitors (some of whom were his friends).

There was Jimmy Monaco, currently billing himself grandly as 'James V. Monaco' and this because he was up in the *Billboard* Top Ten with a ballad, a raggy one but a ballad just the same: 'You Made Me Love You – I Didn't Want to Do It'. Joe McCarthy, a good boozer and an all-round good fellow, had written the masochistic words and Joe stayed 'Joe' on the credits.

1913 was certainly their year for ballads. Sticking with the bleeding-heart theme, they squeezed hard in 'I Miss You Most of All' (with the splendidly anthropomorphic line: 'The chairs in the parlour all miss you, the pictures all frown on the wall') and 'I'm Crying Just for You' (with the mixed-up kid line: 'I ought to hate you but I love you, love you, love you'). These were the kind of saloon songs that caused crying in prostitutes and made Al Jolson, that fast-rising star, lust for Monaco/McCarthy songs as much as for Berlin songs.

Jolson, a Russian-Jewish emigré like Berlin, had risen from minstrel shows to Broadway revue. On stage he wore his heart on his sleeve, pleading on his knee for one-way love. Off stage he wore a frown and sometimes a glare, and he ate up songs and show girls like there was no tomorrow. He was queer for these Monaco/ McCarthy weepers: a sea of self-pity and what a great way to drown! Mr Monaco could accompany the World's Greatest Entertainer to the race track any day.

Only a few years ago James V. Monaco had been plain 'Ragtime Jimmy'. Born in Genoa, Italy, he was raised in Albany, New York. By the age of seventeen he was playing his self-taught ragtime piano on the honky tonk circuit of Chicago. The city fathers were saloon keepers and, as in the Bowery of Izzy Baline, they organized politics and crime from their saloon back rooms while out front the likes of Ragtime Jimmy kept the customers in a happy jagtime haze. Jimmy got into the saloon business himself and soon found himself paying protection money to such city fathers as 'Bathhouse John' Coughlin and 'Hinky Dink' Kenna.

Forking out for these micks made him feel bad and when Jimmy got mad he looked very dark and very Italian. So it was lucky for all concerned when, with the help of Edith Maida Lessing, he placed a hit with old Will Rossiter, the Chicago publisher who'd long ago been Charles K. Harris's mentor. 'Oh! You Circus Day' soon spread all round the nation and Jimmy entrained for New York and the Alley. In 1911, following 'Alexander', he one-fingered 'At the Ragtime Ball' to words by Roger Lewis (about honeybabes taxi-ing to the ball where there'd be much animal dancing and prizes to be won). In 1912 he scored a whopper with 'Row, Row, Row' (words by Billy Jerome) in which Johnny Jones, a weisenheimer, romanced his girlie in a boat far from the ragging crowds. Then, in 1913, he picked up his mandolin and, possibly filled with the spirit of old Genoa and probably remembering the harmonies and melodies that forced tears from tough tarts in dingy saloons, he plucked out 'You Made Me Love You' – and a career in balladeering began.

James V. Monaco was the melodist supreme at the Broadway Music Company (run by Will Von Tilzer, one of Harry's many brothers). He was also known as the 'Beau Brummel' of the Alley because of his beautiful suits and ties. His only sartorial rival was Lewis F. Muir, another self-taught melody man who couldn't read a note. Muir specialized in dazzlingly white high collars and equally dazzling multi-coloured ties in horizontal stripes. With a brace of ragtime hits to his name he was lately to be seen closely escorting a real foreign blue-blood, Miss De Sorel – daughter of a Spanish count and granddaughter of Gustave David, the noted French painter.

Time was when Muir, by his own admission, had been a tramp. Time was, not by his own admission, when he'd been Louis Meuer, born in New York to German-Jewish parents. For five years, at the turn of the century, he'd bummed around the South and Mid-west as an itinerant pianist, playing that underground circuit known to Scott Joplin, Ben Harney and numerous forgotten ragtimers. In 1904, like Joplin, he'd played the midway fun area at the St Louis Exposition and, no doubt, had been exposed to grander ragtime than that which he'd picked up and performed in the low joints of his tramp years. For a while he was a member of the Lew Dockstader minstrel troupe, a fine training ground for commercial songsters. Al Jolson was a fellow member. Then he became a travelling salesman for the J. Fred Helf Music Company of New York.

In 1910 he first turns up in print, under the J. Fred Helf banner. By this time he was a seasoned piano man – with no legitimate schooling and only the key of C but also with a head full of ragtime folklore – strong, shared melodies, a heap of tricks and licks and riffs, a memory of animal dances in the raw. With various helpers on the lyrics 'Lewis Muir' emerged with 'The Oklahoma Twirl' and 'Oh, You Bear Cat Rag'. None of them hits but both published a year before 'Alexander's Ragtime Band'.

In 1911, at J. Fred Helf's offices, he met Irving's one-time partner Edgar Leslie. They wrote 'Texas Tommy's Dance' to no avail. Then they got real cheeky with 'When Ragtime Rosie Ragged the Rosary'. F.A. (Kerry) Mills chose to publish this novelty and, in December, with Irving being acclaimed as Ragtime King, Kerry Mills took an ad in the *New York Clipper* (a trade paper) to boast: 'There is no use going into endless conversation about this song. It is simply putting everything else out of business.'

L. Wolfe Gilbert was a man about Tin Pan Alley. He'd been born Wolfe to parents fleeing an anti-Jewish pogrom in Odessa, Russia. In America he had a vaudeville act and he wrote songs. He was good with the patter and his gossip column in the *Clipper* was lively and sometimes controversial. 'Ragtime Rosie' spelled sacrilege to Wolfie Gilbert. In his column he chastised Leslie and Muir for travestying the sacred 'Rosary'.

Wolfie was making the rounds of the publishers a few days later when he was confronted by Lewis Muir: 'Who are you to criticize my song? Did you ever write anything yourself?' Wolfie cited 'Mammy's Shufflin' Dance' and 'The Texas Prance'. Snorted Muir: 'I never heard of them. But if you're a songwriter why don't you and I get together and write one?'

After a hard night's work they'd produced a couple of

150

numbers and next day they demonstrated them with gusto to Kerry Mills. Now Mills had been one of the first composers and publishers of cakewalk ragtime back in the nineties. His 'At a Georgia Camp Meeting' and 'Whistling Rufus' were respectful and folksy. He told Gilbert and Muir that the ballad 'stinks' and the Dixie song was 'out-of-date'. As he showed them the door he told them to 'get the knack' of today's pop by studying some of the F.A. Mills professional copies.

Wolfie stormed out. But, later, he remembered he'd forgotten the promised song copies. When he returned to the reception lobby he heard Mills shout out from somewhere: 'Just a minute, Gilbert! Let me hear that "Robert E. Lee" again. Can't get the darn thing off my mind.'

'Waiting for the Robert E. Lee', a striding ragger about shuffling daddies and mammies down on the levée in old Alabammy, was an immediate hit. Wolfie joked about having never been near the South and Muir told him he was lucky. Al Jolson was the main pusher of the song. He knew it was in his handwriting the moment Wolfie first demonstrated it to him. Wolfie had stretched his arms and bent his knees while Muir drummed the transposing piano and all the while a Mills plugger stood by waiting for the command for the lever to be pulled, thereby releasing the verse in C to the chorus in F.

'OK. I give in!' said the grim-faced Jolson. 'Gimme an arrangement in F sharp.' Did Wolfie's Alabammy evoke memories of Russia? Or did Jolson feel he could ride this one like a winning jockey? At the Winter Garden he sat on the 'Robert E. Lee', imprinting his mark everywhere. At the end of a performance he'd point at the darkness and thump his chest and tell the world: 'Don't you just love Jolie? Don't you just adore me?'

But 'Waiting for the Robert E. Lee' was not Jolson's property. The song hit a chord of familiarity in millions of hearts and many had a go, including Guards bands and organ grinders. In Britain the song seemed more American than 'Alexander'. In *The Times* article on ragtime (the one Irving had read) 'Robert E. Lee' was musically analyzed in detail. Britain was, it seemed, tired and jaded and dying to

151

be peacefully invaded by the siren of American ragtime and ragtime America (the clothes, the slang, the posture, the outlook). Yankee modernity would wash away the sludge of music hall with its trapped cast of mothers-in-law, kippers, ale, tripe and onions. 'Hitchy Koo' would be the war cry.

'Hitchy Koo' a new song by Muir and Gilbert with a little help from Maurie Abrahams, was a jaunty catch-phrase that could mean whatever you wanted (but especially 'It'). In the summer of 1912 there was much 'hitchy-kooing' going on in New York when British impresario Albert de Courville arrived. He was in the market for genuine American rag acts to appear at the London Hippodrome, his current venue for novelty and revue. William Morris, his New York connection and a foxy agent, led him down to Coney Island, the loudest place on earth.

Coney Island was the favourite resort of New York's masses. Along the boardwalk of Surf Avenue were assorted amusements – dance halls, Greek picture houses, the haunted house, the steeple chase, sawdust cafés and cabarets, Bozo the Wild Man from Borneo and the Biggest Hot Dog in the World – plus assorted personalities, including some gangsters, plenty of drunken sailors, painted ladies, and drooling old varmints. Coney Island was always lit up sharp and stark. It was perfect for ragtime.

Kelly's Cabaret was a typical blood-and-sawdust saloon. But Albert de Courville's eyes were on the antics of a male quartet who were flinging themselves through ragtime songs and dances. He hired them for London. At the College Inn (an 'upholstered sewer' according to Wolfe Gilbert) the impresario was welcomed by Wolfie himself and seated in a reasonably clean seat. Wolfie had lately been using this dump as his song showcase. William Morris had tipped him off about the Englishman's visit. Wolfie was ready with a bunch of vaudeville singers hastily grouped together to knock the pants off the buyer.

Flushed with drink and the chance of a break, the ad hoc act raced through a selection of Muir & Gilbert numbers, all action and big gestures. De Courville bought the show. He then augmented the three singers and their pianist

Melville Gideon with the Kelly's Cabaret quartet. They were henceforth to be the American Ragtime Octette and they were to get ready for a foreign trip, a friendly invasion. The Octette arrived at Southampton in September 1912. They were to be the show-business sensation of Britain. They helped set the scene for the appearance of Irving Berlin, the Ragtime King, in the following year. But they were not the first American ragtimers to invade Britain, nor were they the first manifestation of American syncopation in those isles.

We have already seen how minstrelsy became popular among the British – how some even claimed to be perfectors of the genre, how the Prince of Wales took banjo lessons from the Negro picker Bohee, how high society, clerics, children, all loved their golliwog Sambo.

By the early 1900s local minstrelsy was considered polite entertainment for the middle classes – at the seaside show, the charity concert, the children's party. Banjos had become a national instrument for the amateur gentleman. American virtuosos were much in demand as trainers. Following the success of the Bohee brothers and James Bland in Victorian times, Vess Ossman, a German-American, was invited to tour Britain at the behest of Clifford Essex, a local banjo nut and a Pierrot star. Ossman duly made the rounds of the usual hotels, town halls and floral halls, finishing up by playing some duets at the Palace with Edward VII (the erstwhile Prince of Wales).

But by now there were British banjoists who could give the Americans a run for their money. Olly Oakley, though his name has a Yankee ring, was born Joseph Sharpe in Birmingham, England. He became a prolific banjo recording artist. Charlie Rogers, born in Shepherds Bush, was known as the Banjo Boy Wonder of Clifford Essex's Royal Pierrots. At the age of fourteen he was recording cakewalks and plantation numbers.

The Coon Song craze had not missed Britain but the inhabitants chose to treat the subject with more respect, going about the job with the sort of meticulousness that they usually reserved for their gardens. Military and 'silver' (brass) bands recorded many versions of 'The Darkie's Dream', and another favourite was 'Down South – American Sketch' which came with a detailed description of the cakewalk, sand dance, big-boot step, and humming necessary for complete performance. Elite regiments were permitted to join in the examination of authentic ragtime: HM Band of the Coldstream Guards recorded 'A Coon Band Contest' in 1905 hoping to equal the sales of 'Shuffling Jasper' by their rivals the Grenadier Guards. In 1908 the City of London Police Band attempted to balance the picture with some local colour by recording 'Lancashire Clogs'.

On the stage there were coon songs by local composers, Leslie Stuart being the best ('Lily of Laguna'). His pastoral whimsies were opposed by the raucous (but never nasty) coon songs of Kate Carney, the Cockney comedienne, who appeared with her own company of East End cakewalkers and recorded 'Liza Johnson' in 1903. *In Dahomey* (with Williams & Walker) had, of course, inspired many local acts to modernize their minstrelsy. And there were blackface ragtime specialists like 'The Chocolate Coloured Coon' (G.H. Elliott), a Lancastrian with American experience, introducing the Latest American ragtime songs into the music halls.

But, generally, in this period of early ragtime the response of British music hall (a powerful institution, yearning for respect and respectability) was to laugh it off. Alec Hurley (a husband of the saucy comedienne Marie Lloyd) had established himself as a Cockney costermonger and he delighted audiences of 1900 with his satire of the American craze by appearing as a 'ragtime navvy' and surrounding himself with fellow workers, armed with pickaxes and singing:

> Don't know much about this here ragtime,
> But me dinner time I never, never miss.
> I'm a pic-piccaninny and I must have been a ninny
> When I picked upon a job like this!

British comedians, viewing foreigners suspiciously from over the garden wall, grew shrill and bitter in their funny songs as time went by and ragtime made itself at home. By 1912 and the Ragtime Invasion of Britain the local songwriters were bashing the Americans with such reactionary songs as 'If They'd Bury Alexander's Ragtime Band', 'The Death of Ragtime' and 'Who Killed Ragtime?'

But the civilization presented in music-hall songs appeared stagnant, grimy and parochial. Characters seemed to be stuck in the mud of poverty: 'The Girl in the Clogs and Shawl', 'At Trinity Church I Met My Doom', 'Boiled Beef and Carrots'. The words were often very clever and ironic ('I Live in Trafalgar Square – with four lions to guard me') but the static insularity of a sodden land full of nagging wives and in-laws and over-cooked dinners, and place names like Slough and Wigan, made ragtime America seem very alluring. Ragtime America had 'dolls' and 'honey lambs' cavorting in sunny and musical places like Alabama and Tennessee. You could do the turkey trot in your street clothes instead of evening dress. You could follow your betters, the upper classes, as they staggered to a ragtime tune into a future in which anything might happen. It's important to remember that the upper classes still set the trends; their young people, especially in Edwardian times, were hungry for the exotic because they were thoroughly over-civilized.

Music hall got its seal of approval and doom in July 1912 with the first Royal Command Variety Performance at the Palace Theatre. A good healthy vulgar act like Marie Lloyd was excluded – and so was ragtime. The prehistoric wheezes and conventional hilarity of British music hall had received their just reward – a Royal pat on the back and the approval of the clergy. The Reverend Arnold Hole told the *Era:* 'The atmosphere of beer and tobacco has given place to the cultured and refined artiste. Now a pater familias need never be afraid of taking his children to the Halls'.

But the people who went to the halls were, like their betters, tired of the dumpity-dump 6/8 rhythm of so much local music and ready for the up-to-date new city ragtime of Irving Berlin and the Alleymen. On these same respectable music-hall bills of 1912 – among the farmyard imitators, lightning calculators, human hairpins and Charles Coburn

155

singing 'Two Lovely Black Eyes' for the umpteenth time – were to be found a few music-hall stalwarts having a go at the latest American ragtime. George Lashwood, known usually as a smart dresser, was doing 'Alexander's Bagpipe Band' clad in kilts. Wilkie Bard, famous for his pantomime dame, was trying out 'You've Got to Sing in Ragtime', making the song local and topical by referring to the current wave of strikes and suffragettes.

Just as in America, the new ragtime meant Our Times which meant chaos round the corner and sometimes on our doorstep. In February the title of a revue by George Grossmith, Jnr, expressed the general bewilderment: *Everybody's Doing It Now*—there was hardly any ragtime music in the show but plenty about odd goings on in Hyde Park and the Albert Hall. In April ragtime was reported as present when the world's first unsinkable ship went down in the Atlantic with the loss of 1,517 lives. As the *Titanic* had slipped into the icy depths the ship's orchestra, reportedly, had kept on playing. Much of its repertoire had been cheer-up ragtime songs by Irving Berlin and his colleagues. Within weeks of the tragedy Poole's Magnificent Myrioramic Productions was offering an act showing the liner sinking with full sound effects as, centre stage, the conductor exhorts his players:

> Please to mark the time, boys,
>   Please to watch the score.
> Never heed the wavelets
>   Sobbing down the floor.
> Play it as you played it
>   When with eager feet,
> A hundred pair of dancers
>   Were stamping to the beat.
> Stamping to the ragtime
>   Around the lamp-lit deck
> With shine of glossy linen
>   And with gleam of snowy neck.

But apart from ragtime as the musical accompaniment to contemporary events there was, of course, ragtime for its own sake. And here the Americans were paramount. No

British acts could compete with the Yankee invaders who started arriving in the spring of that year, 1912. One of the most impressive acts was the Hedges Brothers & Jacobson. Freddie and Elven Hedges behaved on stage like hyperactive teenagers, while Jesse Jacobson, the pianist, looked and sounded like their uncle. Dressed in white tie and tails the trio nevertheless assaulted their audiences with the latest Alley product (usually courtesy of Bert Feldman) in a frenzy of movement that left many customers begging for more, addicted to the new music. J. B. Priestley never forgot them and later reckoned that they were harbingers of the First World War and all future topsy-turviness. Guy Grenville, a public schoolboy at the time, wrote in the 1950s about his conversion:

I instantly became, at a callow 16, an avid fan of the real American ragtime. Not for me the wet and weedy British imitations! When those Hedges boys let loose with their eccentric hand gestures and torso gymnastics I had to be physically restrained by ushers so excited had I become. Why, these lads were no older than I! There and then I wanted to talk American, walk American, and dress American.

After their vigorous exercise at the Tivoli the boys set off to tour Britain. They so enjoyed themselves that they decided to settle there; Jesse Jacobson became quite an expert on heraldry. Willie Solar, with a scratchy voice and scat-song style, followed in their wake at the Tivoli. At the same time Carlisle & Wellman were presenting their *Ragtime Revelry* at the Oxford Music Hall nearby. Maude Tiffany was reported to be conquering Manchester with her rag medleys of Irving Berlin songs. In June Albert de Courville brought the stentorian Emma Carus to his Hippodrome. Famous for her version of 'Alexander's Ragtime Band', she made as much noise as the Hedges Brothers & Jacobson. Commented the *Era:* 'She belts out her rags and seems to enjoy her jokes as much as, if not more than, her audience.' In July she was relieved by the famous Broadway star Ethel Levey, ex-wife of George M. Cohan. Miss Levey was armed with ragtime songs and Bert Feldman

157

weighed her down with more. 'Take these to Newcastle with you and they'll shower you with affection – they only throw coal at the English acts.'

Albert de Courville opened his American Ragtime Octette at the Hippodrome on 23 September. The ground had been prepared for the new city-slicker ragtime to be presented by these eight brazen Yankee invader-traders. *Eight* ragtimers spreading and smearing the word, well-choreographed, well up in the latest pops, well-versed in dealing with the press. And the press fed off them voraciously. With the world turning upside down and yet always wearing the right colour of shoe, the timing was perfect for a mess of manic American boys in formal evening clothes.

The *Era*, being for the trade, was the calmest of the papers, trying to assess the boys as just another act: twenty-one minutes, three bows, booked for a five-week run. Advertised as 'dancers' and sharing the bill with a trick cyclist, a trapeze act and the maestro Leoncavallo conducting his new one-act opera *I Zingari*. But the reporter had to admit that the Octette, on opening night, 'caused a perfect furore'.

'On stage, in a foreword, they tell us that ragtimers are born, not made. It is utterly beyond the powers of the British, who cannot cultivate it.' Then the stage darkens until it is lit solely by a high 'amber pin light' under which a young man starts to sing the verse to 'Hitchy Koo'. Gradually the Octette members amble in from either side to join the weird refrain: 'Oh, every evening hear him sing . . . It's the cutest little thing . . . Got the cutest little swing . . . Hitchy Koo, Hitchy Koo, Hitchy Koo!' When the whole crew is assembled they form a semi-circle, 'swaying and gesticulating wildly in their regulation soup and fish dinner suits'. At the end of their ring shout they flop into gold chairs 'leaving a few "hitchy koos" lingering in the air for good measure'.

'Ragging the Baby to Sleep' was soloed by a member in the *bouche fermée* style (whatever that is) while the others ran down into the aisles to coax the audience to join in the second chorus. The grand finale was 'Waiting for the Robert

E. Lee' in which the entire company was expected to sing along while the Octette went into an orgy of finger-snapping alternated with hand-clapping, back-slapping and close-clinched dancing with each other. Afterwards a disgusted Leoncavallo told management they could count him out of this 'exhibition'.

'I do not care for the new music,' he told the press but they had plenty to express in their own way. The *Daily Sketch* published a full-page picture-spread headlined 'Ragtime Craze Hits London: Real Hustle Music from America'. The queer gestures of the Octette were juxtaposed with an article on the opposite page: 'Art Gone Mad' – the 'queer perversions' of the fauvist movement, the 'cult of the ugly as perpetrated by M. Matisse and M. Cezanne. Shouldn't art be beautiful?'

The *Evening News* man cast his vote against the Octette, offended by 'their shuffling to and from, arms jerking frantically to and from'. He doubted the authenticity of their ragtime since it lacked points of negritude: 'Are we supposed to look upon them in a negro light? It is hard to imagine the negro village and the light-hearted childlike blacks when the octette men are all in evening dress . . . It is also very hard to believe the reality of the "Robert E. Lee".'

The *Daily Mail* man placed ragtime beyond negritude (and Jewry, for that matter). Ragtime was America – 'The child song of the child people. It is just an overgrown nursery rhyme . . . The Octette behave like dancing dolls . . . The audience is hustled into appreciation . . . Hustle set to music, energy chained to a rhythm.'

The *Daily Telegraph* was more charitable. The Octette were fun and good for the children and there was nothing to get worried about: 'They are as jolly as sandboys and as merry as crickets. They sing and dance and chortle and whoop with the exuberance of youth. If you can imagine the old Christy Minstrels brought up-to-date, vitalized and Americanized, you have them in a word. They are on the friendliest terms with the audience. They should make a host of friends.'

And so they did. Several of the Octette settled down in

England, some even dying there. Melville Gideon, having informed the press that 'no-one is playing ragtime properly over here', went on to accept gigs around town – conducting dance orchestras in West End restaurants, supervising recording sessions, writing revue scores. By the 1920s he'd turned native, owning a country cottage and wellington boots, offering up songs with such lines as: 'How can a guinea pig show he's pleased if he hasn't got a tail to wag?' Ragtime had served its purpose for him.

Meanwhile, back in 1912, the invasion was gathering momentum. Albert de Courville decided to gather the craze elements together and dish them up in a baked Alaska: in November he announced an extravaganza starring everybody and a lot of expensive sets. The show would open just before Christmas. He was going for the gold and the chic. Therefore, to be in the fashion, to attract the smart set, the new show must be a revue: *Hullo, Ragtime*, snappy title. There wasn't much time. Max Pemberton wrote the script in one night, bringing in scenes involving Peter Pan, performing seals, Lloyd George and Winston Churchill. Topical. Imported from Broadway, at great expense, was the show craftsman, Louis Hirsch. Schooled at a German conservatory, up in the latest styles in song, Hirsch was made musical director and chief composer. His first contribution, 'How Do You Do, Miss Ragtime?', with its characteristic minor dips, suitably sent Miss Ragtime America through schule without destroying her corn-fed eyes. From the best drawing-rooms of Park Avenue came Jack Mason. He was booked to teach the cast how society was dealing with the ragtime animal steps. Jack claimed he'd taught New York's 400 a version of the turkey trot which still left them looking classy. Jack caused a stir when walking down the Strand in his snap-brim hat, drape jacket and peg-topped trousers. He was the latest. So was the cast – friendly invaders, recently arrived: Ethel Levey played a princess; Willie Solar played a ragtime yokel. He made 'You Made Me Love You' sound racy; she made 'Snooky Ookums' bubble. New songs, late-breaking hits, could be inserted any time and any place in the show.

Hullo, Ragtime opened on 23 December and at once

160

became the talk of the town. *Everybody* had to see it. Rupert Brooke, the poet and beauty, took parties over and over. The revue ran into several editions. News of the day was mixed with hits of the day. *Everybody* was saying 'Hitchy Koo!', even the parrot at the Cheshire Cheese in Fleet Street. And so it was that *The Times* took notice of the seriousness of ragtime and on 8 February 1913 there appeared the article that Fred Day later gave Irving Berlin: the 'rhythmic subtleties' of ragtime 'can only be paralleled in the motets of the early contrapuntalists'. The anonymous writer went on into the realm of culture and nationalism: 'Nor is this syncopation a mere academic accomplishment; it connotes a special frame of mind, an eagerness, a desire to be beforehand which is eminently characteristic of the nationality of its performers.' Finally: 'America has waited too long for her own music. Her serious musicians must cease to look abroad for their inspiration and turn their faces homeward.'

The Times writer's musical examples were drawn from the material of the American Ragtime Octette and *Hullo, Ragtime*. And so it was the songs of Alleymen like Lewis Muir, Wolfie Gilbert and Irving Berlin that aroused the interest of European music critics. Of Scott Joplin they knew nothing. When Stravinsky and other art-music composers dabbed a little ragtime into their work it was the 'swing' and 'tingle' of Tin Pan Alley that had inspired them.

Early in 1913 the *Era* announced that 130 American rag acts were planned for visits during the year. Among them would be Irving Berlin, the acknowledged King of it All. There seemed to be something for everybody – from Franco Piper playing fifteen banjos whilst rotating at 350 revs per minute to the Real Ragtimers, a band of Negroes sent over by the Clef Club of New York and advertised as 'Every Member a Full-Blooded Negro from the Southern States'. Joining *Hullo, Ragtime* at the Hippodrome was Tucker, 'The Ragtime Violinist & Singer', playing both a man and a woman by means of vocal trickery and a costume whose left half was a lady's evening gown and whose right half was a man's evening dress. 'He stands in the necessary position for each role,' pointed out the *Era*. Meanwhile, at the Finsbury Park Empire, Gene Greene was scat-singing his way nightly through his big American hit, 'King of the Bungaloos' to the car-chase rag piano of Charlie Straight of Tin Pan Alley. At the Empire were the gee-whiz kids, Jay Whidden and Con Conrad, with their *Ragtime Royalty* act. Their natty clothes and accents had even Jack Mason beat. Old-timers complained to the *Era* about the uncouth manners of the American upstarts: too much 'dis' and 'dat' and 'Boy did we tar 'em over with the *jasbo*'; too much concentration on speed – resulting in old-timers being ordered by management to hurry up their routines, to cut out the second and third verses, to cut down the patter about the meat pie. Alfred Butt, one of the leading employers of American talent, retorted: 'They [the Americans] are sober, reliable – and always inserting new songs.'

Among the invaders was a young man who, though he sang out of the side of the mouth and wore his slouch hat at a devilish tilt, was no Yank-on-the-bounce. Nat D. Ayer was born and bred a gentleman and did much to repair the damage done to foreign relations by some of his compatriots. 'I know how you feel, believe me I do,' he'd say softly to bruised local talents. He oozed charm and had a lovely silver cigarette case. Bert Feldman adored him. When he arrived in London in March for a date at the Tivoli he was already known to Bert as a successful songwriter: 'Oh, You Beautiful Doll' was much loved by the British. The song had brought Feldman's plenty in royalties. Bert asked Ayer up to his North London home to discuss future plans, in the manner of gentlemen. *Hullo, Ragtime* could do with some new blood.

Ayer accepted Bert's sherry. He then told Bert a little about his background. His father, a prominent Boston doctor and a Harvard graduate, had entertained Sousa at his home, and the Barrymores, 'and so on'. Young Nat had attended Haverford College where he'd mostly studied 'pieces of female fluff' and party piano. Friends told him he was a jolly good entertainer. So he ambled up to Broadway, residing at the Chandos, a very comfortable hotel for theatricals. Dad was footing the bill and Nat also had a lot of

162

Dad's connections in society and the theatre. A connection invited him to one of the exclusive Sunday concerts at the Green Room Club. When called on to perform he entertained at the piano with some of his own college songs and skits. The appreciative audience included top impresarios Klaw & Erlanger, and Edward Albee. Cards were exchanged. George M. Cohan offered his congratulations. Pretty soon Nat was winning his spurs playing burlesque houses and Coney Island. A little later he was getting booked at decent vaudeville theatres in New York.

One day, at the Chandos, he got chatting with Seymour Brown, an actor and lyricist who was currently writing sketches for the Ziegfeld Follies. Brownie said Ziegfeld was airing an idea for a big production number and maybe Nat would like to help realize the boss's dream. See, President Roosevelt, the famous conservationist, has been big-game hunting in Africa—it's all over the papers—and we have a jungle ballet number with the girls dressed as animals. Must have a big finish with a lively, timely song. What about seeing the slaughter from the animals' point of view? Nat and Brownie wrote the song at Remick's on 41st because the atmosphere was pipe-smoky like a men's club and old man Remick was a cinch for advances.

'Moving Day in Jungle Town' was a hit and helped make Sophie Tucker a sensation at the opening of the Ziegfeld Follies of 1909. Mr Remick invited Nat for a round of golf and Nat made sure he let the publisher win. Next day, Ayer and Brown had a contract and a friend. The old man took life easily, letting the hits roll in or not, more interested in golf and books; used to be in the dairy business in Detroit, a gentleman of the old school, not like that abrasive Isadore Witmark.

However, the song bug soon bit Ayer & Brown, the new team. They got to thinking pop night and day. They were dining at Rector's – the fashionable bohemian restaurant, just pricey enough to keep out the riff-raff – when Rector commented about the present rage in Paris being dinner music and dancing. 'Gee, I Like the Music with My Meals'. said Brownie. Back at Remick's the team soon had the whole song together and it was a smash. Brownie then read

163

in the paper about a husband getting beaten up by his wife
for saying 'Mabel!' in his sleep when the wife's name was
Gladys. 'If You Talk in Your Sleep, Don't Mention My
Name' was a good seller.

To test their new songs Ayer & Brown hit the vaudeville
circuit. Sometimes the wives came along, sometimes not.
Mr Remick only published the songs which clicked. When
they were playing the north-east the boys would put in an
appearance at debutante parties and stay at Nat's parents'
home with the famous names. Old man Remick, who had
a country place nearby, liked to pop in for a drink. It was
all very convenient.

In Seattle, riding the Orpheum circuit, they fell in with
some naval officers. Over mixed drinks the captain of the
crew invited Nat to write a jaunty tune to inspire his men
to speed up during morning physical jerks. Nat obliged with
a thing he called 'The Texas Tommy'. Then Ziggy Ziegfeld
cabled for an instant production number, on the lines of
'Jungle Town', something to fit a barnyard scene based on
Rostand's story of Chanticleer, something melodramatic,
fast. Brownie devised a bloodthirsty tale of a thieving mouse
getting sentenced to death at the court of the big boss
rooster. 'King Chanticleer' was a hit of the Follies, a best-
selling Victor record and the background music to many a
1930s movie. A classic.

One hot afternoon in St Louis, Missouri, in July 1911 the
two vaudevillians were relaxing outside the theatre after a
matinée. A nice bit of fluff sashayed by, causing an electrician to pronounce spiritedly: 'Say! – there's some
beautiful doll! I'd like to get my limbs round her!' The
boys went to work and before the evening show they had
completed a future evergreen: 'Oh, You Beautiful Doll'.

But the song required some push in order to settle on the
public's mind. When Nat first played 'Doll' in the act he
stressed the long verse, slipping in some ragtime tricks and
slides. The framework of that verse was the Negro 'blues'
and Nat was the first Alleyman to use the blues, although
the stuff had been lying around for years, albeit underground in honky-tonky town. Nat had only discovered
ragtime the year before, in 1910. He'd been frequenting an

after-hours dive called Jenny's in New York's Darktown where the fried eggs were spicy and the band was six darkies called the Hot Babies from Alabama who moaned and groaned as loud as they played but, boy, did they play splendidly! Spicier than the eggs. Nat studied the pianist's style intently. By July 1911 he figured he was every bit as nifty as the Alexander about whom big-chested lady singers raved. However, at the evening show in St Louis the audience didn't exactly go nuts over 'Oh, You Beautiful Doll'.

Three months later and Ayer & Brown still weren't getting any sparks from 'Doll' so they shelved her. But at the Lamb's Club one afternoon Nat was playing pool with A. 'Baldy' Sloane, the veteran Alley composer, arranger and general card. Baldy casually asked Nat whether he had a stop-gap song for killing time between scenes in some show he was involved with.

At rehearsal Baldy put twelve leggy chorus girls to work, kicking and chanting 'Doll' while the scene-shifters laboured behind the curtains. It was all routine till one of the lovelies, bending over the front stage to make lovey-dovey talk to a fiddler in the pit, rested her foot on the footlights. By happenstance an electrician suddenly switched high these lights, throwing the girl's legs and thighs and torso into silhouette. Strong stuff.

Baldy's show, *The Red Rose*, hadn't been doing so well but now all that was to change. Twelve chorus girls were discovered straddling the blazing footlights in an orgy of hot crotch. 'Oh, You Beautiful Doll' was the hit of the show and got an average of ten encores a night. And after they got over the excitement of the flaming bodies people realized they liked the song. 'We made $24,000 off that in one year,' said Nat proudly and Bert felt Nat was starting to talk like him. Bert said that 'Doll' was doing very nicely for his company over here. The Octette had practically adopted it as their theme. Bert thought 'hot crotch' was a bit much but he didn't say anything, just poured more sherry. These Americans are a funny lot. Then, pulling himself together, Bert asked for 'something topical' for the next edition of *Hullo, Ragtime*, something straight from the headlines. 'Your Seymour Brown can surely come up with the goods.'

'You can't whistle the words,' replied Nat stiffly, becoming the patrician again. 'And anyway, I now work with Harry Williams.' 'Excuse *me*,' said Bert and made a mental note not to invite Mr Ayer up for drinks again. Still, Nat did get together with Harry Williams and they came up with 'That Ragtime Suffragette' ('Ragging with bombshells and ragging with bricks, haggling and naggling in politics'). Ethel Levey did a good job on the number in the third edition of *Hullo, Ragtime*.

But this edition had a speciality that was to eclipse anything of Nat D. Ayer's: the man who started it all, the Ragtime King himself – was scheduled to appear in the show for the first week in July. Mr Irving Berlin, said the notices, will be accompanied by his musical secretary, Mr Cliff Hess. He will be receiving the gentlemen of the press at his Savoy Hotel suite between three and four p.m. on 19 June. All other enquiries to be made to his personal representative, Mr Albert de Courville.

Nat D. Ayer should make such an entry!

The Irving Berlin publicity machine was by this time working extremely smoothly. The press got exactly the copy they wanted. It was a beautiful relationship, it made for beautiful writing. On 20 June, the day after the Berlin reception, the *Daily Express* went to town on 'the boy genius':

> In every London restaurant, park, and theatre you hear his strains; Paris dances to it, Berlin sips golden beer to his melodies; Vienna has forsaken the waltz, Madrid has flung away her castanets, and Venice has forgotten her barcarolles. Ragtime has swept like a whirlwind over the earth and set civilization humming.
>
> Mr Irving Berlin started it.

This was so simple, so neat. What a trick! American ragtime reduced to the Great Man theory. No bothersome history of Negroes, Irish, Jews, Scots, Germans; no immigrants, poverty, brothels. No trouble at all.

The Great Man ('He looks nineteen') explained his song-writing technique with modesty: 'I hum the songs, that's all.

166

Hum them while I am shaving, or in my bath, or out walking. I hum them and fix my own words to them until they're fixed clearly in my mind; and when I have got the rhythm I want I call in an arranger. I don't know anything about harmony, but I can make tunes.' Cliff Hess agreed, adding that when he offered a selection of chords from which to choose, Mr Berlin uncannily always chose the right one. Then Mr Berlin revealed his current project: 'I am making an opera now – a grand opera in ragtime. Not a musical comedy, mind, but a real opera on a tragic theme. Why not?'

Unlike Nat D. Ayer, or Gene Greene, or the Hedges Brothers & Jacobson, or any of the other American invaders, Irving Berlin was dignified with a whole review to himself in *The Times* (8 July 1913):

> Mr Irving Berlin is the inventor – or at least the adaptor-in-chief – of rag-time. To Mr Irving Berlin Eastern America and England owe rag-time; and to announce that he is in London is to give a hint to many that here is their wished-for chance of having Mr Berlin's blood. Yet once they have seen and heard him on the stage, only the most truculent could wish to have Mr Irving Berlin's blood. It is not only that he sings his rag-time songs with such diffidence, skill and charm. In his mouth they become something very different from the blatant bellowings that we are used to. All their quaintness, their softness, their queer patheticalness come out; they sound, indeed, quite new, and innocently, almost childishly, pleasing, like a negro's smile.

Once again *The Times* was very perceptive on ragtime and ragtimers. Irving's intimate performances were indeed unique in those pre-microphonic days when acts tended to punch their songs across. 'You had to hug him to hear him,' said Joe Frisco, the vaudevillian. The only recording of Irving during this period is 'Oh, How That German Could Love', a comedy waltz number of 1910 – but it reveals an impeccable sense of vaudeville timing coupled with a winning insouciance.

IRVING BERLIN
IRVING BERLIN
IRVING BERLIN
KING OF RAGTIME
KING OF RAGTIME
KING OF RAGTIME

– screamed the ad for *Hullo, Ragtime* in the otherwise staid *Daily Telegraph*. From the stage one night the King asked his subjects for requests (meaning, of course, his own songs) and he was surprised to be inundated with requests for 'The Robert E. Lee', 'The Beautiful Doll', and lots of 'Hitchy Koos'. Publicity had worked its trick most efficiently. Irving Berlin was believed to be the source of all ragtime.

The King regarded the world at large. A new and all-embracing rag song was gestating. Perhaps he was inspired by the reference to the international appeal of his songs in the *Daily Express*, perhaps he was responding to the current use of the word 'rag-time' as synonymous with chaotic times (mass strikes, problems in Ireland, the Balkan wars, suffragettes, crazy modern art), perhaps he just chose the word 'international' because it was buzzing about lately in the papers. At any rate, while staying at the Savoy, he produced a brand new number: 'The International Rag'.

The song blames America for making nations into jumpers: London has lost its dignity and also France and Germany; even dukes and lords and Russian Tsars are throwing up their shoulders to ragtime. On his final night at the Hippodrome Irving introduced his new song and he received a standing ovation. It had been a satisfying foray.

By 25 July he was back at work at Waterson, Berlin & Snyder. Ted had been looking after the shop because Max Winslow and Henry Waterson had also been away on various bits of business. Now they all took a meeting. Ted announced that, as usual, Tin Pan Alley was speed and change: raggy material was in even more demand but you had to be careful because racy songs had been ordered out of all public places by the mayor and Waterson, Berlin & Snyder were tops on his hit list. So nothing changes, said

Henry – and immediately called his lawyer and ordered an injunction. Ted went on to say that their pluggers had been banned from certain music stores for annoying the female sales staff. So what's new, said Max, and went into a huddle with Irving at the piano while Henry took an early lunch. Ted was getting the feeling he was redundant.

Max didn't even enquire about Irving's English trip. He was anxious to hear the new material: 'International' was knockout. The topical one's good, too – what a title: 'I Was Aviating Around'! Then Irving muddled through 'The Ragtime Soldier Man' and Max, although he was beginning to think they all sounded like expiring frogs, reckoned they were winners. Irving shot back that he'd written a lot of dogs and don't you forget it! Whatever happened to 'The Apple Tree and the Bumble Bee' or 'Abie Sings an Irish Song' or 'Jake-Jake' or 'Yiddisha Professor' or 'Goody, Goody, Goody, Goody, Goody Good'? Dogs, all dogs. If you say so, said Max. And Ted kept quiet.

In October there were three 'firsts' for Irving. (1) His first Broadway stage score: he was to write all the music (no interpolations by other writers) for a new musical to be produced by the great Charles Dillingham. No title as yet. (2) He published a song with another company: 'There's a Girl in Arizona' was given to the Harry Williams Company. No comment from the offices of Waterson, Berlin & Snyder. (3) He was honoured with a 'roast' at the Friar's Club.

What an honour! To be eulogized – albeit, with some joshing – by one's peers! The Hotel Astor's banquet room was full, so even were the balcony boxes. Friar Abbot Rumsey was in the chair. Judge McCall, a candidate for mayor, made an excellent speech. But the big thrill for Irving was to get a glowing tribute from his mentor, George M. Cohan:

Irvy writes a great song. He writes a song with a good lyric, a lyric that rhymes. And good music – music you don't have to dress up when you go to listen to it but good music just the same. He has become famous and wealthy, without wearing a lot of jewelry and falling for funny clothes. He is uptown, but he is there with the old

169

downtown hardshell. And with all his success, you will find his watch and his handkerchief in his pockets where they belong.

When it came to his turn Irving was very nervous. Unlike Cohan and the candidate for mayor, he was no orator. But he'd arranged to respond in song.

> Friar Abbot! Brother Friars! Ladies and Guests!
> Don't expect too much of me,
> I'm confined to melody.
> And furthermore, I must confess,
> I don't know just how to confess
> The depth of my appreciation . . .

And so on, in high croak.

Afterwards the band played for dancing. At first they played nothing but Waterson, Berlin & Snyder but as the evening wore on they started sneaking in some Leo Feist and some Shapiro-Bernstein. Max was furious and rushed over to the bandleader to remonstrate. But Irving didn't mind. He was fascinated, watching the people trying to master the latest steps and making a mess of it.

But help was on its way. In 1914 an instruction book was published which showed Americans (who wanted to be American) exactly how to dance to ragtime without resorting to Afro-Americanism. *Modern Dancing* by Mr and Mrs Vernon and Irene Castle denounced the ragtime animal dances as 'ugly, ungraceful' and, far worse, 'out of fashion'. No home was complete without *Modern Dancing*. No song was complete without a dancing capability. The Castles regulated the beat.

They were now America's No. 1 Couple. Irene was a willowy beauty from New York; Vernon was a sliver of air from Norfolk, England. When they danced together they became a floating love match, pure and white and married and beyond sex. Imagine! A man dancing with his wife and making a beautiful picture! No camel walks or chicken struts for the Castles – instead, they introduced a new animal dance which, in time, consumed all the other bush steps:

the fox trot, a brisk walk in straight time and any fool could do it. In the years to come the foxtrot was to evolve into the quickstep or the 'businessman's bounce'. During the 1920s, the jazz age, the foxtrot was to be virtually the only dance step permitted by the dictatorship of the dance bands. By the 1950s this walk (or bounce or stagger) was still the standard beat and when 'Rock around the Clock' by Bill Haley & the Comets was first released the label described this anthem of rock'n'roll as a foxtrot.

Vernon liked to tell how Jim Europe's blues piano-playing had led to the development of the foxtrot. Vernon was absolutely sold on Negroes as source-beat musicians and he insisted on employing them, with Europe doing the hiring. The only condition asked for by Vernon was that he be allowed to bang along on drums. When Jim and his Society Orchestra played 'Memphis Blues' and 'St Louis Blues' and other down-home specialities they employed a syncopated dotted rhythm that was reminiscent of the old schottische reels but was now real modern. This rhythm was to remain the basic pattern for most dance music for the next quarter of a century.

The foxtrotting kingdom was headquartered at Castle House, opposite the Ritz-Carlton in New York. A marble foyer with fully operational fountain, paintings of Irene's bogus ancestors on the wall. For business, two long, mirror-lined rooms – one for tango, maxixe and other Spanish-tinged dances, to a string orchestra; the other for ragtime dancing, to one of Jim Europe's fevered ensembles. The Castle Empire included Castles-in-the-Air (on a New York roof-top) and Castles-by-the-Sea (on Long Island) as well as a string of franchised instruction ballrooms across the country. Vernon and Irene couldn't be everywhere but they tried. People wanted to see what they were wearing, not only what they were dancing. They were style-setters, they were a social index – just like best-selling pop songs could be. On whirlwind tours they showed themselves off to All America, (travelling in a special train with a special Pullman car for the Europe band). In 1914 they were reckoned to be the highest paid act in vaudeville.

Taking a break from their hectic schedule the couple

171

returned to France, the scene of their first dancing triumph. Anything originating in Paris was très chic in New York. They were spending a lazy August, visiting old friends and receiving compliments, when the Great War broke out. Vernon wanted to do his duty and report to Britain for service. But Irene's tears persuaded him to come back with her to America. Specifically, there was a big chance in the offing: Charles Dillingham had invited them to star in his new musical, *Watch Your Step*, a festival of ragtime. Irving Berlin was the sole composer and lyricist. He had already completed twenty-two numbers. Irene might be allowed to sing one. The couple would certainly be able to show off their dazzling technique in such production numbers as 'The Syncopated Walk', 'Look at Them Doing It', and 'Show Us How to Do the Fox Trot'. The ballads, such as 'Lead Me to Love' and 'Settle Down in a One-Horse Town', would be in the capable hands of Elizabeth Brice and Charles King. It was a rich score, a varied score: 'Play a Simple Melody' had a devilish clever counter-melody in raggedy time, possibly a Broadway first; 'Opera Burlesque' required seventeen pages of music. You know Irving – once challenged, there's no stopping him! No more of this high-flown talk about writing a serious grand opera. Irving was doing what he did best (even if unnaturally): ragtime songs and dances matched by ballads of deep yearning, almost wailing.

On 8 December, 1914, *Watch Your Step* opened on Broadway 'at the worst time of the worst season' (according to *Variety*). 'The First Syncopated Musical' had been pared down to a slick and speedy machine in out-of-town performances. Anything that slowed the pace was eliminated, e.g. a sketch starring W. C. Fields. The sets and the girls were gorgeous. But most of the success or otherwise of the show was riding on the Berlin name.

There was no need to worry, all was well. *Variety* with, as usual, eyes on box office and not artistic appeal, marked the show as a 'terrific hit' from opening night alone. Sime Silverman, the big man at the paper, wrote:

Irving Berlin stands out like the Times building does in the Square. That youthful marvel of syncopated melody

172

is proving things in 'Watch Your Step', firstly that he is not alone a rag composer, and that he is one of the greatest lyric writers America has ever produced . . . Besides rags Berlin wrote a polka that was very pretty, and he intermingled ballads with trots, which, including the grand opera medley, gives 'Watch Your Step' all the kind of music there is.

Let's look now in some detail into Irving Berlin's musical and lyrical progression since those first days at Waterson, Berlin & Snyder. Although he professed to know nothing of harmony his songs reveal an instinctive grasp of important elements. What would 'When the Midnight Choo-Choo Leaves for Alabam'' be without that lonesome railroad *whoo-whoo* on the diminished seventh chord? 'When I Lost You' would lose much of its heart-tug if there was no elevator drop from the initial C chord to the B7 on the word 'roses' as in 'I lost the sunshine and *roses*' (whoosh! – and the hearts flutters). 'He's a Rag Picker' (1914) would lose some interest if the moving harmony line on the 'rag' of 'He's a rag picker' wasn't there as an under-melody. But it's blinkered work using technical lingo to describe the emotional effect of music – suffice it to say that Berlin knew enough about chord sequences and their effect to be able to manipulate the public's heart while appearing to have hummed up the music in the natural habitat of the bath-tub. Cried the man-in-the-street: 'That's how I feel, that's how I'd make up songs if only I had the time!'

Also: Berlin knew enough about harmony not to let the power of chords arrest the flow of the melody. The sense, the story, must come first, must flow naturally like a river; the chords must remain as support for the tune river, colouring and shading the landscape like a sky that smiles one minute and frowns the next. Take two songs from *Watch Your Step*, one raggy, one pastoral, both with the same striking characteristic: 'The Syncopated Walk' and 'Settle Down in a One-Horse Town' have sudden changes from major to minor, sometimes within a short phrase. It's as if the singer is experiencing a mood swing, like we do in real life. This is natural, conversational music at its best. This is

173

the way good popular music should be – the vernacular of the everyday modern but set to music that takes it off from the street like a plane.

Now to Berlin's use of words ('lyrics' seems too high-flown to me, part of the artiness that crept into show-tune writing from the late twenties onwards). His easy expertise in the use of everyday American speech patterns show him to be the best, but not the only, East European immigrant practising to be the real live nephew of Uncle Sam. Berlin was always picking up the talk rhythms of the street, the beat of twentieth-century America. He crystallized catch-phrases into song form: 'Come on and hear!', 'It's a bear!', 'Cut it out!', 'Look at them doing it!' – all those ejaculations, like the speil of a lapel-grabbing fair barker.

Berlin understood that syncopation is most effective when it's not used as a device or trick, but when it springs naturally from conversation and, more especially, from the push and pull, parry and thrust, punch and duck, chatter battle of basic New York Swinglish-English. In accents other than American the ragtime song sounded unnatural. In English-English it sounded ridiculously stiff and starchy. Cockney might have got by but it has unfortunate guttural edges that can scrape and spoil good syncopation. And so from 1912 onwards, after the Invasion had conquered, British singers who wanted to ride American songs tended to adopt an American accent.

Berlin's simple vaudeville humour is to be cherished in this period for it was to disappear during the twenties and thirties, thanks to a pseudo-sophistication demanded by over-educated theatre writers. In these teen years of the century his wit was his strongest point, he was still thinking like a singing waiter who specialized in parodies. The moon-June love song was parodied into 'Snooky Ookums' in which an apartment dweller is kept awake by the baby talk of the couple behind the wall: he's only four foot but she's a giantess and they get along so well with their 'mushing' that you'd never know they were man and wife. 'The Old Maid's Ball' is a return to the cruel humour of Chinatown saloons: four old maids burst into tears when the band plays 'Here Comes the Bride'; someone then mentions that there's a man outside and that breaks up the old maid's ball. Early Irving, like an unspoilt child, loved playing with the sound of words: 'to us' is rhymed with 'St Louis' and in 'I Want to Go Back to Michigan' we miss the rooster that 'use-ter' wake us up, and we'd love to 'fish again' in Michigan. 'I Want to be in Dixie', not necessarily for Mammy, but certainly for to see hens which are 'doggone glad to lay scrambled eggs in the new-mown hay'. Even with straight love songs Berlin would sometimes have fun in order to avoid the slush: 'If I Had You' (1914) then we wouldn't envy Carnegie or Rockefeller with their tons of troubles and 'automobubbles'.

However, there was a side of Berlin that tended, at times, towards the pretentious. In 1911 and 1912 he had occasionally published 'song poems' full of leaping arpeggios and orders to go *andante moderato:* 'My Melody Dream' and 'Spring and Fall'. Maybe he was only trying to answer a demand in the marketplace; maybe he craved a respectability he'd never get with ragtime songs. We've already heard him tell reporters of his plan to write a grand opera in ragtime. And in *Watch Your Step* there was a second-act finale, 'Old Operas in a New Way', where the ghost of Verdi begs the cast not to rag and thus ruin his classical music. Maybe Berlin was getting a conscience about having had his first hit through a raid on Mendelssohn's 'Spring Song'?

At Waterson, Berlin & Snyder there were rumblings that the boy genius was finding it irksome to have to keep turning out journeyman pop songs. He was spending more and more time away from his office and away from the Alley.

On 5 December 1914 papers were filed in Albany, New York, declaring Articles of Incorporation for a new company called Irving Berlin, Inc. This corporation would publish his scores for the musical theatre. Pop singles, one-offs, would remain with Waterson, Berlin & Snyder. But what did the future hold for Waterson, for Snyder and for Max Winslow and Cliff Hess, not to mention a bevy of female stenographers?

Irving wasn't saying. He was so very elusive these days. After the wonderful opening night of *Watch Your Step* he'd shunned the champagne supper party and midnight frolics in the roof garden. Instead he'd slipped away to his apartment on West 71st St with only his mother and sisters and Cliff Hess for company. After the family had said goodnight Irving and Cliff Hess got down to work on song revisions for the show. Round about 3 a.m. a bunch of merry friends came knocking and Irving took this opportunity to demonstrate the improved songs and also to show off some new acquisitions to his collection of fine art and rare chinaware.

After *Watch Your Step* had laddered him up onto Broadway Irving could be expected to stay in that heady theatre atmosphere. But, surprisingly, for most of 1915 he stuck to single pop songs – and to tailoring special material for two special customers: Belle Baker and Al Jolson. Both knew that Berlin could deliver but they had to wait and be patient – he would soon come up with a blockbuster ballad amidst the ethnic comedy stuff ('Cohen Owes Me 97 Dollars'). Both needed fire songs like a baby needs milk. Both pushed their songs home with a deal of Hebraic passion, sometimes teetering on the cliffs of near bathos, sometimes falling over to thrash around in the syrupy mud. But both had the ability to quickly pull themselves out with a bit of humour and a bit of dirt. Belle Baker (born Bella Becker to Russian-Jewish immigrants) redeemed herself from bathos by eye-rolling and cries of 'Oy!'; Al Jolson (born in Lithuania) would stick his tongue in his cheek and open wide his banjo eyes. Baker and Jolson shot vaudeville through with their pizzazz, a precious shiny metal that also came with a razor edge. They were generous with their hearts and their talent – so long as there was an audience and it was a one-way love affair. At home, things may have been very different.

Jolson, starring in revues that needed new songs almost every week, was a prime customer for the Alleymen – *they* came to *him*. But with Berlin it was different. Jolson had a habit of calling up at odd hours (like in the morning) to announce: 'Jolie needs a sob song and fast!' If Irving had one ready he'd sing it over the wire. 'I have to make them cry,' said Jolson. Then he'd stomp off to make love to the world in public for he was, as he said himself, the 'World's Greatest Entertainer'.

Belle Baker was different. Since his earliest hits Irving had been close to this pudgy, dark little lady. She had once been a protégé of the esteemed Jacob Adler of the New York Yiddish Theatre but she'd gone on to wider projection, her stage persona ricocheting off the back wall of the gallery. She valued songwriters greatly; she valued Irving the most. And, in turn, he recognized her power and her friendship and made sure she got a goodly supply of songs. Recently, as a headliner at the Palace, she had taken to performing Berlin songs exclusively, with subjects ranging from the 'Wop' and the 'Yid' to rousing crowd-pleasers concerning the trouble in Mexico. But her favourite subject was ragtime.

By 1915 Belle Baker was practically the only vaudeville star specializing in rag songs. And Irving dutifully produced the goods for her. He was even known to pipe up from the stalls with a couple of verses at Belle's Palace appearances. Of course, she'd prompted him, coaxed him, begged him. He had a funny way with his ragtime, something special.

But there were those in the trade who felt ragtime's days were numbered. The *New York Dramatic Mirror* put it bluntly: 'The trend has been distinctly away from the rag. The noisy singer of this sort of song is disappearing.' Belle Baker was urged to develop a fuller, more rounded style. Mankind, and that certainly included Miss Baker, cannot live by rag alone. Mankind needed moments of reflection.

Belle Baker agreed. Couldn't Irvy come up with something meaty that she could get her teeth into? Something poetic, along the lines of Jerome Kern, a comparative new boy in town. Kern had learned his craft in the London musical theatre, hob-nobbing with those elegant Oxford composers of lilting fluffy-ruffle songs about skittish girls with curls. He'd returned to New York with a nice style in understated but strong and haunting melodies – like the current hit, 'They Didn't Believe Me'. Couldn't Irvy produce something slow, dreamy, even philosophical?

He did. 'When I Leave the World Behind' was just the ticket. But Al Jolson grabbed it first and then a mad dash

177

of vaudevillians, including Miss Baker, went for this brilliant piece of altruism. The way Irving saw it, you couldn't keep a good song from the world at large. Belle understood. Let Jolie be first if that's what gave him comfort. God knows he needs it.

'When I Leave the World Behind' was a monster. The idea had come from Wilson Mizner, the playwright and character, and a pal of Irving's. Mizner had spun him a yarn about a crazy lawyer, one Charles Lounsbery, who was eventually locked up in the nuthouse. There he died – leaving nothing but a unique will:

> ITEM – I leave to children exclusively, but only for the life of their childhood, all and every, the dandelions of the field and the daisies thereof, with the right to play among them freely, according to the custom of children, warning them at the same time against the thistles . . .
> ITEM – To lovers I devise their imaginary world, with whatever they may need, as the stars of the sky, the red, red roses by the wall, the snow of the hawthorn, the sweet strains of music, or aught else they may desire to figure to each other the lastingness and beauty of their love.

And so on.

Far from seeing this as a conceit Berlin took Mizner's tall tale as the inspiration for an inspirational song, a chance to be reflective, philosophical, poetic. The Berlin song has the singer as gold-less but willing the sunshine to the flowers, the springtime to the trees, the night time to the dreamers, and song birds to the blind. The lovers get the moon. The tune moves at a stately pace, building up to a big finish, sounding a little like a sacred piece. It was 'Respectfully dedicated to the memory of Charles Lounsbery whose will suggested the theme for this song'. It was a smash, travelling the western world and even making progress in India and places further east. 'When I Leave the World Behind' was a lovely thought, deeper than ragtime, especially appreciated by a world locked in a Great War.

Later, when a publisher invited Wilson Mizner to write his memoirs, the reply was: 'It would be blowing a police whistle.' Irving soon discovered he'd fallen for a prank: the

178

Lounsbery will had been written for a banker's magazine by someone calling himself Willston Fish. But the last laugh was on Irving because, from a base of deceit, he'd moved the world. And Irving would continue to bring on the roses when he felt the market would buy them.

Meanwhile, back in 1915, the theatre proper was calling to Irving for more. On 2 September *Billboard* announced that he had been engaged to write the score for a new production, *Blow Your Horn*. On 11 December the score was ready and the show was now called *Stop! Look! Listen!* And on 27 December the musical, a comedy in three acts, opened at the Globe Theatre. Gaby Deslys, the French personality, was the star, with Harry Fox and Blossom Seeley in support. Most of the show was fast and raggy with lots of girls and opulent sets. But there was room made for a sweet tune, a production number called 'The Girl on the Magazine Cover' sung by Joseph Santley in front of a backdrop painting of a *Vogue* cover. The melody sails along, sometimes choppy, sometimes smooth, always harmonious, and with new musical thoughts all the way.

But the main emphasis was on ragtime. There was a 'Ragtime Melodrama' and an extravaganza revolving around a 'continuous piano of six divisions and players spread across the stage' (according to *Variety*) in which, somewhere in the middle of the mêlée, Harry Fox sang a ragtime song called 'I Love a Piano'. Irving was very proud of this number, stating that it was his best so far (and in the 1960s he still felt the same way). A sturdy tune with a catchy opening phrase that gets repeated, the chord sequence is almost a blues. The rhymes are very keen and busy – you've just finished saying 'how clever!' to one rhyme when another one hits you: the singer says he used to love bands but – 'Today, when they play, I could hiss them; Ev'ry bar is a jar to my system' because the singer loves only pianos now and 'I know a fine way to treat a Steinway.' Gaby Deslys continued the ragtime obsession with a Gallic comment on the crazy USA: 'Everything in America is Ragtime'. A land riddled with syncopation, a million acres of shoulder shakers dancing to composers, 'just as thick as bees, writing raggy melodies'.

Ragtime and more ragtime! While Sime Silverman, in *Variety*, wrote that the show was 'corking all-round enter-tainment' there were others who were critical of the samey-saminess of the score and the constant harping on tired ragtime. Said the *New York Dramatic Mirror:* 'There is no glowing, sensuous, extravagant appeal . . . It is wholly ragtime, noisy, overdone ragtime from the opening chorus to the final number, which describes our only passion as a "fashion of snapping fingers".'

During 1916 Irving continued to manufacture pop songs in the style and subject matter of the day, sometimes inspired, sometimes run-of-the-mill – songs about Honolulu, bamboo shacks, Florida and then more ragtime. But he knew that there was more to life than ragtime. He liked the idea of working with Victor Herbert, the Operetta King, on the *Century Girl*. This was class – but again the *New York Dramatic Mirror* put him back in his place: 'As might be expected when Victor Herbert and Irving Berlin collab-orate, the music is a mixture of tuneful sentiment and ragtime.'

Ragtime, ragtime! Would he ever throw off its bear hug? I like to imagine him, at this period, up in his tastefully-furnished apartment with his fine art objects and his great literature, sitting at the special piano, hunting and pecking for new hits, having second and third thoughts about ragtime, about pop music in general. There lay the flimsy sheets of Irving Berlin songs, printed on cheap paper; there sat the thick volumes of Shakespeare, printed on creamy art paper. Much time to think and ponder and come to conclusions. After all, no decent song is long in the making. Over-done omelettes are lumps. He must have had a lot of time on his hands. Did he go dancing, did he go gambling, did he read his Shakespeare all the way through?

I like to imagine that he sometimes reflected on what he had wrought. His rags were truly international, ringing round the world and making folks dance and sing and whistle and be happy. Off out in Russia a military band bearing the Tsar's name had recorded 'Alexander's Ragtime

Band'. That was something to ponder! But did Irving ponder – or did he just hunt and peck, hunt and peck, hunt and peck and worry?

Were the Cossacks who'd burned his family home now shouting 'It's a bear!'? Were they doing their squat-down dance steps to 'Snooky Ookums'? Was the Tsar himself leaping about under the personal direction of the Mad Monk?

Let us now leave the Alley of Ice Cream Songs and visit the Empire of Ice.

7

Russian Rag

Whether Tsar Nicholas II ever danced to ragtime is not documented – but the thrall of syncopation was to contribute to his downfall. The vision of 'The International Rag' presaged the revolutionary potential of American pop. This deadly package, this culture bomb, was to help lure Rasputin to his assassination. And as the hypnotic monk was then the virtual ruler of Russia and as, a few months later, the dynastic empire fell and Communists began their takeover, we can conclude that pop music had made its first contribution to the course of world history.

The following is a hitherto unknown chapter in modern history.

Russia, like Europe, had been very receptive to American entertainers since the 1850s when 'nigger minstrel' troupes arrived. White and black, the burnt-cork songsters and dancers were particularly popular with, and patronized by, the Russian nobility and wealthy landowners. In the banjo-and-bones numbers they found novelty value, the spice of a faraway place; but in the plantation ballads they recognized a melancholy similar to that which lined the Russian soul.

By 1900 a theatre circuit had been established from St Petersburg, the most westernized city, up to Novgorod. But the great mass of Russia, the hinterlands, was left untouched by the spicy American invaders. In salons, mansions and palaces, the blacks found a refreshing absence of prejudice. They met black jockeys, barmen, Shakespearean actors. Tsar

Nicholas II employed a black page. When the cakewalk craze swept through Europe the black vaudeville team of Charlie Johnson and Dora Dean, as American champions, were much in demand. Then, from 1907–11, they found a home in Russia, touring the new theatre circuit. They were there when the ragtime animal dances arrived – the turkey trot and bunny hug, etc. – and they knew these steps of old. But they soon had competition: schools of 'modern dance' sprang up in St Petersburg, the best ones having real black instructors. In 1910 the city welcomed, hot from America, Garland's Opera Troupe with the all-black production of A Trip to Coontown.

Local music publishers contributed with home-made inter-mezzos like 'Holiday of the Negroes'. And there were dozens of record labels (for Russians took the gramophone very seriously) which were prepared, in between releases of more high-brow and folksy music, to insert such novelties as 'The Darkie's Dream', recorded in Warsaw by the Stella Rekord Concert Orchestra. Or cakewalks, two-steps and 'character-istic plantation coon frolics' played by a number of Royal military bands. These local efforts were all rather formal, singularly lacking the necessary punch of lasciviousness.

For the real thing – American imports – the syncopation buff had to have contacts at the local offices of Edison or Victor records. The wealthy buff could travel to the West and there experience American music in the burgeoning new nightlife of the big cities. Cosmopolitan café society was in swing by 1913: in New York, London and Paris the 'International Set' could be seen bunny-hugging and tangoing. Robber barons, English lords and Russian aristo-crats were in the thick of the dancing.

The Russians, it was noticed, seemed to fling themselves into the ragtime beat with an abandon bordering on mania – like a display of medieval religious frenzy; some seemed to be doing a dance of death. Lady Diana Manners, at a London ball reviving the Age of Chivalry, was escorted by Prince Felix Yusupov. This young man, a recent Oxford undergraduate, had an impeccable Russian noble lineage: a descendant of Frederick of Prussia, he was heir to the largest estate in Russia, he would be richer than the Tsar. He was an equisite, heavily bejewelled, but Lady Diana was irritated by his 'wriggling around the ballroom like a demented worm, screaming for "more ragtime and more champagne"'. She also noticed that this exquisite smelled strongly of scent and that there was mascara on his cheeks.

The Prince was fond of dressing up in women's clothes. He'd done this publicly since the age of twelve; once he was almost picked up by the Prince of Wales because he looked so girly-girly; at a St Petersburg night club he'd appeared as a 'French' cabaret singer. Lately, he'd been expressing an ambition to be a 'coon shouter', all dolled up as a black drag queen.

He was an expert on coon shouting as he was on most matters pertaining to American music and manners. He was Russia's most devoted syncopation buff. And he, of course, had the money to indulge this passion. The Yusupov family owned two palaces in St Petersburg and the bigger one had three ballrooms with a large private orchestra on call. The family had owned an orchestra since the eighteenth century but, in the ragtime years, the Prince had augmented the traditional strings and flutes with a six-man saxophone section, the only one in Russia. While 'Too Much Mustard', a current hit, fluttered from the saxes (transcribed from an imported record of the Six Brown Brothers, black American saxomaniacs) Prince Felix performed a one-step with his bride, Princess Irina, daughter of the Tsar's sister. She was also a cousin of the Tsar's nephew, the Grand Duke Dmitri Pavlovitch. And he was Felix's best friend since childhood and his fantasy lover.

When Felix explained that he was 'shaking the blues away' he wasn't only referring to that latest American music form. The word 'blues' had been used in Russia to describe deep depression since the end of the eighteenth century. The mood itself went back to before Ivan the Terrible. It was the heart of the Russian soul: black, bitter, fatalistic. Prince Felix, Grand Duke Dmitri and all their rich cosmopolitan friends, were tired of the weight of the Russian blues. Ragtime for them was a light in their country's doom-gloom, a beacon in the vast darkness of the eternal tundra. Since the seventeenth century, when Peter the Great had attempted to Europeanize

184

Russia, the local 'westerners' had periodically tried to bring daylight into the stagnant medievalism of their society.

But in 1916, with Irving Berlin's syncopated revues on Broadway, with jazz on the brink, abstract paintings in the galleries, and Freud a household name among the enlightened, Mother Russia was still sunk in the Dark Ages. Superstition ruled, even here in sophisticated St Petersburg: invisible hands played grand pianos in the homes of ladies who presided over table-shaking séances; strange portents were witnessed by filthy, self-styled priests who'd wandered in from the steppes. Scum like Vassily, the itinerant pilgrim, who'd started the rumour (among his lady admirers) that the anti-Christ had been born in May 1912 (a year after the publication of the American hit, 'When Ragtime Rosie Ragged the Rosary') and that this evil baby was known by his full set of iron teeth and gruff bass voice. Vassily could often be seen lugging his fifty-pound cross onto city trams, his pockets stuffed with publicity brochures about himself or about the evils of ragtime (an American-Jewish conspiracy, he claimed). As he clambered onto the tram, clusters of penitentials, with their steel caps and their heavy chains, had to make room for this thrusting star.

Vassily had been known to get replies to some of the numerous telegrams of advice he sent to the Tsar. Nicholas II, that subservient ikon-worshipper, cut off from the real world by his obsession for the family circle, was ruled by his imperious wife – probably in touch with the Germans and certainly under the spell of the peasant priest Rasputin, currently styling himself 'Grigori Rasputin-Novykh' in a pathetic attempt to sound British and thus classy.

Early on the morning of Friday, 29 December 1916 – too early for Prince Felix – Rasputin phoned to confirm, rather egregiously, his appearance at the Prince's palace tonight in response to his kind invitation. Then he added: 'Providing there is no urgent Imperial business.' The words were slurred, probably due to vodka.

Felix was furious. The conspirators had to be certain of Rasputin's appearance. Tonight was the night set for the *wretch's murder. All was being arranged: the chocolate-cream cakes, the sweet wines; even now workmen were starting to lay carpets and fit new doors in the palace basement, a fashionable decorator had been hired to take care of the furnishings. No expense had been spared to turn the empty space into a well-appointed drawing-room. The doctor had the poison.*

And now this upstart serf was putting the plan in jeopardy. It had been hard enough just finding a murder night, so full was the Prince's appointment book with parties and things. This 'Imperial business' nonsense was really very irritating . . .

But an hour later the problem was solved. Dmitri phoned in high excitement: the test pressing had arrived from America! The record of this new spasm music, this 'Jass'. Dmitri said he'd already played it and he pronounced the music was as insane as the current state of the Empire. But with more frenzy than any of the ragtime Rasputin had soaked up ever since the Prince had first addicted him.

When, later that morning, Felix at last played the battered and scratchy shellac disc labelled 'Test Pressing: Original Dixieland "Jass" Band' he certainly agreed with the Grand Duke. Insane – but also imbued with a terrific swing. He played the record five times, relishing the hot sweet fever of the "jass" that batted the high window looking out onto a blanket of snow which had silenced St Petersburg on this vile, black-sky morning. Felix felt certain that Rasputin, arch-syncopation fanatic, would kill to get the record.

'Rasputin,' said Felix slowly and low, incanting the name as if it was the curse laid on Russia since her birth. Rasputin – who had ordered the Tsar's Volhynia Life Guards to play more ragtime after he'd learned that a hated rival, the Sumskoi Hussar Regiment, had hit with their version of 'Alexander's Ragtime Band'. Rasputin – the Siberian peasant who now, with the Tsar away at the war front, had hypnotized the Empress into letting him and his Jew cronies run Russia. Running her from bath houses and night clubs, from the telephone in his flat in the slum part of town, sometimes even from the Empress's bedroom as he lanced the little

haemophiliac son and heir with his glinty eyes so that, by some devilish magic, the bleeding ceased.

RASPUTIN – the name connoted sexual appetite unlicensed, and gross appetite, too: rasputstvo.

In his great black boots, gallumphing round Drew's English Tea Shop snatching bath buns, with his wake of twittering society women. 'Entertaining' them at tea in his flat by getting them to lick the jam off his fingers, wipe the madeira from his beard and fondle his enormous organ as he lay on a rug listening to one of his lady disciples banging her way through a rag. 'Love is God', he liked to croon, 'And I am God' and then, in the bedroom (if you could call it that), while the others chatted of table-rapping and ouija boards, he'd 'relieve' a fan or two of their Original Sin, using his sin to drive out theirs by thrusting with his infernal engine and stimulating them into such wild shrieks and gestures (due partly to the wart strategically placed on his primeval tree-trunk) that they often fainted clean away, but then he'd bring them back alive by silken whispering in a relaxed and rhythmic chant he'd learnt from the gypsies in the wood. The gypsies, he was always with the gypsies, slipping off at dawn after orgies at the Aquarium night club where he'd grabbled with the roast meats, never using cutlery, and sucked noisily at his favourite fish and vegetable soup, almost drowning out the string orchestra which may very well have been trying out the new American import, 'Gee, I Like the Music with My Meals'.

Gypsy songs and dances intoxicated Rasputin like vodka. Sometimes, in the night clubs, he would be so carried away by a gypsy air that he'd dance spontaneous steps, as he squatted with legs shooting and arms folded in the stubborn peasant fashion, until he passed out. Felix had witnessed such exhibitions and been both repulsed and attracted. And Rasputin had been captivated by Felix's sweet way with a guitar and his febrile singing of the gypsy ballads. Eventually Felix was persuaded by the beast to perform privately for him and, in return, the beast had tried to cure the beautiful Prince of his homosexual tendencies. Bending over him as he lay prone on the bed, Rasputin murmured remedies and then ululated eery modal folk melodies with goldfish breath, his clotted beard so close it scraped the youth's babycake cheeks. Yet Felix was transfixed – because a delicious, warm bath current was wrapping his body while his soul seemed illuminated by an ancient electricity radiating from Rasputin's razor-sharp, black diamond eyes.

Afterwards, after the scented rose bath, Felix showed Rasputin the palace's main ballroom and told him that sometime soon he'd invite him to take a tango tea and maybe two-step with his wife to the strains of the famous private orchestra and its saxophone section. To hold Irina, the Princess of ineffable beauty and sophistication! The beast was thrilled.

And, as time went by, and as he took modern-dance lessons from a black instructor, Rasputin grew to admire the new American music. Felix plied him with imported rag records and he liked to swivel his head, eyes like moons, watching the spinning disc. He was becoming addicted. Sometimes, the effect of a rhythm could be violent: he shivered and roared and then collapsed. A much stronger effect than his beloved gypsy music, the old refrains. For ragtime was the twentieth-century extension of the old faithfuls, now motorized and filled with promise. And Rasputin, with the war going badly and his enemies encircling him, responded to ragtime, the Alice tonic, like a teenage boy to his first dose of heavy-duty hard rock.

After breakfast Felix called 646-46. He had to fight through several officious, female phone-call fielders before reaching Rasputin. He spent some time elaborating on 'jass', as if it was some new wonder drug. He soon had Rasputin excited. Imperial business or no Imperial business, he'd definitely be at the party tonight. But, he added, the Prince himself was to pick him up, in a bullet-proof Packard limousine, after midnight at flat 20, 63–64 Gorokhavaya St. Come up the backstairs and bring in the dustbins. Felix took a deep breath and agreed. Magnanimously, or perhaps in the intoxication of relief, Felix told Rasputin he'd give him the jazz record as a gift.

What was this record that helped change the course of history?

In the Chicago of late 1916, the Dixieland Jass Band, five white lads from New Orleans, had been creating sensational press copy. Playing brass-band ragtime indoors, with a perverse and abandoned individuality bordering on anarchy, they soon attracted the attention of New York cabaret bookers, hungry for novelty. The Reisenweber restaurant chain, urged on by Al Jolson (who'd actually seen the band in action), made the best offer – with the proviso that they must submit to an audition. In November the little band came to New York and, to an enthusiastic audience led by Jolson and his cronies, they won a booking at Reisenweber's Columbus Circle branch, starting in January 1917.

Also at the audition was a talent scout for Columbia records and he offered the band a test recording session. As material, Jolson suggested a song by his pal Irving Berlin: 'Everything in America is Ragtime'. The band played by ear and not by the book; their method was to go wood-shedding secretly till they'd worked out their individual parts and sewn them together into a seemingly crazy quilt that could razzle-dazzle an enervated world. After a few weeks' work the Dixieland Jass Band was ready to deliver the Berlin number in their very own style of controlled chaos.

But the Columbia recording executives, used to sedate orchestras and precise military bands, were appalled by the performance. They considered the test master to be un-releasable, they scratched it from their matrix files, they wanted no evidence of this crazy racket that sounded like the Western Front in full battle.

But Al Jolson kept a copy. As the 'World's Greatest Entertainer' (this was how he was currently billed), he had acquired many VIP contacts, some were even fans, and he thought of a certain gentleman who'd get a big kick out of this rare record: Grand Duke Dmitri Pavlovitch. Jolson, like Berlin, had been a victim of the Imperial anti-Jewish policy – but show business success can override such matters of the past. Jolson, now an American businessman with powerful connections, knew how to get the record to Russia despite the fact that the nation was at present locked in battle with the Central Powers on the Eastern Front. In fact, the Grand

189

Duke himself was supposed to be at the Tsar's side as one of his aide-de-camps.

Jolson knew better. Through his friendship with Viscount Bryce, the British Ambassador in Washington, he had learned that Duke Dmitri, or 'Dimmy' as Al called him, was actually safe at home in St Petersburg – roaring around in his 100 horsepower car and annoying chauvinist Russians with his snooty Oxford accent and baggy Scottish tweeds.

Jolson gave Bryce the record and Bryce promised to pack it straight off to the Duke. Despite the war big business was operating as usual, over and above matters of national pride. Through the good offices of an international bank 'Everything in America is Ragtime' was eventually delivered by sleigh to the Duke's winter palace within the month.

Felix had been bothering Dmitri for weeks about the record. He'd been reading stories of the new jass in the American trade papers. He was itching to hear the new music. Felix was a music appreciator, while Dmitri was a good-time noble who used entertainment as a diversion from the dreariness of Russian life. It had been fun a few years ago in Paris when he'd danced the bunny hug with lovely Irene Castle and she'd written out the words to 'When the Midnight Choo Choo leaves for Alabam' so that he could later dash over to the Ritz and sing it to his father, Grand Duke Paul, the Tsar's uncle and a devoted Irving Berlin admirer.

But today, with Russia in mortal danger, this ragtime or jass appeared nothing more than a jangle of trivial nonsense. If Felix believed a record could lure the beast to his death then he'd certainly go along with the murder plot. Right at present he was more interested, aesthetically, in the Frank Cooper Oxford marmalade that he was carefully spreading on his breakfast toast.

There was precious little pleasure left in life for Rasputin. So American music had become an obsession, a bright dream out of the white night glare of contemporary life. A few days ago he'd informed their majesties that he was certain he'd be killed before 1 January 1917. To the protesting Empress he prophesied that if he was murdered by nobles then there would follow a civil war in which the Tsar and his entire family would be wiped out.

Today, on this freezing December morning, he had only the Prince's party and the record to look forward to. Heavily guarded, he stumped out of his pokey flat, pushed past the washing on the backyard line, and finally stopped at the gate to issue instructions to his daughter, Maria, who was on her way in with the mid-morning shopping. Take in the laundry, do the dishes, fend off the disciples. And take no phone calls – except from 'the little pretty one', his nickname for Prince Felix.

Then he went to church, changed his clothes, visited the bath house, changed his clothes, held court back at the flat (telling a woman occult writer that his end was very near), had a shower, told Maria to keep those fool female fans away, got a fit of depression and was drunk by one o'clock. He slept through the afternoon while the snow plumped down monotonously and the sky grew angrier.

At around four o'clock Maria woke him up to announce tea but he wanted Scotch. He told her of his dream, a telescope parody of his life: the Siberian villagers crashing drunk around him, accusing him of having a third eye and a nose for smelling out guilt and a stump for the village girls; as a strannik *priest he was wandering through his beloved steppes speaking in tongues, talking in riddles, quoting the Bible indiscriminately, in such a state of ecstasy that he neglected to change his underpants for six whole months; in a cave with the Khlysty sect he took part in the circle dancing with its face and thigh slapping, followed by the brief encounters against the walls; and finally, and triumphantly, he was a* real start *using his tower of power to prove that we are the product of lust, that sex is a liberating force, releasing the goodness that lies within the bosom. By making love to one another we are worshipping Him. But, lately, dullards, plodders, material men, have got in his way. Only through what's left – the music and dance used as an elevator to heaven – can true freedom be realized. This Jass record sounded like the answer. An elevator to the plateau of eternal ecstasy!*

191

As arranged, Prince Felix picked him up at the flat just after midnight. Maria, in tears, told him her forbodings and begged him not to go. Felix said that Irina had a headache and needed Rasputin to use his healing powers. At the Moika Palace he was listening to the Dixieland Jass Band on the big horn gramophone at the top of the basement stairs when he was offered the poisoned cakes and the poisoned wine. He ate some cakes and he drank some wine as he considered the record. The jass was certainly very interesting and he should have been really excited. But, tonight, everything seemed of no more consequence than yellow snow and much more tasteless. He took a lot of madeira but neither that nor the cakes nor the wine had any effect. But the record bothered him horribly: it wasn't the answer, there was no question. He was complaining miserably about the record when Felix shot him in the chest. He fell onto a bearskin rug. While he was grunting there the Prince started fooling with his penis and he tried to strangle the little pretty one but the slippery neck escaped him. The Prince fled upstairs to his parents' quarters. Rasputin, bitterly disappointed by this betrayal of his spiritual brother, clawed up the stairs and out into the courtyard where he cried, 'Felix, my poor dear!' and other endearments till he was shot twice by the politician Purishke-vich. Meanwhile, Dmitri was hiding close to Felix. When it was safe Felix inspected the body, making sure by beating it on the head with a blackjack. At 5.30 a.m. the assassins stuffed the corpse into a gunny sack, dumped it in the boot of a car, drove to the Petrovsky Bridge and heaved it into the icy river. At the post mortem it was declared that death was by drowning.

In March 1917 the Romanov dynasty fell. In April Woodrow Wilson, US President, declared war on the Central Powers and Lenin arrived in St Petersburg to lead the Bolsheviks in the struggle that eventually brought them to power.

The Bolsheviks were against ragtime and jazz and any popular culture not instigated and controlled by them. So after the revolution they shut down all the record companies – except one: Pathe was to continue business by pressing the recorded speeches of Lenin and other selected revolution-

192

*aries. The music of real revolution and revelation was offici-
ally banned.*

*Prince Felix fled to Paris. In later years he'd sometimes
visit America and spend time in Florida with Grand Duke
Dmitri, who was then working as a champagne salesman.
Maria Rasputin eventually settled in Hollywood where she
often dined out by amusing movie people with a slide show
of her father and his royal friends.*

*The test pressing disappeared in the disruptions of 1917
and has never surfaced since.*

8

Mr Jazz Himself

On 1 April 1917 Scott Joplin died in the Manhattan State Hospital. He was mad. His publisher, and other supporters, had long ago titled him 'King of Ragtime Writers'. Not till the 1970s did the world recognize this title.

On 1 April 1917 President Woodrow Wilson sat nurturing his ideals alone in his study in the White House, a sort of hot-house. Looking at the world through stern rimless glasses, this academic was nurturing away while humming a popular tune. He liked vaudeville, the acts took one's mind off affairs of state, the women were comely and the songs could elevate one far above the unfortunate squalor of everyday life.

'When I Leave the World Behind' . . . Maybe they'll remember me for making that world safe for democracy by sending out a crusade of young Americans to fight without rancour, and without selfish object, seeking nothing for their country but what they shall wish to share with all free peoples . . .

The following evening he delivered the finished War Message to Congress. The beleaguered Allies would be rescued from the evil Central Powers by a noble American game-plan and a barrel of morals. This was the wrap-up:

> To such a task we can dedicate our lives and our fortunes, everything that we are and everything that we have, with the pride of those who know that the day has come when America is privileged to spend her blood and her might

for the principles that gave her birth and happiness and the peace which she has treasured. God helping her, she can do no other. (Wild cheers and much stamping.)

The whistle was blown, the game was on. There must be no shirkers or doubters in the team. Americans must pull together as one man or else. Said President Wilson: 'Woe to the man or group of men that seeks to stand in our way in this day of high resolution!' Irish-Americans, Italian-Americans, Jewish-Americans, and, especially, German-Americans must now be plain, straight-ahead Americans. There followed an Americanization campaign of Prussian thoroughness. James Gerard, the recently-recalled US ambassador to Germany, spelled out his plan for recalcitrant German-Americans: 'There is only one thing to do with them and that is to hog-tie them, give them back their wooden shoes and the rags they landed in and ship them back to the Fatherland!' Wagner was banned; sauerkraut was re-named Liberty cabbage. There was jail for any who dared to mock any American military uniform. There was a ten-year jail sentence for Mrs Kate Richards O'Hare: she suggested, in print, that women should avoid bearing sons because the government would only use them as cannon fodder.

Words had become weapons. Propaganda made its first appearance. A federal agency, the Committee on Public Information, was established in order to foster the correct war spirit. Its slogans – the old 'catch-phrase' now politicized – were spread via poster, magazine, newspaper, motion picture, stage show, Liberty Bond rally and song sheet. Over the German lines were air-dropped condensed versions of President Wilson's speeches, translated into German and printed in Gothic type. Tin Pan Alley songs were occasionally dropped: 'We'll Knock the Heligo-into Heligo-out of Heligoland!'

George Creel, the whizzy newspaperman who ran the American propaganda factory, was all in favour of singing soldiers, providing they sang the right stuff. To that end he'd appointed Army Song Leaders (one of them, Geoffrey

O'Hara, contributed 'K-K-K-Katy'). Creel also looked to another factory to aid him in this worthy cause.

Tin Pan Alley was ready to do its duty and some business too. The Alley sold more sheet music than ever before. The War Industries Board supplied plenty of paper because, as the slogan said: 'Music is essential to win the war'. In a gesture towards war economy the publishers shrank their tall sheets and they stayed that way even after the war.

But beyond such practical matters there was the larger issue of freedom or tyranny and the Alley responded with all the art it could muster. Here was an international cause that paled the sugar babes and honey lambs and made irrelevant any midnight choo choos leaving for Alabam. First off was George M. Cohan – quite rightly – with 'Over There'. The Yanks were coming to finish off this dirty business. A stirring tune with a bugle-call motif that was reminiscent of 'Alexander's Ragtime Band'. Still, you can't copyright a bugle call of ancient days, and anyway George and Irving were friends. Other Alleymen were not far behind in this hour of need: 'Just Like Washington Crossed the Delaware General Pershing Will Cross the Rhine'. Washington would be followed by many pop-song characters, specially mobilized: Dixie darkies went to war with Alexander leading the ragtime band while, at home, a baby telephoned Central to ask for her daddy in No-Man's Land.

Where did Irving Berlin stand amidst all this war fever?

Of course, his last name was out-of-style. But although the British royal family changed their German name to 'Windsor' Izzy Baline stuck fast to 'Berlin'. 'Irving Washington' or 'Irving Delaware' didn't sound right. On the matter of war Irving Berlin had always been dead centre, marching along with the public. In 1912, at a time when full-blown war was but a distant memory, he'd written comic songs about soldiery. 'A True Born Soldier Man' grows up on pistols, goes to war as a young man, comes home and gets married – and keeps fighting at home for the rest of his life. In 1914, with America staying firmly neutral in the quarrel over there, Irving had the Devil advising his impatient son to 'Stay down Here Where You Belong'. Up above, said the Devil, the world's gone mad and 'don't

196

know right from wrong'. This was good pacifist material and Irving was right on course, even ahead. Next year a song with even stronger pacifist sentiments sold over a million copies: 'I Didn't Raise My Boy to Be a Soldier' (written by Al Bryan to a tune by Al Piantadosi, Irving's early song rival). But later, with the press reports of terrible slaughter on the Western Front, Irving proposed using ragtime as a cultural weapon for peace: Kings, Tsar and Kaiser laid down their swords to toast each other 'While the Band Played an American Rag'. Shortly after publication there appeared a song with a similar idea: 'We're Going to Celebrate the End of War in Ragtime (Be Sure That Woodrow Wilson Leads the Band).'

So often was Irving the first out with a new idea, words and music. Much copied, never copying. But, as we've seen, George M. Cohan, Irving's mentor, had won the war race with 'Over There'. Still, Irving wasn't far behind: 'For Your Country and My Country' – we must speak with the sword not the pen to show our appreciation to America for opening up her heart and welcoming every immigrant group. Next, Irving joined with George Meyer and his old colleague Edgar Leslie in a song that demanded an end to ethnicity: 'Let's All Be Americans Now'. But Irving hadn't lost his sense of humour, nor discarded his race genre: a proud Irish-American mother, after watching her soldier boy on parade, comes home to tell the neighbours – 'They were All out of Step but Jim'. Here was the war humanized.

Irving had handled the war with both message and joke. War business as show business as sales. And still he had time to write 'Cinderella Lost Her Slipper' and 'Letter Boxes' and 'Way down South', etc. The patriot-comic was running around more than ever, always turned out in a smart dark business suit. Business as usual at Waterson, Berlin & Snyder – but special business for a special time and Mr Berlin could get shirty, even harsh and tough. No – he won't appear at that theatre, nor this one. No, he won't write a song for your benefit, even for your mother. No, he won't take the call. He's tied up in the office. He's not at the office. Mr Berlin agrees to auctioning two of his war songs at the Palace Theatre providing proof is shown that the money goes straight to the war effort . . .

In the winter of 1917 business as usual stopped at Waterson, Berlin & Snyder when Irving got drafted into the army. He was to report to Camp Upton at Fort Yaphank on Long Island. Soon he was a number, swabbing down floors, making up his bunk, counting blankets, eating crude food and getting woken rudely at five in the morning by a bugle call that wasn't a song quote. As a professional insomniac and night person who was finally getting straightened out into normality, he really resented that bugle call. Also, his nervous indigestion was playing up crazy. And there wasn't a nice, quiet, small private space for him to pace up and down in and worry. And, on top of this, to take the biscuit, there wasn't a darn thing to worry about because the army took care of every moment.

Private Berlin became Sergeant Berlin. The US Army swelled to 4 million men, 2 million of them eventually getting to Europe (where 20 per cent had been born). One day, in 1918, General Bell, commanding officer of Camp Upton, gave Sergeant Berlin an order. He would put on a show, an all-soldier revue, to raise money for building a community house. All performers will be male. No females in this show. If there is to be a song involving a woman then that woman will be played by a soldier. And this show will be the best damned show ever.

Irving was free to get worried again. To pace miles on carpets, smoking furiously as he frowned up his songs on the special piano. Three officers at his beck and call, 300 soldiers under his stage command. Only an entire score to write.

After try-outs at Camp Upton, to an audience that included Al Jolson and Eddie Cantor, *Yip, Yip, Yaphank* opened on Broadway at the Century Theatre in late August. Said the *New York Dramatic Mirror:* 'The contingent is stationed at the Seventy-first Regiment armory, Park Avenue and Thirty-fourth Street, and will march to and from the theatre every day in military formation. They will be under military discipline while in the city.'

But there was nothing stiff and starchy about the show.

198

Nothing amateurish either. Sergeant Berlin had drilled his 300 soldiers mercilessly and the result was a hit show with hit songs. Something for everyone, even some cross-dressing. A minstrel-show sequence contained an amusing throwback to the coon-song craze: 'The Ragtime Razor Brigade' would cut off the Hun's retreat – old-fashioned subject matter but funny as hell. Old-fashioned too, but heart-warming, was 'Mandy', a close harmony minstrel number sung by Private Murphy to Private Healy (who looked very comical as Mandy). Poor Private Johnson was given a hard time when he attempted to sing 'I Can Always Find a Little Sunshine in the YMCA'. Lots of catcalls and Bronx cheers. *Yucky* – the Sergeant's off the mark. Lucky he'd cut that big patriotic number from the finale! 'God Bless America', sung by a bunch of soldier lugs, would have been way over the top. Put it back in the drawer. Use 'We're on Our Way to France' – straightforward and sensible.

The Sergeant himself came on stage all bedraggled and put-upon, in a sack-shaped military tunic. He sang-whined 'Poor Little Me—I'm on KP' and 'Oh; How I Hate to Get Up in the Morning'. These were two from the heart and the audience went along with his grouses. He was back on the track – and what an ingenious punch line! He's going to murder the bugler for waking him up at such an ungodly hour – and then he'll get the other pup: *the guy who wakes the bugler up!*

At the grand finale the soldier-actors marched up a gang-plank and into a great troop carrier set in a foggy bay. They sang 'We're on Our Way to France'. Tumultuous applause. General Bell made a thank-you speech from his box; Sergeant Berlin, on stage, declined to utter a word. The cast then carried off their little producer like he was victor ludorum. The producer's mother, Leah Baline, having seen her son perform for the first (and last) time in her life, was shocked all over. What have they done to my son to make him look so woebegone? Are they taking him away so that they can shoot him?

Yip, Yip, Yaphank had originally been scheduled for eight performances. But such was the response it ran for six weeks, raising over $80,000 for the new hall or whatever it

was that the General had in mind. What did that matter?
A hit is a hit is a hit. And what a tremendous morale
booster! George Creel and President Wilson thoroughly
approved. Send them across with a smile and song. At the
music counters in department and five and ten-cent stores
the Berlin soldier songs were selling briskly.

The thirty-second performance saw an amazing pay-off.
Under orders from the War Department Sergeant Berlin
led the entire cast, plus the backstage crew, off stage during
the finale. Down the aisles they marched, singing 'We're on
Our Way to France'. Out into the street and away to their
waiting troop carrier. Tin Pan Alley had joined hands with
real life. But two months later, on 11 November the armis-
tice was signed, the war had been won and so that part of
real life ended happily. Signs on shop doors said: 'Too
happy to work; come back tomorrow'.

Another part of real life, deadlier than the war, had opened
in September at Camp Devens, near Boston. A terrible
influenza pandemic, already killing millions around the
world, made its first American appearance at this army
camp. The recruits were soon spending a good deal of their
time burying fellow soldiers. Intestines were placed in steel
buckets and conveyed to the incinerator; the disembowelled
cadavers were then lined up under canvas, awaiting coffins.
Soon all America was infected by the flu; 4500 deaths a
week was the record in New York. Within nine months
550,000 Americans had died. Among them was Henry
Ragas, pianist with the Original Dixieland Jazz Band.

He died on 18 February 1919 and the band was scheduled
to sail for England two days later, for a tour. There was
much palaver. Who could possibly replace Henry? A master
of the new jazz music with his marching and strumming left
hand and his dancing and jumping right. Who knew the
secret of the jazz, save these sprightly boys from New
Orleans? They were the 'Creators of Jazz' and 'Assassin-
ators of Syncopation' – or so their publicity claimed.

A search turned up J. Russel Robinson, a seasoned
ragtime composer, songwriter and piano-roll cutter.
Recently he'd joined the ranks of the Alleymen. Robinson

200

knew the new music, the new rhythms, the new harmonies, the new melodies and the new poses for the papers. He knew the new music of old because he'd been playing the honky-tonk circuit for years, around the South, in California, all over the bohemian twilight time. Now he was anchored in New York and of course he knew the jazz – he and a whole mess of Alleymen with similar credentials. And the others were learning fast. Since the end of 1917 'jazz' had become the IT word in popular music and dancing. The very latest in pep and fizz. In the biz you had to know the jazz or you were dead. You were in a jazz band, you fronted a jazz band, you owned a jazz band, you at least wrote songs about jazz bands and jazz babies. A new kind of Dixie had come to New York and this jazz baby was making Miss Ragtime look like an old maid.

Sophie Tucker had quickly learned the new lesson. 'The Mary Garden Of Ragtime' was now 'The Queen of Jazz' backed by her 'Five Kings of Syncopation'. These boys, all young and fine looking, she kept in line, smacking them down when necessary. And absolutely NO DRINKING. But keep that spontaneity cooking when on stage. Audiences liked that these days, a sense of danger. Since the war there'd seeped in an 'emotional tensity. Folks were keyed up;on edge.'* Jazz was the tonic for the time being. A new trick, a new angle on the old situation. But the crucial question was: does it have human appeal? Is it the kind of thing everybody will laugh at?

Sophie Tucker, like Al Jolson and a host of other acts, had made it pay off plenty. Sophie's old booker, back in her ragtime days, was Max Hart, a jumping bean. He'd been first off with the Original Dixieland Jazz Band, spotting their laugh potential right away, even when they were small-potato 'jassers' in a Chicago café in 1916. Back then it was spelled 'jass' and 'jasz' and meant a fuck or a woman as cunt and cunt alone. To Max Hart the word spelled 'bank rags' if he could play his cards right. In 1916 people were still talking ragtime, even Irving Berlin, *especially* Irving

---

* Sophie Tucker writing in her life story, *Some of These Days*, New York, 1945.

Berlin. But Al Jolson had cabled Max about the band in Chicago who'd made him cry and Max had journeyed all the way to this crummy café to see what Al was shouting about. Max knew at once that these Southern fire-eaters could be a talking point in the columns, laugh-getters in cabaret, maybe directors of a new way with dancing. Max took out an ad in the trades stating that the band was 'The Sensational Amusement Novelty of 1917' – quite a claim because the year had hardly begun. But Max was always full of hunches and Al was usually right and anyway the band had a tight contract with Reisenweber's, a top nightery.

Reisenweber's went to town too with their ads: 'Untuneful Harmonists Playing "Peppery Melodies".' The band would help open the '400 Room' at the new Reisenweber Building. Max told the press that his boys would give modern dancing a new life and a new thrill. Mr and Mrs Castle had better watch out.

On opening night, 27 January, Max didn't worry when it wasn't socko from the start. The little five-piece Dixieland band had dashed into their very own 'Tiger Rag', raising a ruckus louder than a full military band. But the public had forgotten their cue, sitting firm on their asses, some with arms folded, some shouting directives like 'Send those farmers back to the cotton fields!' No, Max wasn't fazed – he just got up and, with a cocky hip wriggle he'd learned from Al Jolson, he told the public: 'This music is for dancing.' Then he started demonstrating. And soon the mugs got the idea. And then there were lines round the block. And then high society got involved and that's never bad – they held private parties that sometimes went on till noon. And then the press got into the act, spreading the gilded word: 'Gingery, swinging music is what the dancers want,' said *Variety* in March.

Late in the morning the jazzers go to work and the dancers hit the floor, to remain there till they topple over, if the band keeps on playing. It leaves no question but what they like to dance to (is) that kind of music and it is a 'kind'. If the dancers see someone they know at the tables, it's common to hear 'Oh, boy!' as they roll their eyes while floating past, and the 'Oh, boy!' expression probably describes the Jazz Band music better than anything else could.

'Oh, boy!' music was interpreted by New York's dance-orchestra leaders as meaning high-speed cacophony. These establishmentarians, mostly classically trained violinists in charge of over-stuffed ensembles, did not understand the finer points of the Original Dixieland Jazz Band – that this band was truly original, very musical, very exciting and impossible to imitate accurately. The orchestra leaders, running with the spirit of the times, analyzed the seemingly random hot licks and flames and wild raspberries of the boys from New Orleans and deduced that the secret of jazz was noise. Bassoons and oboes were banished, tin cans and temple blocks were ushered in. Corrugated iron in the jungle.

How did the members of the Tempo and Clef clubs – those organizers of Negro musicians – deal with this latest manifestation of wild sounds from the Old South? It had been embarrassing enough when That Creole Band, an off-key and crude black band from New Orleans led by Freddie Keppard, had infested New York vaudeville houses between 1915 and 1917. Billed as 'rubes' and trailing turnip greens and cotton balls when they harmonized to 'Old Black Joe', such ill-educated country boys were destroying the status achievements of the ever circumspect Negroes of New York.

But now here were the whites obsessed with the word 'jazz' – an unfortunate piece of Negro argot, embracing jelly rolls, shimmy-sha-wobbling, and other details of the sex life. Why must American Music be so tied to dirty habits?

Nonetheless and notwithstanding, the Grand Plan must continue to be pursued: accommodation within the white man's world (at least where money is concerned); and, at the same time, a strict adherence in the concert hall to classical Negro music – spirituals and work-songs, tone poems, etc. – for the glory of the soul and for posterity. But commercial considerations to the fore: the fad of the hour being this so-called 'jazz' transmogrified into music, the members of the Clef and Tempo clubs must needs determine to go 'primitive', shedding skins of good taste and conservatory training, catering to those crazed white girls who yell, 'Oh, boy!'

James Reese Europe was particularly depressed by this sudden return to musical crudity. The originator of both the Clef and Tempo clubs, a glowing and glowering example to rising Negro musicians, Europe had taken great pains in the selection and training of his pride and joy, the Negro Symphony Orchestra. The British regiments being so skilled at training natives, he had sent to South Africa for French horn players and to the Sudan for his oboists. In the field of commerce he had supplied the Castles with refined ragtime orchestras and bands – ensembles stressing massed banjos and mandolins all strumming chords with which to accompany rows of melody instruments playing in unison. A triumph of precision. And no cutting loose. 'Our people are not naturally painstaking; they want, as they put it, "to knock a piece cold" at the first reading,' James Reese Europe told the *Evening Post* in 1914. 'It takes a lot of training to develop a sense of time and delicate harmony.'

And now this 'Oh, boy!' music, with its emphasis on anarchy and improvisation, had forced him to advertise his prize sixty-piece brass band as a jazz outfit. But, mercifully, by the autumn of 1918 he was proudly serving his country out in France as Lieutenant Europe, leader of the Hellfighters, the 369th Infantry Band. His mission was to provide marches, ballads, waltzes and a complete vaudeville show for the American soldiers and the war-weary Allies. A morale booster, a good advertisement for Uncle Sam. 'But where is the jazz?' asked his General. 'Where is my "Army Blues"?' Lieutenant Europe obeyed with alacrity, sending back to New York for men with a suitable rough edge to their playing. Build for the future, go with the Man.

Meanwhile, in New York, Europe's colleagues were doing the best they could. Ford Dabney, the man with royal credentials, had been conducting a large syncopated orchestra for Ziegfeld's *Midnight Frolics* on the Amsterdam Roof—a decent, well-paid job—when the jazz craze broke out. He soldiered on, regardless. Joe Jordan, highly trained

and a fine conductor, had just returned from a successful
stint in Britain where he'd delighted with his ragtime compositions. He was galled to find his 1909 copyright, 'That
Teasin' Rag', turning up uncredited on the first recording
released by this Original Dixieland Jazz Band. How dare
they call their number 'The Original Dixieland One-Step?'
But Joe was a quiet and level-headed man and he set about
getting his royalties in the proper way. He came up against
a brick wall. The Alley made the rules. Jim Europe had
explained the status quo in an interview with the *New York
Tribune* in 1914:

> The music world is controlled by a trust, and the negro
> must submit to its demands or fail to have his compo-
> sitions produced. I am not bitter about it. It is, after all,
> but a small portion of the price my race must pay in its,
> at times, almost hopeless fight for a place in the sun.
> Some day it will be different and justice will prevail.

Someday, when the clouds roll back, and what a mighty day
that will be! Jim was tireless at explaining the position to
his brothers. Some found the position unacceptable. Will
Marion Cook and a few others later took off for the
comparative freedom of Europe. Will was still smiling but
the smile never reached his eyes. Of the other songwriters:
J. Leubrie Hill had enjoyed some success in the real world
with 'At the Ball, That's All' because Mr Ziegfeld had
borrowed it from Hill's Harlem revue and placed it in the
Ziegfeld Follies where sales followed but there was little
follow-up; Jim Burris and Chris Smith had hit in 1913 with
'Ballin' the Jack' and were awarded correct royalties;
Spencer Williams and Dave Peyton came under the
umbrella of white man Roger Graham to produce 'I Ain't
Got Nobody' in 1916 and 'Shim-Me-Sha-Wabble' in 1917;
Canadian-born Shelton Brooks had come up all on his own
with 'Some of These Days' in 1910 (Sophie Tucker's theme
song) and 'The Darktown Strutters' Ball' in 1917 (which
everybody performed, including the Original Dixieland Jazz
Band); W. C. Handy, stenographer of the blues, was to
open a music-publishing office in the Alley in 1918, hoping
for a place in the sun but, at first, that place turned out to

be the pavement in front of the door where W. C. and his partner Harry Pace wouls stand and drum up business with passersby. Prior to joining the Original Dixieland Jazz Band, J. Russel Robinson had been manager of Pace & Handy's. He was used to listening to Harry Pace's rhetorical tirades against the music business and its boycott on blacks.

But in February 1917 Henry Ragas was the pianist with the Dixielanders and they were recording for Victor Records, after the débâcle with Columbia. 'The Original Dixieland One-Step', with its uncredited rag strain from Joe Jordan's 'That Teasin' Rag', was released with 'Livery Stable Blues' (another disputed copyright) as the other side. Together these numbers constituted the first jazz record. By year's end 2 million copies had been sold and more releases had appeared: 'Indiana', 'Tiger Rag', 'At the Jazz Band Ball'. Not only did these records provide novelty music for dancers whipped up by war frenzy and the craziness of life in general, but the New Orleans jazz ensemble playing of the Dixieland Band laid down the patterns, phrasing, rhythms and hot licks for embryonic classic jazzmen: Bix Beiderbecke, Benny Goodman and Louis Armstrong were but a few of the youngsters inspired to take up jazz after hearing records by the Dixielanders. And after the inspiration smoke had cleared they settled down to some hard studying, playing the records over and over, learning all the licks and tricks.

But as far as the general public and the industry was concerned these pioneering jazzers were just another flash, as good as their last record or publicity stunt. Soon they were to be overtaken by slicker operators like Paul Whiteman and Ted Lewis. But the records of the Original Dixieland Jazz Band remain as testimony that they were the genesis of traditional dixieland jazz. They were proof, too, that it was possible even in Teutonic America to be a player in the clockwork team and yet remain an individual. This surely was democracy at work!

In a wider angle, the band was the essence of the feeling of the times. Nick La Rocca, the feisty cornet-playing leader, had described their neat working system: 'You see

I cut the material (Larry) Shields (clarinet) puts on the lace, and (Eddie) Edwards (trombone) sews it up.' But Edwards, mything, said with glee: 'None of us knows music.' Actually, he was musically literate but the world wanted musical anarchy, notes that bashed into each other as they shot down from the angry heavens, notes that might pierce the howling earth. Change and destruction: after the Great War there was no more Holy Roman Empire and the unholy Bolshevik Empire was rising ugly. A Devil who never knew God was stalking the map, threatening Western Civilization. New World Civilization already had plenty to cope with – race riots in Chicago, strikes everywhere (even among the actors, even among the police), inflation, unemployment, an invalid President (with his wife running the White House). Godlessness was hovering over God's country: in 1919, that horrid violent year that should have seen the dawn of the millennium, the American Communist Party was founded and it was rumoured that this was their fraternal yell: 'Bolshevik, Bolshevik, Bang!'. One of these American Communists (oxymoronic!) was reportedly using the Stars & Stripes as his lavatory floor rug.

How did Irving Berlin react to all this intrusion? He wrote 'That Revolutionary Rag' (referring to the crimson flag that puts fear into kings and queens) and he warned people to 'Look out for the Bolsheviki Man'. As far as the new music was concerned he treated jazz like he'd treated ragtime: he wrote about it. President Wilson (in 1918 still up and about) was advised to 'Send a Lot of Jazz Bands over There' to keep the soldier boys in good cheer. Then he closed in on the saxophone as a symbol of change, describing a young fellow who had 'dusted off the saxophone' and made it modern by giving the world dreamy moans with strange changes in minor keys. We were all invited to shake hands with Irving's new friend, 'Mr Jazz Himself'. Irving was, as usual, making the modern appear OK regular.

But the modern was marching in with monstrous strides. And in battalions, too. As the little Dixieland Band's chirrupy music faded from the main arena so entered the foxtrot dance-band corporations, precision drilled to be the ideal accompaniment to the 'Jazz Age.' From now on the word 'jazz', like 'fascist' in the sixties, was fair game for any interpretation. In the Jazz Age there would be tiers of horns and reeds with shirts gleaming white, chugging relentlessly into the thirties where there would be a pit stop for stream-lining. And all these soldier-worker-players would be under the command of their conductor-boss, standing with his back to the band, dressed like a company director, smiling like Uriah Heep, watching closely the paying customers as they shuffled by.

But though the cold shower punch and eupepticism of ragtime and original dixieland was to disappear, and though there would be technological changes to deal with (radio and talkies), the need for a steady supply of popular songs would continue, would increase. Irving Berlin was looking to this future and to his continuing place in the race. He decided to be his own man. In January 1919 he severed his connections with Waterson, Berlin & Snyder.

He had always been a minority shareholder. Henry was the boss. And Henry understood his friend's ambition. Snowy-haired Henry, with his cowboy hats and his Kentucky Colonel demeanour, wished his boy good luck. In the Alley hangouts there was much gossip about the whiz-kid: he was signing with Harms, Inc., but no, that was unlikely because 'Revolutionary Rag' had flopped and, anyway, Harms were quality publishers, show-score gents and, although Irving had had his fling at show tunes, he was at heart a 10–cent pop-song man; he's told the trade that he demands a guarantee of $75,000 a year plus bonus, and who's fool enough to go for that when he's not got the hold on the public purse that he had a few years back? The cheesecake and strudel were consumed, the gossip kept rolling. And Irving acted.

In July Irving Berlin, Incorporated opened offices on Broadway at 48th St. Max Winslow and Saul Bornstein were installed as company officers reporting directly to Mr Berlin. Publicly, he was to be always referred to as 'Mr Berlin'. To get in to see him a visitor had to negotiate lines of secre-taries, assistants and protectors. One afternoon a newly hired girl actually stood next to him at the water cooler.

Mostly he was invisible. A bodyguard with a police dog, a chauffeur in a bullet-proof Packard limousine, were at his beck and call. Recently, there had been rumours of an impending kidnap. These days, with anarchists roaming around, you can't be too careful.

Somewhere, sometime, Irving Berlin was making songs. The new company had to have a catalogue. Six new songs appeared. Word was that Mr Berlin had hopped down to Atlantic City, holed up in a hotel for three days and come back with some catalogue. 'Nobody Knows (and Nobody Seems to Care)' – maybe a real personal number, he's been a loner lately. 'You Cannot Make Your Shimmy Shake on Tea' – very topical what with Mae West wobbling her assets in the new Hammerstein show, and the Volstead Act making liquor prohibition a reality.

The shimmy number could also be right for the new Ziegfeld Follies. Ziggy wants material now, like yesterday. Pressure, pressure. Irving can certainly produce under pressure. And at the moment he's on a definite writing streak. Eddie Cantor needs special material? The boss has come up with a boffo: 'You'd be Surprised'. So it's a bromidic phrase, a commonplace – but listen to the switch: 'He's not much in a crowd, but when you get him alone – ' Dramatic pause and the boss's shoulders sway ever so slightly and he telegraphs the hint of a wink – 'You'd be surprised'. Everybody in the office agrees it's a knockout. What about the big ballad production number? Ziggy's got truckloads of dames with swell threads and great gams and he'll send them perambulating around the stage like a dog-show parade. He wants a song to suit.

Irving whispered and banged out 'A Pretty Girl Is Like a Melody'. The inner circle of Winslow and Bornstein applauded and broke out the cigars because they knew that, despite the boss's performance, the song was right on the money. Ziggy thought so too. He had his lovelies criss-crossing the stage all stately and all dressed as famous classical melodies like 'Spring Song' and 'Barcarolle' and that sort of thing. Talk about class . . .

Nothing can stop the boss. Now you see him, now you don't. Mostly you don't – except in the papers or on the stage. Here we are in October and he's headlining at the Palace for a tidy sum. Bee Palmer and Her Jazz Band close the first half and she's a vision of loveliness in her diaphanous white gown but does she become a wild, wild woman when she cuts loose on the shimmy shaking? I'll say she does! In the second half all we need is the Irving Berlin name flashing on the board to raise a round of applause. He tries out a whole slew of numbers but he seems to only feel serious about 'Nobody Knows (and Nobody Seems to Care)'. He has a neat and timely number about the jazzing lovely: 'Oy, Mama, Bee Palmer Has Got Becky Shimmying Now'. Then, at the end, he's going into 'You'd be Surprised' when who should step on stage to join the master but Eddie Cantor himself! Quips Eddie: 'Let's be friends, Irvy. You write great songs but let somebody else sing them!' Big laugh. Show biz is a fine fraternity and they do a lot of charity work. Irvy's a big star, no question. And, they say, a helluva nice fellow if you know him . . .

He slipped off after the show without anyone knowing. Could be at the office worrying about catalogue, about whether we have enough waltzes to balance the foxtrots and jazz novelties. Could be up in his apartment with his art treasures. Could be writing cheques to settle Mike Salter's debts. Old friends will always get quiet attention.

We're told it's a magnificent apartment. Paintings by great American artists and carved figures from France and the Orient—these are but a few of his latest acquisitions. In the book cases there are bound original manuscripts by President Lincoln himself, and all kinds of music textbooks and a rhyming dictionary and a thesaurus.

Four in the morning and way up there is that yellow smudge, the only light in the building. The snow continues to fall without imagination, ending its journey with a dull *phutt* on the pavement below Irving's castle.

He was riding around New York for the hell of it. Christmas was near and so the snow was welcome, at least from the viewpoint of the warm interior of the long sedan. Up front, separated by a glass partition, sat the chauffeur and the bodyguard. Between them squatted a German shepherd dog, ears pricking, hyperventilating from anticipated violence. The trio was at all times prepared for the moment when matter meets anti-matter. Anarchy was in the air, according to the newspapers. There had been another rumour of a kidnap operation on the boss.

Wrapped in his polar-bear overcoat, sunk into the cushions, happy in the enveloping smell of seasoned leather, Irving Berlin was pure thought. He was thinking about 'Oh! How I Hate to Get up in the Morning' and, in particular, the guy who wakes the bugler up. What about the guy who wakes the guy who wakes the bugler up? And, tracing the mystery to its source, what about the guy who makes the stars which make the galaxies which make the universe? What about the Man Upstairs? Too much pure thought chasing round and round and getting nowhere. Maybe a ghetto legacy. Look up the answers at home. Home?

Meantime, better to look out at the passing show – the general public slogging through the snow. Mostly office people rushing to lunch, to buy gifts, to perhaps purchase a song. At a stop sign there was an unpleasant occurrence. A threatening person, probably displaced, in a threadbare overcoat and a slouch cap pulled low, rapped hard on the hood of the sedan. As he rapped he glared, squashing a beetroot-veined face against the front window.

The chauffeur pulled away fast, ignoring the red light and leaving the person in a swirl of snow. What had the person wanted? Was it Irving or the idea of Irving? And would such a person leave the sunshine to the flowers and the songbirds to the blind?

Was Irving Berlin music any more than jingle-jangle, a pleasant escape from the thudding here and now? Was it all just a joke and was somebody up there laughing? Or was Irving Berlin music – and all music – a telephone line to heaven? And is the public ready for another telephone song?

The person in the slouch cap was long gone, rubbed out by the winter and the city. The sedan took a bit longer to vanish but it vanished all the same. And then everything was white and still and only the songs remained.

211

Bibliography

Anderson, Jervis. *Harlem: The Great Black Way (1900–1950).* London: Orbis, 1982.

Berlin, Edward A. *Ragtime—A Musical and Cultural History.* Berkeley and Los Angeles: University of California Press, 1980.

———. *Reflections and Research on Ragtime.* New York: Institute for Studies in American Music, 1987.

Blesh, Rudi (and Harriet Janis). *They All Played Ragtime.* New York: Oak Publications, 1966.

Brunn, H.O. *The Story of the Original Dixieland Jazz Band.* London: Sidgwick and Jackson, 1961.

Castle, Mr. and Mrs. Vernon. *Modern Dancing.* New York: Harper & Brothers, 1914.

Charters, Ann. *Nobody—The Story of Bert Williams.* New York: The Macmillan Company, 1970.

Charters, Samuel B. (and Leonard Kunstadt). *Jazz: A History of the New York Scene.* Garden City: Doubleday & Co., 1962.

Gilbert, Douglas. *Lost Chords: The Diverting Story of American Popular Songs.* Garden City: Doubleday, Doran and Co., Inc., 1942.

Gilbert, L. Wolfe. *Without Rhyme or Reason.* New York: Vantage Press, 1956.

Goldberg, Isaac. *Tin Pan Alley: A Chronicle of the American Popular Music Racket.* New York: The John Day Company, 1930.

Hamm, Charles. *Yesterdays: Popular Song in America.* New York: W. W. Norton & Company, 1979.

Harris, Chas. K. *How To Write A Popular Song.* New York: Chas. K. Harris, 1906.

Howe, Irving. *World of Our Fathers.* New York: Harcourt Brace Jovanovich, 1976.

Jay, Dave. *The Irving Berlin Songography (1907–1966).* New Rochelle: Arlington House, 1969.

Johnson, James Weldon. *The Autobiography of an Ex-Colored Man.* New York: Alfred A. Knopf, 1927.

BIBLIOGRAPHY

Kahn, E. J. (Jr.). *The Merry Partners: The Age and Stage of Harrigan and Hart.* New York: Random House, 1955.

Marks, Edward B.(as told to Abbot J. Liebling). *They All Sang: From Tony Pastor to Rudy Vallee.* New York: The Viking Press, 1935.

Oliver, Paul. *Songsters and Saints: Vocal Traditions on Race Records.* Cambridge: Cambridge University Press, 1984.

Stearns, Marshall and Jean. *Jazz Dance: The Story of American Vernacular Dance.* New York: The Macmillan Company, 1968.

Toll, Robert C. *Blacking Up: The Minstrel Show in Nineteenth Century America.* New York: Oxford University Press, 1974.

Waldo, Terry. *This Is Ragtime.* New York: Hawthorn, 1976.

Whitcomb, Ian. *After the Ball: Pop Music From Rag to Rock.* New York: Limelight Editions, 1986.

Witmark, Isidore (and Isaac Goldberg). *From Ragtime To Swingtime: The Story of the House of Witmark.* New York: Lee Furman, 1939

Woollcott, Alexander. *The Story of Irving Berlin.* New York: G. P. Putnam's Sons, 1925.

Note: For detailed information on ragtime consult *The Rag Times* founded in 1967 and still going strong. Published bi-monthly by The Maple Leaf Club, 5560 West 62nd Street, Los Angeles, California 90056.

Index

Abrahams, Maurie, 32, 139, 152
Adler, Jacob, 177
'After the Ball', 56–8, 60, 98
Albee, Edward, 163
'Alexander and His Clarinet', 70–1
'Alexander's Ragtime Band', 2, 67, 71, 74–81, 142, 144
Alger, Horatio Jr, 19
American Ragtime Octette, 153, 158–60, 165
Armstrong, Louis, 206
Ayer, Nat D., 162–6

Baker, Belle, 32, 176–8
Baker, Ray Stannard, 111
Baline, Leah, 17, 23, 144, 199
Baline, Moses, 17–23
Ball, Ernest, 77
Banneker, Ben, 97
Bard, Wilkie, 156
Barlow Brothers, 87
Barnum, P. T., 88
Barron, Ted, 30
Beiderbecke, Bix, 206
Bell, General, 198, 199
Berlin, Dorothy, 140, 143–4
Bernard, Mike, 122
'The Best of Friends Must Part', 32
Biller, Johnny, 117
Blake, Eubie, 5

Bland, James, 96–7, 153
Blow Your Horn, 179
Bohee Brothers, 95–6, 153
Booth, Edwin, 88
Bornstein, Saul, 208
Botsford, George, 71–2, 77, 138–9
Braham, John, 129
Brattain, Walter, 3
Brice, Elizabeth, 172
Brooke, Rupert, 161
Brown, Seymour, 163–5
Bryan, Al, 197
Bryce, Viscount, 190
Burris, Jim, 135
Butt, Alfred, 162

Cahill, Marie, 32
Callahan's, 23–4, 25, 29
Callendar, Charles, 93
Cantor, Eddie, 198, 209, 210
Carlisle & Wellman, 157
Carney, Kate, 154
Carus, Emma, 79, 157
Casey, Hobnailed, 28
Castle, Irene, 190
Castle, Vernon, 170–2
Cave, J., 88
Century Girl, 180
Chappells, 74
'Christmas Time Seems Years and Years Away, 69

214

Christy, Ed, 50–1, 84, 89
'Cinderella Lost Her Slipper', 197
Clef Club, 134, 203, 204
Clorindy, 128–30
Cohan, George M., 26, 29, 44, 55, 76–7, 163, 169–70, 196
Cohan, Jerry, 88
'Cohen Owes Me 97 Dollars', 7
Cole, Bob, 128, 132, 134, 136
Collins, Lottie, 108
Connors, Babe, 106
Connors, Chuck, 25–6, 27, 29, 69
Conrad, Con, 162
Cook, Will Marion, 98, 126–31, 133, 205
Coughlin, Bathhouse John, 148
Creamer, Henry, 134
Creel, George, 195, 200
Crow, Jim, 87

Dabney, Ford, 134, 204
Danks, Hart, 52
Day, David, 141
De Courville, Albert, 152, 157–8, 160
De Sorel, Miss, 149
Dean, Dora, 99, 183
Delys, Gaby, 179
Dibdin, Charles, 88
Dickens, Charles, 49, 54, 101–2
Dillingham, Charles, 169, 172
Dixieland Jass Band, 189, 192
'Do It Again', 147
'Do Your Duty, Doctor', 69
Dockstader, Lew, 79, 150
'Dorando', 34–5
Dowson, Ernest, 1
'Dreams, Just Dreams', 74
Dresser, Paul, 52, 123
Dresser, Theodore, 52
Dunbar, Paul Lawrence, 98, 127, 129, 131–3

Eardley-Wilmot, D., 73–4
Edward VII, King, 133, 153

Edwards, Larry, 207
Edwards, Leo, 78
Elliott, G. H., 154
Errol, Leon, 137
Essex, Clifford, 153
Europe, James Reese, 134, 171, 204, 205
'Everybody's Doing It Now', 138, 143, 145, 156
'Everything in America Is Ragtime', 179, 189–90

Farrell, Kid, 134
Feist, Leo, 123, 170
Feldman, Bert, 72–3, 141–2, 157, 162, 165–6
'For Your Country and My Country', 197
Foster, George, 102
Foster, Stephen, 47–51, 64
Fox, Harry, 179
Francis, Day & Hunter, 73, 141
Freedman, Max, 76
Friar's Club, 76, 169
Frisco, Joe, 28–9, 167
Frohman Brothers, 93

Georgia Minstrels, 92–3
Gerard, James, 195
Gideon, Melville, 153, 160
Gilbert, L. Wolfe, 14, 150–2, 161
Gilbert, W. S., 77
'The Girl on the Magazine Cover', 179
Gladstone, William, 88
'God Bless America', 199
Goetz, E. Ray, 143, 144
Goodman, Benny, 206
Gotham-Attucks, 81, 134–5
Graham, Charles, 52
Green Harry, 117
Greene, Gene, 162
Greenup, Bruner, 116, 118
Grenville, Guy, 157

'The Grizzly Bear', 71–2, 138
Grossmith, George Jnr, 156

Hague, Sam, 92, 94
Haley, Bill, 76, 171
Handy, W. C., 205–6
'Happy Days Are Here Again', 14
Harding, Frank, 52–3, 55, 61, 116–17
Harms Inc., 208
Harney, Ben, 55, 99–100, 112–19, 120, 122, 124–5, 149
Harrigan & Hart, 53–4
Harrigan, Ned, 54
Harris, Charles K., 55–60, 64, 69, 123
Hart, Max, 201–2
Haverly, Colonel Jack, 87, 93–6
Hayes, Jimmy, 34
Hedges, Elven, 157
Hedges, Freddie, 157
Helf, J. Fred, 150
Herbert, Victor, 31, 74, 180
'He's a Rag Picker', 173
Hess, Cliff, 140, 166, 167, 176
Hicks, Charles 'Barney', 92, 94–5
Hill, J. Leubrie, 133, 205
Hill, Strap, 113–14, 119
Hirsch, Louis, 160
'Hitchy Koo', 152, 158, 161
Hoffman, Aaron, 78
Hoffman, Frederick, 110
Hoffman, Max, 52, 122
Hogan, Ernest, 120–2, 128, 130, 131–2, 136
Hole, Arnold, 155
Hurley, Alec, 154

'I Can Always Find a Little Sunshine in the YMCA', 199
'I Love a Piano', 179
'I Want to Go Back to Michigan', 175
'I Was Aviating Around', 169

'I Wish That You Were My Gal, Molly', 69
'If I Had You', 175
'If I Thought You Wouldn't Tell', 69
'The International Rag', 168, 169, 182
Irina, Princess, 184, 188
Irwin, May, 57, 111–12, 114, 120
Israels, Mrs, 147

Jacobson, Jesse, 157
Jagger, Mick, 84
James, Henry, 110
Jefferson, Gene, 119
Jerome, Billy, 149
Johnson, Charlie, 183
Johnson, J. Rosamond, 128, 132
Johnson, James Weldon, 98, 128, 132, 134
Jolson, Al, 14, 20, 79, 148, 150, 151, 176–8, 189, 198, 202
Jones, Irving, 59, 61, 108, 111, 112, 122–3
Joplin, Scott, 60–1, 75, 99, 136, 149, 161, 194
Jordan, Joe, 134, 204–5, 206
Jose, Dick, 57
'Just Like a Rose', 32

Kelly, Jimmy, 31–3, 34
Kenna, Hinky Dink, 148
Keppard, Freddie, 203
Kern, Jerome, 14, 177
Kersands, Billy, 94–5
'Ki-Yi Yodeling Dog', 138
King, Charles, 172
Kipling, Rudyard, 20
Klaw & Erlanger, 163
Kutchinsky, Kutch, 28

La Rocca, Nick, 206
Lane, William Henry (Master Juba), 101

Lashwood, George, 156
Lasky, Jesse, 71
Leavitt, M. B., 87
Lee, Philip, 89–90
Lee, W. H., 92
Leoncavallo, Ruggiero, 158, 159
Leslie, Edgar, 33, 36–7, 139, 150, 197
Lessing, Edith Maida, 149
'Let's Face the Music and Dance', 9
'Letter Boxes', 197
Levey, Ethel, 157–8, 160, 166
Lewis, Roger, 149
Lewis, Ted, 206
Libbey, J. Aldrich, 57
Lloyd, Marie, 155
Lodge, Henry, 77
Löhr, Hermann, 73–4
'Look Out for the Bolsheviki Man', 207
Louis of Battenburg, Prince, 29
Lounsbery, Charles, 178–9

McCarthy, Joe, 148
Mackney, E. W., 88
McPherson, R. C., 134–5
Mama Lou, 106–7
Manhattan Minstrels, 90
Manners, Lady Diana, 183–4
'Marie from Sunny Italy', 30–1
Marks, Ed, 58, 135
Marks and Stern, 123
Mason, Jack, 160, 162
Mason, Lowell, 46
The Merry Whirl, 77–9
Metz, Theodore, 62
Meyer, George, 197
Michaelson, Nick, 27–8, 30
Mills, F. A. Kerry, 150–1
Mizner, Wilson, 178
Monaco, Jimmy, 148–9
Moore, Tom, 48, 49
Mora, Helen, 57

Morris, William, 152
Muir, Lewis F., 149–52, 161
'My Melody Dream', 175
'My Wife's Gone to the Country', 65–7
'That Mysterious Rag', 80, 143

Negro Symphony Orchestra, 204
'Next to Your Mother, Who Do You Love', 69
Nicholas II, Tsar, 182–3, 185
'Nobody Knows', 209

Oakley, Olley, 153
'Oh, How I Hate to Get Up in the Morning', 199
'Oh, How That German Could Love', 167
'Oh, That Draggy Rag', 70
'Oh, You Beautiful Doll', 164–5
O'Hara, Geoffrey, 195–6
O'Hare, Kate Richards, 195
'The Old Maid's Ball', 140, 174
O'Malley, Frank Ward, 15
'Opera Burlesque', 172
Original Dixieland Jazz Band, 200–3, 205, 206
Ossman, Vess, 153

Pace, Harry, 206
Paderewski, Ignacy Jan, 107
Paine, John Howard, 49–50
Palmer, Bee, 210
Pastor, Tony, 115
Pavlovitch, Dimitri, Grand Duke, 184, 186, 189–90, 192, 193
Pavlovitch, Paul, Grand Duke, 29, 190
Peel, Robert, 88
Pelham, Dick, 89
Pelham Café, 26–31
Pemberton, Max, 160
'Piano Man', 70
Piantadosi, Al, 29, 32, 66, 197

Pietri, Dorando, 34
'Play a Simple Melody', 172
Plunk Henry, 99
'A Pretty Girl Is Like a Melody',
  209
Priestley, J. B., 157
Primrose, George, 96

'Queenie, My Own', 32

Ragas, Henry, 200, 206
'Ragtime Melodrama', 179
'The Ragtime Soldier Man', 169
Rasputin, 185–92
Rasputin, Maria, 191, 192, 193
Rector, 163
Remick, 163–4
'The Revolutionary Rag', 207
Rice, Ed, 129
Rice, Thomas, 86
Roberts, Robert, 119
Robinson, J. Russel, 200–1, 206
Rogers, Alex, 133, 134
Rogers, Charlie, 153
Ronklyn, Georgie, 29
Roosevelt, Theodore, 110, 163
Rosenfeld, Monroe, 60–3, 79
Rossiter, Will, 56, 149
'Rum Tum Tiddle', 138
Russell, Henry, 50
Russell, Lillian, 115

'Sadie Salome, Go Home!', 9, 36–7
Salter, 'Nigger' Mike, 26–31, 210
Santley, Joseph, 179
Sayers, Harry, 107
Schwartz, Jean, 76
Seeley, Blossom, 179
'Send a Lot of Jazz Bands over
  There', 207
'Settle Down in a One-Horse
  Town', 172–3
Shapiro-Bernstein, 58, 170
'She Was a Dear Little Girl', 32

Shields, Larry, 207
Shipp, Jesse, 133, 134
Shrady, Dr, 69–70
Silverman, Sime, 172, 180
Six Brown Brothers, 184
Sloane, A. Baldy, 59, 165
Smith, Chris, 135
'Snooky Ookums', 138, 140, 174
Snyder, Ted, 33–4, 35, 64–72, 74,
  79, 80, 168–9
Solar, Willie, 157, 160
Spaeth, Sigmund, 57
'Spring and Fall', 175
'Spring Time', 69
'Stay down Here Where You
  Belong', 196
Sterling, Andrew, 62, 123
Stern, Joe, 30–1, 58
Stop! Look! Listen!, 179–80
'Stop, Stop, Stop', 70
Straight, Charlie, 162
Stravinsky, Igor, 161
Stuart, Leslie, 5, 72, 123, 154
Sweet, Jubal, 28
Swope, Herbert Bayard, 29
'The Syncopated Walk', 173

Tempo Club, 203, 204
Temun, 16–18
Thackeray, William, 88
That Creole Band, 203
'That Mesmerizing Mendelssohn
  Tune', 69
'There's a Girl in Arizona', 169
'They Were All out of Step but
  Jim', 197
'They've Got Me Doin' It Now',
  139
Thomas, Hannibal, 110
Thornton, Bonnie, 78
Thornton, James, 51–2, 78
Tiffany, Maude, 157
Travers, Duke, 122
Trevathan, Charles, 111

INDEX

'A True Born Soldier', 196
Tucker, Sophie, 14, 20, 163, 201, 205

Vassily, 185
Victoria, Queen, 95
Von Tilzer, Harry, 24–5, 31–3, 39, 40, 58, 62–3, 81, 133
Von Tilzer, Will, 149

'Wait, Wait, Wait', 33
'Waiting for the Robert E. Lee', 151, 158–9
Walker, George, 125–6, 128, 131–4, 136
Warfield, David, 37
Washington, Booker T., 109–11
Watch Your Step, 172, 175–6
Waterson, Berlin & Snyder, 80, 139, 147, 168–70, 175, 197–8, 208
Waterson, Henry, 33–4, 35, 37, 72–3, 80, 142, 168–9, 208
'Way down South', 197
'We're on Our Way to France', 199, 200
West, Mae, 72, 209
'When I Leave the World Behind', 177–9
'When I Lost You', 8, 138, 140, 144, 147, 173

'When the Midnight Choo-Choo Leaves for Alabam', 143, 173, 190
Whidden, Jay, 162
Whiteman, Paul, 206
Whiting, George, 65–6, 68
'Wild Cherry Rag', 69
Williams, Bert, 125–6, 128–9, 131–5, 136–7
Williams, Harry, 166, 169
Wilson, Woodrow, 194–5, 200, 207
Winslow, Max, 31–3, 77–8, 168–9, 170, 208
Witmark, Isadore, 55, 58–9, 116–17, 118, 120, 121, 124, 129–31, 163
Witmark, Julius, 55, 58–9, 88, 116–17, 118, 120, 124, 130
Woollcott, Alexander, 15
Woodward, Willis, 107–8

Yellen Jack, 14
'Yiddle, on Your Fiddle, Play Some Ragtime', 69, 73
Yip, Yip, Yaphank, 198–200
'You Cannot Make Your Shimmy Shake on Tea', 209
Yusupov, Prince Felix, 183–93

Ziegfeld Follies, 163, 164, 205, 209